British Army Communications
in the Second World War

Birmingham War Studies (BWS) is a series of works of original historical
research in the area of History and War Studies. The works cover
all aspects of war in the nineteenth and twentieth centuries, with the focus
primarily, but not exclusively, on the British experience.

Series Editors: Gary Sheffield, Chair of War Studies and Director
of Military History and Jonathan Boff, Lecturer, both
University of Birmingham, UK

Series Associate Editor: Dan Todman, Senior Lecturer in History,
Queen Mary, University of London, UK

Also in the series:
The British Army in Battle and Its Image 1914-18, Stephen Badsey (2009)
The Human Face of War, Jim Storr (2009)
Red Coat, Green Machine, Charles Kirke (2009)
*The Leadership, Direction and Legitimacy of the RAF Bomber Offensive
from Inception to 1945*, Peter Gray (2012)

Forthcoming titles in the series:
Changing War, edited by Gary Sheffield and Peter Gray (2013)

British Army Communications in the Second World War

Lifting the Fog of Battle

Simon Godfrey

BIRMINGHAM WAR STUDIES SERIES
Series Editors: Gary Sheffield and Jonathan Boff
Associate Editor: Dan Todman

B L O O M S B U R Y
LONDON • NEW DELHI • NEW YORK • SYDNEY

Bloomsbury Academic

An imprint of Bloomsbury Publishing Plc

50 Bedford Square
London
WC1B 3DP
UK

1385 Broadway
New York
NY 10018
USA

www.bloomsbury.com

Bloomsbury is a registered trade mark of Bloomsbury Publishing Plc

First published 2013
This paperback edition first published 2014

British Library Cataloguing-in-Publication Data
A catalogue record for this book is available from the British Library.

ISBN: HB: 978-1-44119-039-0
PB: 978-1-4725-9133-3
ePUB: 978-1-44118-143-5
ePDF: 978-1-44110-892-0

Library of Congress Cataloging-in-Publication Data
A catalog record for this book is available from the Library of Congress.

Typeset by Deanta Global Publishing Services, Chennai, India

Contents

List of Illustrations

List of Abbreviations

AA	Anti-aircraft
ACAB	Allied Central Air Bureau
ACV	Armoured Command Vehicle
AD	Armoured Division
AFHQ	Allied Force Headquarters
AFV	Armoured Fighting Vehicle
ATIP	Army Training Instruction Pamphlet
ATM	Army Training Memorandum
ATS	Auxiliary Territorial Service
BAFF	British Air Forces in France
BEF	British Expeditionary Force
BRA	Brigadier Royal Artillery
C2	Command and Control
C3	Command, Control and Communications
C3I	Command, Control, Communications and Intelligence
C in C	Commander in Chief
CIGS	Chief of the Imperial General Staff
CO	Commanding Officer
CRA	Commander Royal Artillery
CSO	Chief Signal Officer (of Corps or Division)
DAK	Deutsches Afrika Korps
DF	Direction Finding
DMI	Director of Military Intelligence
DR	Despatch Rider
DRLS	Despatch Rider Letter Service
FOO	Forward Observation Officer
FSP	Field Service Pocketbook
FSR	Field Service Regulations
G1	As for GSO 1
G1098	A term describing the level of equipment in a mobilized wartime unit or formation. It increased over the period of the Second World War

GHQ	General Headquarters (of BEF)
GOC	General Officer Commanding
GPO	General Post Office
GS	General Staff
GSO 1/2/3	General Staff Officer Grade 1/2/3
HF	High Frequency
HMS	His Majesty's Ship
HP	High Power (Wireless)
HQ	Headquarters (of Corps, Division etc)
I (tank)	Infantry tank
ID	Indian Division
IHR	Institute of Historical Research
IWM	Imperial War Museum
J	Wireless Intercept of Own Troops
Kcs	Radio frequency – Kilocycles per second
LAD	Light Aid Detachment
LCV	Lorry Command Vehicle
LHCMA	Liddell Hart Centre for Military Archives
LO	Liaison Officer
L of C	Lines of Communication
L/T	Line Telegraphy
MBSO	Main Beach Signal Office
MCO	Motor Contact Officer
Mhz	Frequency – Megahertz (=1000 Kcs)
MTP	Military Training Pamphlet
NAM	National Army Museum
NCO	Non-commissioned Officer
OC	Officer Commanding
OCTU	Officer Cadet Training Unit
OODA	Observation, Orientation, Decision, Action
OP	Observation Post
PIAT	Projector Infantry Anti-tank
PSC	Passed Staff College
Q	Abbreviation for Quartermaster stores
QMG	Quarter Master General
RA	Royal Artillery
RAC	Royal Armoured Corps

RAF	Royal Air Force
RAM	Royal Artillery Museum
RASC	Royal Army Service Corps
RE	Royal Engineers
RHA	Royal Horse Artillery
RTR	Royal Tank Regiment
RSM	Royal Signals Museum
R/T	Radio Telephony
RUSI	Royal United Services Institute
SAD	South African Division
SEE	Signals Experimental Establishment
Sigint	Signals intelligence
SO in C	Signal Officer in Chief
S + S	Speech plus Simplex
SR	Supplementary Reserve
STC	Signals Training Centre
STM	Signals Training Manual
TA	Territorial Army
TACR	Tactical Reconnaissance
TCP	Traffic Control Point
TM	The Tank Museum
USS	United States Ship
VHF	Very High Frequency (waveband)
V/T	Visual Telegraphy
WDF	Western Desert Force
WO	War Office
W/T	Wireless telegraphy
Y	Wireless Intercept of Enemy Troops
1AD, 2AD etc.	1, 2 etc. Armoured Division
4ID	4th Indian Division

Series Editors' Preface

War Studies is an influential, popular and intellectually exciting discipline, characterized by the broad range of approaches it employs to understand a fundamental human activity. It has the history of war at its heart, but goes beyond operational military studies to draw on political, cultural and social history as well as strategy, literature, law, political theory, economics and social science. *Birmingham War Studies* celebrates this diversity by publishing examples of the discipline at its best, bringing the best academic scholarship on war to a wide audience. The remit of the series is deliberately ambitiously wide, ranging across subjects, methodologies and geographic regions. In this, it takes its cue from the treatment of the subject by the Centre for War Studies (CWS) within the Department of History at the University of Birmingham. The launch of the series in 2008 as a joint venture between Continuum and CWS marked the latter's emergence as a major force in the field, both in the UK and internationally.

'Traditional' military history certainly has its place in *Birmingham War Studies*, but the series' scope is very broad. The high quality of research, analysis and expression will make these books required reading for all those interested in the study of war in general as well as in the topic covered by each volume. In each case, the methodologies used in these specific studies will drive the field as a whole forward.

In many ways, academic study of the British army of the Second World War is now at roughly the same stage as study of its predecessor of 1914–18 was in the mid-1980s. Previously largely the province of memoirists, journalists and popular writers, 'Churchill's army' is undergoing scrutiny based on a patient exploitation of the riches to be found in numerous archives. As this army was effectively an imperial coalition force, relevant material is to be found not just in the UK but also throughout the Anglophone world. In the process, some of the more negative views of the competence of the British army of the Second World War put forward by earlier writers such as Chester Wilmot, Carlo D'Este and Max Hastings have been revised, a process that has curious echoes of the 'revisionist' history of Haig's army. However, although the works of scholars such as David French, Stephen Hart and Niall Barr have laid very substantial foundations on which to build, there is still much to do. There are sizeable areas of the experience of the British army of 1939–45 on which there has been little or no scholarly work.

One of these areas was communications, so Simon Godfrey's work is very welcome indeed. Effective communications are a prerequisite of success on the battlefield, and so it is strange that in general military historians have devoted so little effort to exploring the issue. Dr Godfrey's work, based on his PhD, provides an important corrective to previous neglect. Concentrating on the British army's operations in Europe and North Africa, he begins a process of reappraisal which will hopefully stimulate further research into not only communications in other theatres but also the army's attitude to, and use of, technology more generally. Dr Godfrey convincingly demonstrates that in the area of communications at least, the British army did undergo a learning process, drawing upon experience to produce more effective doctrine and to greatly expand the amount and quality of signals equipment. This is not a Panglossian picture, however; as he makes it clear, in some ways the developmental process was slow, and some problems remained 'intractable'. Dr Godfrey's book is an important addition to the growing scholarly literature on the British army of the Second World War, which deals with a specialized and technical subject in an accessible way.

Gary Sheffield, Editor, *Birmingham War Studies*
Jonathan Boff, Associate Editor, *Birmingham War Studies*
February 2013

1

Introduction

One of the dominant motifs in the history of the British Army on the Western Front between 1914 and 1918 is that time and again senior officers found it impossible to exercise command because once their troops had crossed into no-man's land, the German barrage came down, telephone lines were cut, runners were killed, and communications between the generals and their soldiers were often fatally disrupted. This presented commanders with a unique problem. As Gary Sheffield has written:

> Wellington was able to control his army in person during his battles, which were fought in relatively compact areas. The Iron Duke had been able to rely on a staff of little more than a dozen and had on many occasions been able to ride to danger points to give orders in person, most famously at Waterloo. Even at the time of the American Civil War, generals had been able to exercise a degree of 'voice control'. By the time of the First World War this was no longer possible. Technological developments after 1918 in the form of radios, light aircraft and helicopters were to restore a measure of voice control to commanders. The era of the First World War stands as the only period in history in which high commanders were mute.[1]

This book has two main purposes. First, it will examine the extent to which the British Army did, in fact, succeed in developing communications systems between 1919 and 1945, which lifted the fog that had descended on the battlefield and allowed commanders to exercise a 'measure of voice control'. Secondly, it will explore the ways in which the Army's communications systems contributed to its victories and defeats in the war against Germany between 1939 and 1945. These are contested questions. The official histories of the Royal Signals, published in the 1950s, present a generally positive picture of the work of that Corps, but they were written by Major General R. F. H. Nalder, a former senior Royal Signals officer who may have been more sympathetic to Signals than to the army commanders who were their clients.[2] His view is not shared by many other historians, who have tended to focus their analysis on what they perceive were the shortcomings of the Army's communications, and to pass over in silence their successes.[3] This could be because good news is less interesting than bad news or because it fits with the frequent theme of the British soldier overcoming the obstacles placed in his way by incompetent auxiliary services. Whatever the reason, existing literature gives neither a consistent, objective account of the efficiency of British Army forward communications nor of their impact on the success or failure of operations, nor of the way in which they interacted with command systems.

By making use of original sources, such as the contemporary war diaries of units and formations, the many official reviews of actions and campaigns and the personal records left behind by combatants, this book attempts to establish an unbiased view of how well communications performed and how this affected the overall performance of the Army. It explains the origin of communications doctrine at the start of the war, how the communications system evolved over the following six years, and how it interacted with command doctrine. The focus is particularly on tactical command and communications, at corps level and below, and on communications within the Army rather than between the army, air force and navy.

The book deals with the five main theatres in the land war against Germany – France and Flanders (1939–40); the Western Desert (1939–42); Algeria and Tunisia (1942–43); Sicily and Italy (1943–44) and North-West Europe (1944–45). In addition, the important developments that took place in the Army in the UK – the 'Home Forces' – between Dunkirk and the preparations for the Normandy landings are described. But the signals doctrine used by the Army at the start of the war and the equipment that was provided was consequent to decisions made between 1919 and 1939; this period is therefore covered as a precursor to the main events.

These issues are relevant not only in an historical context, but to the present-day services too. Command systems continue to be a current topic of discussion within UK and US forces because digital technologies have greatly increased the ability to transfer information and because operations have become more complex. Although the rapidity of change is now much greater, the current situation is similar in some ways to that of the period 1919–45, when the improvement in wireless technology offered the potential for commanders to exercise control more easily than ever before. Information technology today similarly allows the possibility of new methods, such as Network Centric Warfare and self-synchronization, which can replace restrictive command systems, and take mission command to its furthest extreme.[4]

To avoid confusion, it is important to make clear that while the main responsibility for communications in the army during the Second World War rested with the Royal Corps of Signals, the Royal Signals personnel themselves normally only provided communications down to the headquarters of cavalry regiments, artillery batteries and infantry battalions. Regimental signallers normally provided the communications below this level on equipment that was generally maintained by the Royal Signals. Throughout the book, 'Signals' is used for the Royal Corps of Signals, while 'communications' is used to describe the system that both the Royal Signals and regimental signallers operated.

Theories of command, control and communications

Command in an army may be defined as the expression of will necessary to accomplish a mission, while Control encompasses the structures and processes needed to ensure that this will is carried out.[5] Command and control (C2) systems in an army can only operate if means exist to communicate information and decisions between personnel. Command, control and communications together are generally known as C3, and with the addition of Intelligence, the system is known as C3I. The capabilities of the communication system place restrictions on the type of C2 that can be operated, though there may be a choice of alternative types of C2 systems that can be adopted with a given communications capability. For example, as explained below, even though its communications systems are more sophisticated than they have ever been before, the British Army currently operates a mission command system whose core principle of devolved responsibility is the same as that of the Royal Navy's command system in the eighteenth century, when communications at a distance scarcely existed.

The ability to communicate has undergone many step changes, each of which has broadened the range of possible C2 systems. As in most technologies, the pace of change has accelerated, with more changes occurring in the last century than in the previous millennium. The main developments and methods have been:

- Messengers carrying verbal or written messages
- Fire and smoke signals

- The telescope, whereby the commander could observe much more of what was happening from a vantage point
- Flag and semaphore systems which, combined with the telescope, enabled messages to be passed over longer distances
- The telegraph and Morse code
- The telephone (*the major new technology in the First World War*)
- Wireless telegraphy and Radio telephony (*the main innovations in use in the Second World War*)
- Satellite telephone
- Email
- The internet and Web-based systems

The means of communication used by the Army during the period of study were line, wireless, written messages sent by the army postal system or by despatch riders (DRs) and personal visits by liaison officers (LOs), who could add verbal explanations as well as deliver messages. 'Orderly' was a frequently used term, and often meant a soldier who delivered verbal messages, somewhere between a DR and an LO. Additionally, commanders themselves frequently travelled to deliver or receive orders personally. Visual signalling by light (visual telegraphy or V/T), flags and Verey pistols was also used, as were carrier pigeons and dogs. Line communications were sent via special field cables or civilian telephone lines, and utilized voice conversations (line telephony) or Morse code (line telegraphy). Similarly, wireless communications used voice conversations known as radio telephony (R/T) and Morse code messages known as wireless telegraphy (W/T). Signal security was an extremely important issue with both wireless and line leading to the use of codes and ciphers. The discovery that line signals could be intercepted by the enemy measuring induction through the earth led to the invention of the Fullerphone in the First World War, which enabled W/T to be operated securely over normal lines and continued to be an important instrument until well after the Second World War.

It is worth considering some of the characteristics of line and wireless methods in relation to one another and to email and Web-based systems since this would highlight the limitations of the methods available during the Second World War and the advantages offered by more modern methods. In the following table, features that may be considered undesirable are given in italics.

It will be seen that the first four modes of communication – the ones that were available in the Second World War – have considerably more limitations and disadvantages than email and Web systems. The telephone is particularly

Table 1.1 Characteristics of communication methods

	Tele-graph	Tele-phone	W/T	R/T	email	Web
Need to know identity of recipient	*yes*	*yes*	*no**	*no**	*yes*	no
Need to know location of recipient	*yes*	*yes*	no	no	no	no
Multiple simultaneous recipients possible	*no*	*no*	yes	yes	yes	yes
Sender and recipient need to be 'online' at the same time	no†	*yes*	no†	*yes*	no	no§
Immediate interaction possible between sender and recipient	*no*	yes	*no*	yes	*no*	*no*§
Written word	yes	*no*	yes	*no*	yes	yes
Audio	*no*	yes	*no*	yes	*no*	yes
Pictures	*no*	*no*	*no*	*no*	yes	yes
Security‡	high	*medium*	*medium*	low	high	high

* This is linked to security. Wireless can be intercepted and received by anybody, including an enemy.
† Although a teleprinter needs to be online to receive the message, the ultimate recipient does not need to be present.
‡ This is somewhat subjective and assumes that with today's technology, email and Web systems are (or can be made) secure.
§ Under usual circumstances.

restrictive although, like R/T, it does have the key advantage of being interactive, explaining why it was and remains a very popular method – for example, the UK's current emergency services communication system is specifically designed for voice communication.[6]

Command systems have been classified into as many as six types – cyclic; interventionist; problem-solving; problem-bounding; selective control and control free.[7] However, this seems unnecessarily complicated for our purpose and two contrasting methods, 'restrictive' and 'mission' command systems suffice. The key distinction lies in the amount of direct continuous control that the commander seeks to impose over his subordinates. In restrictive command systems, the commander formulates a plan and issues detailed orders to his subordinates to ensure that his plan is carried out. Subordinates are allowed little freedom of action and are expected to refer back if unexpected eventualities occur, so that the original orders may be modified by the commander. These processes can only work if efficient communications exist between the commander and the subordinates. In fact, as explained below, the total communications task can be analysed by using the 'OODA' loop. The restrictive command system was used by Wellington in the Napoleonic wars, with the commander himself frequently travelling to deliver his orders and to observe their effect.[8] It was also used by the British Army throughout the period covered by this book, and improved wireless technology was used by the British to tighten the higher commanders' grip on their subordinates.

The principle behind mission command is that subordinates are given the broad objectives of an operation and an outline plan, but not the kind of detailed orders that are issued under restrictive command. All ranks are trained to use their initiative (within defined parameters) in order to carry out their commander's objectives, and to react to events in mutually predictable ways. Instead of referring back to their commander if circumstances make the original plan unworkable, all ranks are expected to adapt the plan as necessary. Quite clearly, this system is theoretically less demanding on communications, and because it removes the need for subordinates to refer back to the commander if circumstances change, an important claimed benefit is that it increases the speed or tempo at which a command system can operate. Tempo has three elements – speed of decision, speed of execution and speed with which a force transitions from one activity to another. If an army's tempo is higher than that of its opponent, it can gain by reacting to events faster, leading to an increased likelihood of effecting surprise, reducing casualties on its own side and increasing casualties on its opponent. Even though they had very similar communications technology to the British, the German Army used mission command at the start of the Second World War, showing that the choice of command system is independent of the abilities of the communications system to a considerable extent.[9]

The British adherence to restrictive command from 1919 to 1939 reflected the British hierarchical social culture and was reinforced by the fact the British had been victorious in the First World War using this system. Moreover, it reflected the Army's fundamental doctrine, which was based upon the fear that unless soldiers were taught absolute obedience, their morale would collapse in the chaos of battle.[10] Restrictive command persisted from 1939 to 1945 for the additional reason that the majority in the Army were conscripts who, left to themselves, would often not have had sufficient training or experience to make appropriate decisions. In the more highly trained German Army of 1939, mission command was feasible, but became less so as the war progressed. From January 1942, as casualties mounted among experienced troops and under the influence of Hitler's strict order to hold positions as the overall situation of Germany deteriorated, the mission-orientated command system was supplanted by an order-orientated one.[11] Mission command is now widely advocated – the modern professional British Army officially replaced restrictive command with mission command in 1987 and proponents of networked information and communications systems are also strong supporters of a fully devolved mission command.[12]

The distinction between mission command and restrictive command is, in reality, more subtle than the descriptions given above. British doctrine in the 1920s and 1930s, as expressed in successive editions of *Field Service Regulations* (*FSR*) and by some senior officers, paid lip service to the need to allow subordinates some freedom of action. But the message was mixed, and the primary emphasis was on the obedience to precise orders and restrictive command.[13] The German equivalent to *FSR*, the *Truppenführung*, published in 1933, was however consistent in its advocacy of giving a free hand to subordinates, while recognizing the complexities of organizing military operations. 'The orders for attack must make quite clear how it is proposed to carry it out. The contents of the order must hold a proper balance between the need for centralized command and the freedom of action of individual units, and must avoid cramping the speed and momentum of the attack by issuing too detailed instructions'.[14] The effect and practice of mission command are less straightforward than at first appear. Tempo in the front line may be increased by mission command methods because the front line can decide what action to take on the spot, without the need to refer back. However, the front line consists of many individuals, and if they need to debate the best course of action, the tempo may be slower than in a more hierarchical structure, even if the ultimate decision is better. Furthermore, the army commander in a mission command system must retain overall control so that he can effect a broad reorientation of front line troops if the overall strategic situation changes; the initiative allowed to the front line must therefore be limited. The commander must retain the ability to communicate with subordinates to allow such reorientation, and so although mission command reduces the frequency with which commanders need to communicate with subordinates, it does not remove the need to provide efficient communications. Another factor is that since it requires the commander to trust his subordinates to act in accordance with his overall aims, mission command is likely to be motivating to subordinates which, in turn, may enhance morale and therefore benefit the ultimate performance. The interaction with logistical services, such as the supply of ammunition and with air support, is also a major issue – the freedom of action of the front line will obviously be severely limited by these matters, which are likely to be controlled by higher command. Overall, mission command is easy to describe in principle, but much more complicated in practice.

Current British Army doctrine addresses these issues, and while making clear that the application of mission command cannot be stereotyped, it enumerates five key elements that are to be used at all levels of command:

a. A commander gives his orders in a manner that ensures that his subordinate understands his intentions, their own missions and the context of those missions. In fact, subordinates must understand not only the intentions of their immediate superiors, but also the intentions of commanders two levels up.

b. Subordinates are told what effect they are to achieve and the reason why it needs to be achieved.

c. Subordinates are allocated the appropriate resources to carry out their missions.

d. A commander uses a minimum of control measures so as not to limit unnecessarily the freedom of action of his subordinates. Decisions should be made at as low a level as possible.

e. Subordinates then decide within their delegated freedom of action how best to achieve their missions.

Nevertheless, the doctrine does recognize that circumstances may arise when the commander has to impose a centralized style of command in order to concentrate forces and to synchronize combat support.[15] The contrast between British Army doctrine today and that operating in the Second World War is therefore one of emphasis – today, it is on delegation of responsibility unless circumstances impose the need for centralization; in the Second World War, the emphasis was on centralization unless this was impossible to achieve, and delegation was necessary.

A useful way of describing a C3 system utilizes the OODA loop, first promulgated by Lieutenant Colonel Boyd, a US Air Force pilot in the Korean War, from analysing his own actions. This may be represented by the diagram shown in Figure 1.1.

The cycle begins with **O**bservations from reconnaissance or other sources. These are then communicated to the commander's headquarters, where they are assimilated and combined with other information, so that an overall picture of the current situation can be communicated to the commander and he becomes **O**rientated with events. He can then **D**ecide what to do, and issue orders for communication to his subordinates. Once they have **A**cted, a further observation

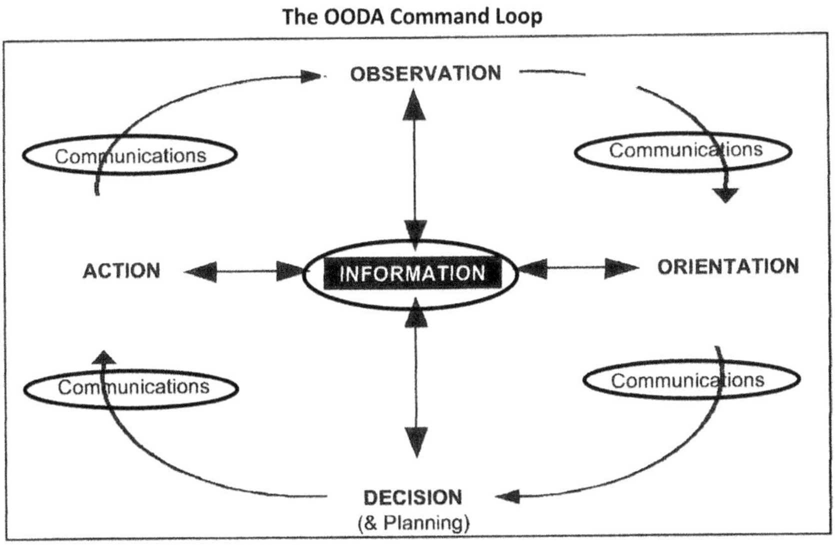

The OODA Command Loop

Figure 1.1 The OODA loop.

stage takes place, and the OODA loop cycles go round again. In this model, there are four points at which efficient communications are needed. The faster the communications take place, the faster the OODA loop can cycle around and the tempo can increase.[16]

The OODA loop concept has limitations; it is only a model of the real world. One limitation is that a decision needs to be taken on what to observe in the first place. The system also becomes more complicated when multiple hierarchical levels of command are in place. The action of the higher level may be the issuing of orders to the lower level, forming an input to its orientation stage. The system therefore involves a hierarchy of interlocking OODA loops (Figure 1.2).

The OODA loop is particularly suited to the analysis of a restrictive command system because of the large number of orders that such a system involves, and it is therefore referred to extensively in this book to identify the points at which communications worked or did not work. It also has application to mission command or even to self-synchronization systems, though in these cases, the ability of the front line to take the initiative without reference to higher command makes it less easy to describe the hierarchical process.

Better communications allow more information to be passed, necessitating a more extensive orientation system to distil the information into an understandable summary. If this distillation process is not carried out, commanders can suffer from an excess of information, possibly leading to confusion and paralysis. For example, if a senior commander's headquarters receives information from every company

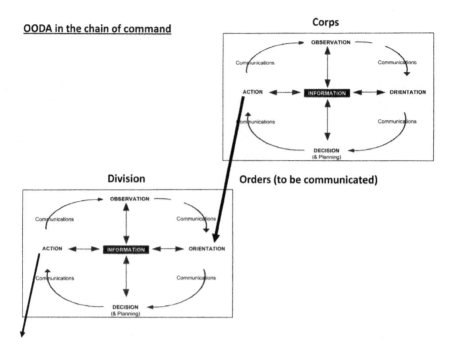

Figure 1.2 OODA in the chain of command.

of every battalion, a large staff (or advanced information technology) is necessary to compile a rapid summary. If this is not provided, increased communication capability may, in fact, lead to a reduction in tempo. It was partly to deal with these consequences of improved communications that the manpower in British formation headquarters increased rapidly during the Second World War. Boyd himself refined the representation of the orientation stage of the process as an interaction between observations and new information with cultural traditions, genetic heritage and previous experience.[17] It is also possible to visualize the OODA loop as operating in three domains – physical, information and cognitive – observation and action take place in the physical domain, while orientation and decision are cognitive. The information domain covers communications and knowledge aspects. These and other related thoughts have meant that the concept of the OODA loop continues to be re-expressed in many ways today.

Overview

One of the main overriding themes of this book is the recognition that comm-unications in an army at war are inevitably liable to interruption by enemy action, by technical failure or by other factors, for example, because formation headquarters have had to make sudden unplanned movements. By far, the most frequent (and often, the only) references to communications in the literature of the Second World War are about the failure of individual links – the breaking of a telephone line by shellfire, for instance, or the breakdown of a wireless set. Unless qualified, this treatment gives the impression that communications totally failed as a result, whereas in many cases, some alternative means was found of getting messages through. It is very important to view and to judge the Army's communications as a *system*, the whole purpose of which was to provide alternative means if one or more methods failed. If such a system of backups was not provided or proved inadequate and this led to a total communications breakdown, then Signals may well be judged culpable, but if, for example, a line was destroyed, but a wireless backup existed to replace it, it should be accepted that the system did not fail and that communications worked satisfactorily.

The evidence presented in this book derives from several primary sources. Chief among these are the war diaries kept by all units and formations during the Second World War, now stored in the National Archive. Their original purpose was to enable the Army to reconstruct events, and hence to learn from experience. Signals units kept their own diaries and these have proved particularly useful. It must be borne in mind that, like Nalder's histories of Royal Signals, Signals diaries may be overly favourable to the Signals point of view. Where appropriate, the staff diaries have also been looked at to verify whether the 'clients' of Signals took the same view; however, in practice, these usually said little, if anything, about communications. As the war progressed, an increasing number of after-action reports were compiled by the staff of formations or by a section of the War Office (often by the Directorate of Military Training or the Directorate of Signals). The accounts of communications in these documents were the result of discussions with, or questionnaires sent to, both staff and Signals, and though they may have had a political aspect, they have often seemed the best source of information. Another major source has been the documents and sound archive sections of the Imperial War Museum, containing the private papers or recollections of individual soldiers. The archives of the National Army Museum, the Royal Signals Museum and the Tank Museum have also been fruitful sources of information.

The communications systems that have been implicated in the defeat of the British Expeditionary Force (BEF) in May 1940 had their origins in the period between the two World Wars, the subject of Chapter 2. Far from ignoring the lessons of the First World War, the General Staff was determined, from 1920 onwards, to avoid a repetition of the attrition on the Western Front, and to utilize the promise of wireless to direct a mobile battle. But, during the 1920s and 1930s, wireless was not developed as much as had been hoped because of a combination of financial restrictions, indecisive political direction, technical problems and concerns about signal security. In the event, the BEF was sent to France in 1939 effectively to conduct a static defensive battle, in which infantry communications were primarily based on line down to battalion headquarters, and messengers below that. Limited wireless backup was provided for the infantry, but there were insufficient sets to take the place of line during mobile operations.

The role that communications played in the battle of France and Flanders, May 1940, is examined in Chapter 3. Contrary to the assertions in some other books, considerable wireless training had, in fact, taken place in the BEF between September 1939 and May 1940, even though the number of sets was too small and there were restrictions on their usage. The concerns about security and the imposition of wireless silence on some occasions were very much part of British doctrine; the restrictions were self-imposed and not forced upon the British by the French. Moreover, highly critical accounts of the performance of communications during the battle itself have been found to be unjustified.[18] Certainly, breakdowns occurred on many occasions during the retreat towards Dunkirk, but communications often worked satisfactorily as well. Given the chaos, it is not surprising that problems occurred, and it has been concluded that most of the problems in signalling were a result of the defeat of the British Army, and not a cause of the defeat.

Two parallel themes are pursued in covering the period between Dunkirk and 1943 – the development of communications doctrine, equipment and training in the Home Forces is examined in Chapter 4, starting with the Bartholomew Committee that was set up after Dunkirk to analyse what had gone wrong; then, communications in the Western Desert, Algeria and Tunisia are examined in Chapters 5 and 6. Both of these sets of experience were synthesized by the Godwin-Austen Committee of 1943, which was charged by the War Office with forming future communications policies. These were the policies that were followed in Italy and North-West Europe, the subjects of Chapters 7 and 8.

The effect that communications had on the major battles of the Western Desert is analysed in Chapter 5. Unlike in France and Flanders in 1940, poor communications were an important cause of the defeat in Operation BATTLE-AXE and of the unsatisfactory progress of Operation CRUSADER. However, the serious defeat at Gazala followed the pattern of France and Flanders in that, defeat caused the communications failures rather than the other way round. These events led the British to change the way they fought battles and the way communications operated, while at the same time, large quantities of equipment were at last becoming available. The subsequent victory at the second battle of Alamein was assisted by these improvements in communications systems, but the failure to destroy the Axis forces afterwards was, in part, due to problems with wireless. Much progress had therefore been made, but communications systems were still imperfect.

Chapter 6 examines the issues that arose during the sea and air landings of Operation TORCH and the invasion of Tunisia by the First and Eighth Armies, along with the difficulties that arose when the two armies linked up. The overall conclusion is that the British Army still had a lot to learn after Alamein. This was not just because the lessons from the Western Desert had not been completely assimilated by the First Army (and Home Forces), but because the methods that applied in the desert did not necessarily work in other terrains, and because the techniques of communications in amphibious landing and parachute operations had not been extensively practised. It was fortunate that the Allies faced a fundamentally weak foe in the Axis forces in Tunisia (weakened by the competing requirements of the Russian campaign and the effectiveness of the Royal Naval and Royal Air Force (RAF) operations against their supply lines). These factors gave another chance for the Allies to improve their performance before they encountered the German Army at full strength.

Chapter 7 describes the Sicilian and Italian campaigns, commencing with the communications training that took place before the invasion of Sicily. The lessons of Tunisia had only partially been absorbed; a start had been made on providing new equipment, but there was insufficient time to complete the process and for units and formations to become familiar with different arrangements. The fact that the Allies suffered setbacks, but no actual defeats in Sicily and Italy, and in the end, achieved victory, suggests that communications, albeit imperfect, were sufficiently successful both in the amphibious landings and on land. Where communications undoubtedly failed, however, was in airborne operations.

With the launch of Operation OVERLORD in June 1944, the main action in Europe switched from Italy to France. Chapter 8 addresses a number of key questions about communications that are posed by the events between the D-Day landings and the pursuit following the crossing of the Rhine in March 1945. Many aspects of communications in North-West Europe worked extremely well, benefitting from earlier experience, the flat countryside and Allied air superiority. But the biggest single factor helping to ensure success was the abundance of materiel and the consequent redundancy that could be built into the system. Communications during the amphibious landings in OVERLORD, the crossing of the Rhine by land forces, the advances across northern France and into Germany, as well as artillery and armoured communications generally, all achieved a high standard. Naturally, there were problems, but they were largely caused by enemy action. More serious endemic failures did occur, however, notably in the airborne operation at Arnhem, with infantry communications generally, with tank – infantry communications in particular, and with wireless security.

In general, the story of British Army communications in the war against Germany is one of an improving signals doctrine, large increases in the quantity and quality of wireless sets and other equipment, more and better trained personnel to operate the equipment and the resultant improved performance. By the end of the war, most aspects of the signals system worked satisfactorily within the limits of available technology, even if failures occurred as a result of enemy action. The systemic problems that remained in front line infantry communications and with security continued for a long time after the end of the war.

The Pre-war Period

As part of the drive to modernize the British Army after its poor performances in South Africa, the Signal Service was created as an independent branch of the Royal Engineers in 1912. At the start of the First World War, however, the Service remained small, and lacked both technical equipment and practical experience. In the opening, mobile, phase of the war, its primary reliance on despatch riders, liaison officers and visual signalling, as opposed to more sophisticated means of communication, such as telephone, telegraph and wireless proved, paradoxically, to be an advantage.[1] By contrast, the German Army struggled to cope because its electronic equipment could not be used on the move and it lacked more primitive, but usable alternatives. Once trench warfare developed in the winter of 1914, however, German communications proved temporarily to be superior. As the British Army expanded in the subsequent years of the war, however, its communications system caught up with that of the Germans – very extensive telephone and telegraph facilities were added and greater use was also made of wireless.

The static trench warfare that dominated operations in 1915–17 allowed reliable line communications to be established down to brigade, and often to battalion, headquarters. Cables were buried deep underground to protect them against damage by shellfire, and grid systems of alternative routes were built so that, if a line was damaged, an alternative was available. Overall, communications at these higher levels of the Army had become satisfactory by 1917, and in this respect, considerable progress had been made since the start of the war.

But the big problem, which remained fundamentally unsolved at the end of the war, was how to get information back from front line troops once they had advanced out across 'no-man's land'. Although cables could be laid behind the advancing troops, these soon became broken by shellfire. As a result, commanders were unable to obtain rapid information on how the attack was progressing in each sector, so they could not judge where artillery assistance should be given and where reinforcements should best be applied. This was an important reason why initially successful attacks failed to be capitalized upon and why a stalemate between the British and German armies persisted for so long.

In the absence of reliable forward line systems, several alternatives were tried. Observation balloons and aircraft were of some help, but suffered from poor visibility as well as problems with their communications to the ground. Visual signalling using flags, flares and lamps was also partially successful, but the former could only convey very limited information, while the latter could only be used from front to rear for security reasons, and were often obscured by smoke and dust. Wireless sets were initially extremely cumbersome, difficult to use and potentially insecure, although their technical performance did improve over time. Another electronic means, the 'Power Buzzer', was simpler to use than wireless, but was equally heavy and insecure. Pigeons were a further possibility, but were only usable from front to rear and were unreliable and inflexible. All of these problems meant that the main method of communication used in the front line was the runner, who was both slow and highly vulnerable. The habit in the infantry of relying on runners for front line communications in the First World War does seem to have been a factor in the reluctance of many infantrymen to embrace more advanced methods during the inter-war period, and indeed for much of the Second World War.

In 1918, the war finally became more mobile, first with the German 'Spring Offensive' and subsequent British retreat, and then during the final 'Hundred Days' British offensive that resulted in the German surrender. How communications coped with this stage is particularly interesting from the point of view of the lessons that were learnt for mobile infantry operations. The Spring Offensive illustrated that, even at the headquarters of senior commanders, the Army could not rely solely on telephones under mobile conditions. As a result of this, coupled with improvements in the technical performance of sets, higher commanders became more willing to accept wireless – by the summer of 1918, sets were issued down to battalion headquarters. Although telephone and telegraph remained the principal means of communication right up to the end of the war, many commanders recognized that other methods, particularly wireless, were essential in mobile conditions. The emphasis placed by the General Staff on pursuing mobility, and consequently, on the development of army wireless during the early 1920s followed directly from the experiences of 1918.

Because of the priority given to mobile operations, the Chief of the Imperial General Staff (CIGS), Lord Cavan, announced 'the abolition of cable' in front of corps headquarters in May 1922, to facilitate communications in such operations.[2] Thenceforth, reliance was to be placed on wireless and messengers. But 18 years later, in May 1940, the BEF advanced into Belgium to establish a static front on the River Dyle, in which communications were primarily to be based on cable, right down to company headquarters. After the crushing defeat of the British and French armies, one of the major conclusions of the Bartholomew Committee of enquiry into the defeat was that wireless had not been sufficiently used.[3] What had caused this apparently paradoxical sequence of events? The changes in communications doctrine that took place during the inter-war period resulted from the interaction of five main influences – army doctrine on such matters as mobile warfare; armoured, infantry and artillery developments; the characteristics of the different modes of communication themselves; financial and manpower constraints; and the technical and production capabilities of manufacturers of signals equipment. The emphases of the technical research programmes were largely driven by the requirements of doctrine, but communications doctrine at the start of the Second World War was primarily influenced by practical issues – in other words, the systems that could be provided. For the sake of clarity, the technical and financial developments over the period are examined first, followed by the doctrinal developments. An examination is then made of communications in practice, during the army training exercises that took place during the 1920s and 1930s, and during Imperial policing activities – the only active operations that took place between the wars.

Technical and financial developments

Electronic methods of communication are inevitably technical and complicated and every effort has been made here to provide simple explanations. However, it is unfortunately necessary to explain some issues in more detail since they had a profound effect on performance. The failure of some officers during the Second World War to make the effort to understand these issues sometimes led to their making impossible demands on their signallers (as arguably occurred at Arnhem in 1944, for example) and in many other cases to their being responsible for serious security breaches.

The momentum of development work at the end of the First World War continued into the immediate post-war period, and a large number of projects were underway in 1919. Thereafter, cuts in budgets and manpower meant that a more modest programme was adopted and the pace was slow during most of the inter-war period.[4] This was a time of rapid development in civilian telephone systems and wireless, but it was found that civilian equipment was seldom appropriate for demanding military conditions. Commercial firms did not find army development contracts attractive because, under the treasury budget system, there was no guarantee of continuity from one year to the next. Therefore, the Signals Experimental Establishment (SEE) found that it had to develop most new prototypes itself, prior to employing outside manufacturers to produce larger quantities, and its limited resources meant that progress in developing military equipment was slow. Army orders for signal equipment were small in commercial terms at this time, and so manufacturers demanded high prices per item to make contracts worthwhile. Furthermore, the rapid advances in electronic techniques made it difficult to decide which designs to mass produce as they became out-of-date before there had been time to make them in larger quantities. There was also some indecision on priorities, which meant that the SEE worked on too many projects and lacked clear directions on technical requirements, such as the range required of wireless sets.[5]

Wireless and DRs were seen as the best means of maintaining communications in mobile operations and, after Lord Cavan's pronouncement in 1922, the main emphasis of the SEE was directed towards wireless improvement and development. Only in 1932 did updating line equipment again become a priority because of slow progress in the wireless development programme.[6] As early as 1919, the SEE had started to design new W/T, R/T and DF sets in the light of experience gained in the First World War, and these became the 'A', 'C' and 'F' sets, introduced between 1922 and 1925. The 120 Watt set, based on the First World War models, also continued in service. Mobile sets ('MA', 'MB', 'MC') were added by 1928. The main characteristics of these sets are shown in Appendix I.[7] Other sets were envisaged, but never produced; the 'D' set, for example, was intended to furnish W/T communications over a range of 100 miles to divisions and flank formations, a technical performance that was still lacking in the Western Desert in 1942.[8]

The sets produced were available in smaller numbers than required in the training exercises that took place, and their performance was less than satisfactory. For example, there were several problems with the MB/MC sets. Valve and other types of failures often occurred with these and it took upwards of an hour to ensure that all tanks were communicating on the same frequency, which would have given ample time for a listening enemy to discover all about the size and composition of a force. The aerial was a thick aluminium tube, eight or twelve feet long, which could easily be seen by the enemy over a skyline, betraying the tank's location and direction of movement. Much less visible 'whip' aerials were introduced around 1930.[9] In addition to sets, the SEE developed the batteries (accumulators and dry cells) that were needed to drive them, and the charging engines for recharging the accumulators. Remote control (by which, wirelesses could be placed some distance away from the operator) was also developed, both to reduce the interference that occurred if sets were placed too close together, and to avoid betraying the location of headquarters through direction finding (DF) or visibility of the aerials.

Technological limitations and production difficulties prevented wireless from fulfilling its potential in the 1920s, but this did not dull the belief that wireless was essential for command and control of all parts of the Army.[10] Impetus was given to the development of wireless by the CIGS in 1929, who appointed Colonel Charles Broad to draw up the specification of a new range of sets (called Nos. 1–6) that would better meet the requirements of the Army.[11] The main features of these and of sets Nos. 7, 9 and 11 that were added to the list up to 1938 are shown in Appendix 1.

Before describing the performance of the new series of wireless sets, it is appropriate to explain various technical issues, which had a considerable impact, both on the development of wireless and on its operational effectiveness. While the sets in the 1920s had operated using medium and long wave, the new series of sets mainly used short wave (high frequencies). One reason for this change was that long wave and lower portions of medium wavebands were congested by civilian stations. The main advantages of short wave lay in its ability to cover large ranges with a smaller expenditure of power compared with longer waves. Its relative freedom from atmospheric disturbance was an additional advantage. However, the range obtainable with any particular wavelength varied during any 24 hour-period and according to the seasons. But by switching wavelengths, at dusk for instance, a practicable service could be maintained over worldwide ranges.[12] In 1936, experiments were carried out using VHF (very high frequencies) – the No 13 experimental man pack set was built, but VHF was concluded to be too affected by the general nature of the intervening country for infantry use and the experiment was discontinued.[13] VHF was later used at high command levels, for example for cross channel communications, but lower level British Army communications remained on short wave throughout the Second World War.

Another technical, but highly relevant, issue is that there are two means, the ground wave and the sky wave, for propagating transmissions at short wave frequencies. The ground wave, in its turn, comprises two main elements – the direct or line of sight wave, the main means of communicating over short distances, and the surface wave, which travels in contact with the earth. The maximum range of the surface wave varies according to the wireless set used, the power of the broadcast, the exact frequency, topography and whether R/T or W/T is used, W/T having a longer range. The maximum range that could be covered by ground wave at this time was about 25 miles, and was often considerably less.

The sky wave, which travels further than the ground wave, reflects off the ionosphere lying high above the earth's surface. The ionosphere changes its characteristics between day and night, and sky wave can be generated with less power at night. For this reason, reception at night is better in that messages are easier to pass over long distances, but worse in that there is more interference from other messages and surrounding objects. Wireless operators varied in their ability to distinguish messages from surrounding interference. The operation of the sky wave varies with the time of day, geographic location, atmospheric conditions, time of year and the intensity of sun spot activities. In particular, there is a maximum frequency beyond which waves pass straight through the ionosphere and the best performance is obtained when operating at around 80 per cent of this maximum. However, the maximum varies considerably in a 24-hour period, for example between 2 Megahertz just before dawn in winter up to 8 Megahertz at midday, necessitating the switching of frequencies.[14] The reflective characteristics of the ionosphere vary in the short term as well, causing fluctuations or 'fading' of reception levels.

Another very important issue is that signals would only bounce off the iono-sphere if they met it at a small enough angle, and this meant that there was a minimum distance away from the broadcaster before sky waves could be received, known as the 'skip distance'. The minimum distance depended on several factors, but 60 miles was typical, well beyond the 25-mile range of the ground wave. Therefore, a signal would not be received by someone in between these two points, for example 40 miles away, but yet received by someone 80 miles away, a source of bafflement to some non-signallers, who usually blamed incompetent signalling rather than accepting it as a consequence of physics. To summarize, ranges of up to approximately 25 miles were coverable by ground wave and from 60 miles plus by sky wave, but there could be a 'dead' range between 25 and 60 miles, which could not be covered by either. Various ways round this inconvenience were discovered over time, as described later, but this skip distance problem often occurred in the first years of the Second World War.

There were limited suitable frequencies in the short wave band, and this restricted the number of channels of communication that could exist in a given area. Rather than having a separate channel between each pair of headquarters, as was mainly the case in the 1920s, it became necessary to establish 'nets' – groups of wirelesses operating on the same frequency. In this way, many more sets could be worked, though this placed a premium on well-disciplined operators to avoid two people communicating at the same time, and demanded accurate frequency control. There was also a trade-off between the weight and range of a set, so that where ease of transport was required, range had to be sacrificed.[15] This became particularly relevant as forward infantry sets were eventually developed during the Second World War.

Altogether, both ground and sky short waves are somewhat fickle and this led to a belief among some officers, who did not understand the issues, that wireless sets were unreliable and, sometimes, that operators were incompetent. To an extent, of course, such beliefs were correct as far as the end result was concerned – communication was often difficult or impossible. But perhaps a more constructive approach would have been to appreciate and allow for the vagaries of a method which, when it operated, gave enormous benefits over the alternatives.

Overall, wireless development made very slow progress in the early 1930s, partly because of the sheer difficulty of solving the technical and production problems, but primarily because of financial restrictions caused by the economic crisis of 1930–31. The amount of money allocated to 'Warlike Stores', which included the funding of the SEE and the provision of equipment of which signalling equipment formed a small part, is shown in the following table. The conversion to current day values makes it clear that, even allowing for the greater purchasing power of money at the time, very small sums were being spent throughout the 1920s and early 1930s.

The allocation of money declined by 20 per cent between 1929 and 1930, from what was already a low level, and it was not until 1935–36 that a real increase in resources was made available. At this point, however, the War Office restricted the development of equipment to items that were sufficiently advanced for them to be issued to troops by a target date of 1 April, 1939. The policy was designed to focus efforts on equipment that could be used to counter the immediate threat from Germany, but it proved to be very damaging as far as the longer term supply of wireless equipment was concerned – several important developments, for example, work on a portable infantry set, were stopped until the restrictions

Table 2.1 Army budget for 'Warlike Stores'

Year	£ million[16]	Approximate £ million in 2010 values[17]
1925	2.8	132
1926	2.4	114
1927	2.1	100
1928	2.1	100
1929	2.4	114
1930	1.9	90
1931	2.2	104
1932	2.1	100
1933	2.3	109
1934	2.8	133
1935	5.2	246
1936	10.7	507
1937	21.3	1010
1938	41.2	1953
1939	56.7	2688

were eased in the summer of 1939, and therefore took longer to reach fruition than might otherwise have been the case.[18]

It might be thought that under the financial restrictions of the late 1920s and early 1930s, the army would have cooperated with the RAF and Navy in the technical development of wireless. Some coordination was established in 1928 between the three armed services in the allocation of call signs, but a committee recommended in 1929 that the services should *not* cooperate on scientific and development work on W/T, on the grounds that their requirements were so different.[19] There was in fact a 'complete lack of inter-service cooperation' at this time and it has to be suspected that this was partly due to inter-service rivalry.[20] The Army did receive some help, however, from the Home Office, which was carrying out experiments with wireless for the police force. The possibility of pooling military resources in straitened circumstances (and maybe of enhancing all-arms cooperation in future battles) was ignored until the Ministry of Supply and Ministry of Aircraft Production assumed inter-departmental responsibility for various aspects of radio production at the start of the Second World War.[21]

Of the sets proposed by Broad, Nos. 1 and 3 proved to be considerable improvements over their predecessors, and their performance was judged satisfactory when they eventually came into service. But major problems were encountered with the No. 2 set, and the No. 4 set was never introduced. The Nos. 5 and 6 sets were only relevant for high-level fixed operations and are beyond the scope of this book. By 1933, only the No. 1 set had been issued for service with an improved version, the No. 11 set, in the planning process. The No. 3 set worked well, but large numbers of trade-produced versions were not supplied until 1937, no less than eight years after the set had first been planned. The No. 7 set for armoured fighting vehicles (AFVs) was added to the list of sets because the No. 2 set was too big for light tanks, but by 1936, there was still no trade-produced No. 2 set and only a few No. 7 sets, mainly because of failure on the part of commercial suppliers. Neither was satisfactory and both were later replaced by the No. 9 set, a sizeable clear space for which (42 × 12 × 16 inches) was left available in the turret of newly designed AFVs.[22] A large commercial order for No. 9 sets was placed; 50 of these were delivered in 1937, with another 200 due in 1938. In fact, 800 No. 9 sets were reported to have been delivered in 1938, a most unusual occurrence of production exceeding expectations.[23] Nevertheless, the number of AFV sets was inadequate to meet demand at the beginning of the war, since the 1 Armoured Division was still deficient in wireless sets in May 1940 because of competing priorities from other forces, such as the future 7 Armoured Division in Egypt.

A major associated area of development work concerned the power supply of wireless sets. For the infantry and artillery, this involved experimentation with different battery charging engines, and improvements in the batteries themselves. Larger sets, such as the No. 3, incorporated their own charging engine as well as batteries, though this added considerably to their already substantial weight. For tanks and armoured cars, there were four possibilities – batteries could be charged by a separate charging vehicle and periodically exchanged; the tank itself could carry a separate charging engine; the wireless battery could be charged by the tank engine; or the wireless could run off the main tank battery. All of these methods had their advantages and disadvantages and were tried out at different times up to and during the Second World War.[24]

In the early 1930s, the international situation became more dangerous. The rolling 'ten year rule' (under which the military was told to operate under the assumption that no major war would occur in the next 10 years) was only abolished in 1932, at least three years too late, and a Field Force Committee was set up to study requirements for a continental war in 1933.[25] It must have been evident that in its then current state of development and availability, wireless would be unable to cope with a high proportion of communications in a major conflict, and it is not surprising that attention reverted back to line communications, regardless of longer term doctrinal objectives. Very considerable advances in civilian telephone and telegraph services had taken place, but the Army's line systems were essentially as they had been in 1919, and were obsolete. It was therefore decided that the SEE should initiate development work to redesign them.[26]

Contrasting with the painful progress of wireless developments, rapid advances in line communications were made by 1934. This was because close cooperation was established with the GPO's development centre at Dollis Hill and because civilian telephone and telegraph equipment was more easily adaptable to Army use than civilian wireless sets. The somewhat unreliable the First World War Fullerphone, a device for transmitting Morse by cable in a secure manner, was upgraded and redesigned for forward use. The new Fullerphone was superior to a stationary No. 1 set in W/T range, and it was simpler, cheaper to make, more secure, more reliable and had a lower power requirement. Figure 2.1 shows a row of Fullerphones being used in the Western Desert, and illustrates their small size and simplicity. By contrast, the short-range No. 1 wireless set was large and

Figure 2.1 Row of Fullerphones.[27]

Figure 2.2 Wireless No. 1 set mounted in a car.[28]

heavy enough to need mounting in a car, as shown in Figure 2.2, and the longer range No. 3 set, shown in Figure 2.3, had to be carried in a lorry.

Obviously, line instruments required lines. Mechanical line layers to replace the horse drawn trailers used in the First World War had been under trial since 1930, and there was the promise that these would increase the speed with which lines could be laid, perhaps giving the impression that line could quickly catch up with events in a mobile operation. The No. 1 mechanical cable layer was able to lay and reel up cable at speeds up to 20 miles per hour, and by 1938, cable could be laid at 30 miles per hour. Rapid methods of connecting cables to junction boxes and switchboards had been developed.[29] Multi-channel line instruments (6 channels of communications on a single pair of lines) and associated high speed teleprinters were under development to deal with the heavy demands of supply routes (known in the Army, confusingly, as 'lines of communication' or 'L of C'). Tests were carried out to assess the message carrying capacity of various line systems, with results ranging between 27 and 60 messages per hour per operator. These numbers were far in excess of what was possible by wireless, and were particularly impressive at a time when manpower was short. It is not surprising that they led to the recommendation for the Field Force to be equipped with teleprinters and high speed Morse as quickly as possible.[30]

At the start of the Second World War, technology had been developed that gave good line communications in the field when circumstances allowed and wireless sets that might fairly be described as basic, but functional. Overcoming

Figure 2.3 Wireless No. 3 set mounted in a lorry.[31]

the technical problems of wireless had taken a long time because of the lack of investment as well as the formidable difficulties that were faced. Moreover, production capability was very limited. These were some of the causes of the lack of sets that was experienced soon after active operations commenced in May 1940. But the main reason for the shortage of sets was the signals doctrine that was adopted in the mid-1930s and the allocation of resources that flowed from it.

Command, control and communications doctrine, and signals security

By the end of the First World War, the British Army recognized that a combined-arms approach and mobility would be two essential elements of success on a future battlefield. It also remained wedded to the restrictive system of command and control through which senior commanders sought to give detailed orders on how operations were to be conducted and to monitor progress.

While it has been argued that restrictive command obstructed mobility, the implications of both objectives on the Army's communications systems were consistent – extensive rapid communications that would operate in mobile warfare were required. Moreover, the Army was keen to embrace technology as a force multiplier and to make up for the drastic cuts in manpower that were being forced upon it. It is not surprising, therefore, that the General Staff enthusiastically promoted the merits of wireless communications from the early 1920s. In recognition of the importance of communications generally, the army Signals Service, previously a section of the Royal Engineers, became the Royal Corps of Signals in 1920.

Every pronouncement on communications by a senior or General Staff officer between 1922 and 1932 recommended the scrapping of cable in front of corps or brigade headquarters. But these seem to have largely been general statements of intent, rather than carefully thought-through policies. Perhaps the aim was to adopt an extreme position in order to force movement in the desired direction. But every time the practicalities of signalling had to be faced, cable was firmly reinstated for use whenever conditions allowed. According to Signals officers and the official War Office publication covering Army doctrine, the *Field Service Regulations (FSR)*, both cable and wireless were needed.

The formulation of a new signals doctrine during the inter-war period began in May 1922, when the CIGS abolished all telephone communications in advance of corps headquarters, apparently without regard to security issues or the volume of signals traffic with which the system would need to cope. The subsequent twists and turns in communications doctrine between 1922 and the most important policy event of the inter-war period as far as communications are concerned – the Jackson Committee of 1936 – are summarized in the table below.

The overall structure of the BEF that went to France in 1939 was determined by a War Office committee that met in the mid-1930s, having the objectives of examining the draft composition of the field force and recommending from time to time what alterations were required. Arising out of this, it was charged with recommending a long-term programme for the force, showing the annual development towards its progressive formation and equipment.[32] However, there was increasing ambivalence among both politicians and the War Office about a continental commitment, to the extent that, in December 1937, the government of Neville Chamberlain allocated a new set of priorities to the rearmament programme. The first priority was now the security of the United Kingdom, particularly from air attack; second was the protection of imperial

Table 2.2 Main developments in communications doctrine, 1919–39

1920	In recognition of the importance of communications, The Royal Corps of Signals is formed as a separate entity.
1922	The CIGS, Lord Cavan, declares that all telephone communications in advance of corps headquarters should be abolished and replaced by wireless.
1924	*FSR* (1924) published. No specific guidance given on communications.
1924	Lord Cavan's policy recognized as impractical because of the inadequacies in wireless performance. Limited forward cable communications reinstated.
1926	The future SO in C during Dunkirk, Major R Chenevix Trench (Royal Signals), publishes a paper advocating a mixture of cable, wireless, visual signalling and despatch riders for forward communications, with duplication on all main links in case of breakdown. He declares that there should not be an argument about line *versus* wireless, but recognition of the merits of each under different circumstances. His logic still held in 1945; it was the inadequacies of wireless technology, lack of resources and fears about security that caused the problems during the intervening period.
1929	Sir George Milne, Lord Cavan's successor as CIGS, sets a long-term policy objective of putting wireless first. He announces the development of a new range of wireless sets (Nos. 1 to 6), each set having a performance and weight designed to suit particular purposes.
1929	*FSR* (1929) includes a complete chapter on communications for the first time.
1930	Senior Royal Signals officers develop Milne's policy, but significantly change the emphasis in infantry communications doctrine back towards line. Wireless is relegated to a standby for use on the move. This is in line with *FSR* (1929). They warn that even this policy will be difficult to implement with existing wireless technology.
1934	The Kirke Committee publishes a report summarizing the lessons of the First World War for army doctrine. The importance of communications is emphasized, but committee members vary in their enthusiasm for wireless because of doubts about its technical capabilities and security. The final report recommends the development of wireless and the abolition of cable in front of brigade headquarters, except for artillery.
1935	*FSR* (1935) adopts Kirke's recommendation for giving responsibility to the higher formation for maintaining communications with the lower formation, but does not adopt his policy on wireless. Communications policy is expressed with much greater clarity than in 1929 and specifies communications doctrine in the attack, the defence and in position warfare. When attacking, communications should primarily be by wireless, supplemented by DR and cable; when defending, both cable and wireless should be provided; in position warfare, the emphasis is on cable. Signals security receives more attention than in 1929.
1936	The Jackson Committee is established to determine communications doctrine and equipment levels for the BEF that eventually went to France in 1939. It recommends the primacy of line communications for infantry, even in mobile operations, going against the spirit of developments in doctrine ever since the end of the First World War.

communications; third was the defence of the Empire; and only fourth was helping to protect the territory of allies.[33] This resulted in a lack of progress in equipping the BEF until after the Munich crisis. Hence, the Signal Officer in Chief (SO in C) could write in March 1940 that 'development of Royal Signals before the war had followed the accepted policy which placed intervention in a European war last among the probable roles for the army', and could give this as the reason for various problems experienced in France during the static period before May 1940.[34]

Another War Office committee was set up to examine the components of the Royal Engineers, Royal Signals, and Royal Army Ordnance Corps within the field force, reporting in June 1935.[35] It was this committee that recommended the reduction of the Royal Signals element and formed a special sub-committee to examine and implement this policy under the chairmanship of Lieutenant General H. C. Jackson, formerly GOC of 50 (Northumbrian) Division in the First World War. Jackson's former command post is significant, since as a result of their experiences in the mobile operations at the end of the First World War, the staff of 50 Division had issued a report in 1918, stating that under mobile conditions, 'the trench warfare methods of laying telephone lines to everyone must be recognised to be impossible . . . and reliance must be placed on wireless, DRs and Liaison Officers'.[36] It is assumed that Jackson was in agreement with these sentiments; yet, as chairman of his committee in 1936, he was responsible for the decision to adopt line as the principal means of communication for the infantry. The possible reasons for this paradox are explored below.

In its briefing to Jackson, the field force committee made specific suggestions about cutting down the number of telephones in use at GHQ and Corps HQ and queried whether multiple means of intercommunication were necessary, 'The importance of reliable communications can hardly be exaggerated, but it is suggested that care must be taken not to add to the means of communications for the sake of convenience only'.[37] Thus, the Jackson sub-committee was given a clear instruction to find ways of economizing on the requirements of Signals. It reported in April 1936, and established the doctrine by which communications in the BEF operated in 1939–40. It recommended the primacy of line communications for the infantry, even in mobile operations, and thus went against the doctrine that had been enunciated by Cavan in 1922, Milne in 1929 and Kirke in 1932; it went against the spirit of the *FSR* published in 1929 and 1935; and it went against Jackson's own experience. Above all, it had a profound negative impact on the performance of the BEF in 1940.

Unfortunately, in spite of every effort, it has proved impossible to find a copy of the Jackson report, though the abstract of its recommendations makes it clear that they were intended for the first contingent of the field force and 'for operations of a mobile nature'.[38] For the detail of the report, it is therefore necessary to rely on the account given by Nalder, the historian of the Royal Corps of Signals, in 1958. He states that the report 'recommended that except in armoured formations, which would rely primarily on wireless, the normal means of communications at all levels would be line telegraphy and line telephony. At the same time, wireless [by which it appears that Nalder meant W/T] should be provided as an emergency method at all levels, with radio-telephony [R/T] facilities in the forward formations and artillery regiments . . . This was an important recommendation since it disposed of the view held by some that infantry brigades and artillery regiments would be able to manage with wireless [W/T] alone'.[39] The Committee also anticipated a bottleneck in the telephone circuits between headquarters at various levels and between the sub-areas of the base, and hence it restricted the number of telephone subscribers to a definite and austere quota for each headquarters exchange.

Judging by his experience in the Second World War, Nalder felt that this doctrine was at fault in three respects. First, there was insufficient emphasis on line and wireless being complementary (but, rather that line should be first and wireless only a standby), so the number of wireless channels was insufficient when line broke down. Secondly, wireless was not sufficient for armoured formations; they also needed line. Thirdly, while it was highly desirable to avoid overloading the telephone system, restricting the number of subscribers was not the best method.[40]

Comparing the Jackson recommendations with *FSR* (1935) leads to the conclusion that the Committee was anticipating position warfare for the field force, or at most, a defensive action. Its recommendations were certainly not in line with communications for an attack, yet *FSR* (1935) had advanced the opinion that 'sooner or later', offensive action would be necessary. Since no updated version of *FSR* was issued before 1940, it is not clear whether a long-term change in communications doctrine was intended, or if the Committee's recommendations were simply a matter of temporary financial expediency.

In the absence of any record of the rationale behind the Jackson Committee's recommendations, the reasons for the switch from an emphasis on wireless in mobile operations to line can only be guessed at. However, given the brief to find ways of economising on signalling and avoiding what was seen as unnecessary duplication, the slow pace of progress in wireless development and the rapid improvements in line communications, it is easy to see why the decision was made. Wireless had technical and supply problems such that even the armoured formations could not obtain adequate supplies – Brigadier Percy Hobart, the commanding officer of the Tank Brigade, complained in June 1936 that he had 'nothing but a few obsolete and worn-out sets' and the 1 Armoured Division was still lacking sets in May 1940.[41] Moreover, compared with line, wireless lacked security, both from interception and DF, was restricted in the number of channels available, was very demanding on battery supplies and the instruments were far more expensive to provide. While line could not work on the move, mechanical line layers held out the promise of rapid connection once halted, and it was probably anticipated that movement would be in 'bounds' with time for line to be laid in between. Under this logic, if emphasis had to be put on one mode of communication, as suggested by the briefing to Jackson, it clearly had to be line. The history of the BEF in 1940 shows that this was a serious error, arising from three sources. First, the brief to Jackson was faulty in that multiple means of communication were precisely what were required – this was not 'for convenience only', but so that one could take over from another when failure occurred. Obviously, lack of money was the driver behind this brief, as it was the cause of the slow development of wireless. Secondly, the extent of the vulnerability of line to bomb blast does not seem to have been properly appreciated by the Army until an analysis of the German invasion of Poland had been made in late 1939.[42] This could partly have been a result of the lack of liaison between the Army and the RAF between the wars, but is nevertheless surprising, given the known effect of shellfire on lines during the First World War, even if bombing from the air was less effective then. Thirdly, the belief (if it existed) that there would be time to lay lines in between 'bounds' proved incorrect because of the rapidity of the German attack. The pace of events had not been foreseen at this stage, nor indeed was it recognized even after the invasion of Poland had been analysed, perhaps because the latter was felt to have had unique characteristics, which would not apply in France.

Whatever the reasons, line was re-established as the primary means of communications down to battalion headquarters, just as it had been in the First World War. Within an infantry battalion, communications remained largely untouched by technology. When operations were imminent, each company commander sent an orderly to battalion headquarters 'to facilitate communications'. Within a company, communications were through orderlies and by visual signalling via lamps, flags and hand signals.[43]

Security was a problem with both line and wireless during the First World War and remained a topic for debate throughout the inter-war period. It was a major factor in determining whether line or wireless should be employed. The issue went wider than the Army. The Strategic Cables Subcommittee of the Imperial Communications Committee, set up in June 1932 and reporting in March 1933, considered whether cable communications must still be regarded as superior to wireless for certain classes of messages 'on account of the superior degree of secrecy over wireless that cable communications are alleged to possess'. As a consequence of the report of this committee, it was concluded that wireless did not provide a suitable medium for secret government communications, including those of the Army.[44] One has only to consider the benefits to the Allies of the breaking of the Enigma ciphers in the Second World War to appreciate that these concerns had some justification; the question that continued to dog communications was how far should caution prevail over efficiency. The War Office challenged the committee's conclusion in 1936, arguing that advances in cipher made it possible for wireless to be used more extensively.[45] But, they later retracted the argument because 'although correct as far as the War Office was concerned, [it] could not be applied to the other services or to Imperial communications in general'.[46]

A pamphlet discussing the security risks of each mode of communication was issued in 1925, and *FSR* (1929) specified that cipher should be employed in wireless communications under most circumstances.[47] It stated that only when operations were in progress could messages in front of brigade HQ be sent in clear (unenciphered), as could other urgent messages when the enemy would not have time to react if they were intercepted. With line, Fullerphones should be used when close to the front. These rules did not change appreciably in *FSR* (1935). The *FSRs* paid particular attention to the issue of wireless silence, something that was to prove controversial during the early years of the Second World War. The rationale for this was that security could be compromised, even when cipher was used, as explained graphically in the memoirs of a signalman at a brigade headquarters in 1940:

> These chaps [the enemy] are no mugs, you know! From the signals they monitor, they can piece together much more than you think. Direction. Location. The number of stations in a group. Even the control station in the group. By timing the transmissions, they can deduce when the next transmission is likely to occur, and in this way detect when units move. Even the daily change of call signs doesn't fool them completely, though of course it helps. You see, tapping out Morse is like handwriting. Each of us has his own particular quirks and style of

doing it. So if you've got a trained ear, you can identify the sender even though his call sign has changed, and detect a change of operator even though the station call sign remains the same.[48]

The report on the 1935 training season discussed the circumstances when wireless silence should be imposed and said that it should normally be observed in reserve formations and during an approach march, but was unnecessary when contact with the enemy had been made. No solution was offered to the problem of how to conceal the movements of a mobile force, but at the same time, control it. The general tone of the instructions was that commanders should use common sense, and indeed they said that the wishes of the commander in the matter of wireless silence were often better in the form of an operation instruction rather than an order.[49] This fairly relaxed attitude had been stiffened considerably by 1938 – restrictive conditions were laid down when wireless could be used in the absence of special orders, 'otherwise wireless silence will be observed'. Use of wireless was generally only permitted by reconnaissance units when no other means were available, by a unit or formation when in contact with the enemy, or in cases of extreme emergency, when no other means were available.[50] When the use of wireless was permitted, cipher was often obligatory, but a report of a training exercise in September 1939 stated that the rules on when to use cipher 'had not been understood' and that very important information was being given away, as a result.[51]

Since army, corps and divisional headquarters usually contained many sets, enemy direction finding could potentially allow them to be located, and then bombed or shelled. The War Office carried out a number of trials in the late 1930s to compute the accuracy of DF at various frequencies and distances, and as a result, Royal Signals believed that fear of DF was much exaggerated.[52] However, the capabilities of enemy DF remained a controversial topic throughout the Second World War with many soldiers believing it to be more accurate than scientific experiments would indicate.

The outcome of all the discussions on security was summarized for the soldier on the ground in the *Field Service Pocket Book* of 1939.[53] It stated that all messages sent by wireless were liable to interception by the enemy, and that an approximate position of the sender could be determined using DF. The following precautions might therefore be necessary:

- wireless silence
- cipher for W/T and restriction for R/T
- periodic changes of frequencies and call signs

Bearing in mind the problems caused by the imposition of wireless silence before and during May 1940, this listing order is relevant. It remained in force until late 1941, when wireless silence was relegated to third place, and an additional statement was added – 'No fixed rules can be given since the importance of secrecy must be weighed against the need for control and information'.[54]

Within overall communications doctrine, very detailed operational procedures were developed between the wars, and published in a series of training manuals. Eight such manuals were created in the early 1920s, after the formation of Royal Signals, which were later reduced in number to six – *Signal Training (All Arms)* covered the individual training of signallers and *Signal Training Volumes I to V* covered the organization of communication in the field as well as technical manuals and procedures for line, wireless and other means. The detailed procedures were only gradually modified – it was the doctrine governing the kind of communications that should be employed in particular circumstances that changed over time, more than the manner in which each type should be operated.

At the start of the Second World War, the official infantry communications doctrine, as expressed by *FSR* (1935), was that both line and wireless were required in sufficient quantities so that one could substitute for the other, depending on whether an attack, a defence or positional warfare was in progress. However, this doctrine had effectively been modified by the Jackson Committee, so that infantry was primarily dependent on line under all circumstances. The desire for economy meant that the amount of wireless equipment available was too little for this means to substitute properly for line, and the rules enforcing the use of cipher and wireless silence meant that the use of even this limited amount of equipment was severely restricted. The hope was that sufficient time would exist for line to keep abreast of any movement of the Army that might take place.

Communications training in the 1920s and 1930s

The Signals Training Centre (STC) was formed in April 1915, and between the wars, its functions were the training of Royal Signals personnel as well as the training of officer and NCO instructors of other arms, who would then pass on their knowledge to regimental signallers. Courses took place at the STC establishment in Sussex, and from 1925 at Catterick. Some live signalling experience was obtained in those units that were engaged in imperial policing duties – for example 12 Lancers were first equipped with wireless while in

Table 2.3 Communications exercises during the 1920s

1921	The Experimental Brigade was established to determine how new technology would affect the structure of Army divisions in the future. Particular emphasis placed on wireless.
1922	Line not used (in accordance with Lord Cavan's declaration). Wireless inadequate, so runners used, but these could not compensate for the loss of line. Consequent recommendation that divisions should be supplied with 15 miles of cable in the future.
1923	Line not re-introduced, not because wireless had improved, but to force the pace of its development.
1924	Re-introduction of line accepted temporarily. But communications still proved inadequate in the summer training exercises because of lack of equipment and shortage of skilled tradesmen in Royal Signals.
1925	Large-scale training programme culminating in a planned three-day corps exercise in September. Three day preliminary communications exercise (without troops) in May, which appeared to run well. But performance in other exercises during the summer was less good and there was 'a danger of serious congestion in communications that would paralyse mobility'. The inadequacy of resources was very apparent in the corps exercise at the end of the season, leading to a recommendation that pending improvements in wireless, the infantry should primarily rely on LOs and DRs.
1926	Wireless also inadequate for tank communications; flag signalling used within tank companies. Experimental wireless sets used for connecting artillery batteries to their OPs also proved unsatisfactory.
1927	The report on the 1927 staff exercises enthusiastic about the potential of R/T, but in reality, wireless was still not available for the manoeuvres of the newly formed Experimental Mechanical Force, leading to its defeat by an unarmoured force.
1928	150 sets issued to the Experimental Force, resulting in a great advance in communications compared with 1927. New wireless sets for the artillery were tried out in the tactical exercises, which demonstrated the potential to speed up the production of a coordinated fire plan compared with cable communications. In reality, mutual interference between sets limited the number that could be employed, leading to poor results.
1929	Some progress made in the use of wireless for tank communications, though there were still many problems. Similarly, the artillery sets linking batteries and OPs were found unsuitable.

Palestine in 1930 – but the points at which communications were tested in an operational context for the majority of soldiers were the Army exercises that took place each year.[55] These varied in scale and realism from large-scale manoeuvres involving troops and all arms (in 1925 and 1935), to separate tank and infantry manoeuvres, down to staff exercises in which officers planned theoretical battles over different stretches of the country, with no troops involved.[56] The lack of funds and limited geographical space meant that training in the inter-war period was mostly on a small scale. The extent to which communications could be properly tested obviously depended on the scale of the exercise, but even in full-scale manoeuvres, peacetime exercises could be misleading – for example, DRs could appear invulnerable in these circumstances, whereas they suffered casualties and got lost in a mobile battle.[57]

Communications advanced very slowly during the training exercises of the 1920s. The Army had a general idea of how things should change – increase the quantity and capability of wireless in order to facilitate mobile operations – but in practice, they had neither the resources nor the technical ability to make this happen. As a result, the situation in 1929 hardly represented an improvement over that in 1919. The table above summarizes the main training events of the period.

After the 1929 season, several Army commands questioned the future of signalling policy, but the General Staff did not really have a satisfactory answer. It recognized that insufficient progress had been made for W/T and R/T to wholly replace line, citing the limited number of wavelengths available as well as the possibility of jamming by the enemy and security problems. Insufficient range was an additional problem. However, line could not cope with the increased mobility brought about by mechanization, and tracked vehicles were liable to cut cables. Therefore, until wireless was more developed, LOs and DRs needed to be used. But, there were insufficient DRs under existing establishments, and owing to financial stringency, no increase in establishments could be sanctioned.[58] Having been forced to confront this unsatisfactory state of affairs, it is easy to see why the General Staff launched a major effort to improve wireless equipment in 1929, even though they may have suspected that the same financial stringencies would lead to slow progress, and were aware that jamming and security issues were endemic to this mode of communication.

Infantry training continued during the early 1930s, even though lack of resources because of the economic situation meant that it was on a limited scale. This was a serious disadvantage since combined training was the only opportunity for staff, Signals and units to practise together. Even when they took place, training exercises were criticized for the unrealistic ways in which civil telephones were sometimes used and commanders drove their cars to the 'battle line' in order to supervise events, as well as for the unreal speed of movements that were possible when assaults were unchecked by bullets.[59]

The desirability for wirelesses to work in nets was emphasized in the report on the exercises in 1930, the advantages being – lower numbers of frequencies employed; the possibility of increased speed, given that messages from HQs were often addressed to more than one recipient; and the reduction in the number of sets at an HQ, bringing more security from DF. The difficulty of nets was to decide where in the chain of command the frequency should be changed, given the widely differing roles of different units.[60]

A signalling exercise by Southern Command in 1931 illustrated the greater speed of mechanical cable layers compared with horse transport, and the long range at which the 11 Hussars were able to send messages by W/T. However, a newspaper report asserted that although 'wireless is working a revolution in army communications . . . the DR still holds his own as the most certain channel.'[61] But the situation was improved with the introduction of new No. 1 wireless sets – a comparable exercise in 1933 found that wireless worked admirably in mobile operations when no cable was used, thanks to the new equipment that was available.[62] The 1 Division exercise in August 1933 provided an interesting illustration of the controversy over whether the higher or lower command should be responsible for keeping higher commanders informed – 'Information! Information! Information!' were the director's final words to the officers of his division after the exercise. The fictional enemy in this exercise were 'hostile tribes' who had carried out 'attacks on oil concessions' – still second class enemies, in the year that Hitler came to power in Germany.[63] The value of apparatus for listening in to enemy wireless communications was illustrated by an exercise in September 1933, as well as the time penalties in using cipher to combat the danger. In one example, a DR delivered a message 35 minutes before the same message was enciphered, transmitted by wireless and then deciphered. However, a large number of DRs were captured, showing that exercises could sometimes give a realistic impression of the difficulties faced in real combat.[64]

The army manoeuvres of 1935 were the largest for 10 years and involved regular and territorial infantry and tanks, the main purpose being to provide higher commanders and staff with practice in handling larger bodies of troops than was possible in normal training exercises. In contrast to the disproportionate size of the opponents in 1925, two complete Army corps were involved in these manoeuvres, this time with mechanized Signals regiments. The weather was as unkind as it had been in 1925, and the manoeuvres did not appear to have been very fruitful in providing useful lessons. As far as communications were concerned, the CIGS wrote, 'In spite of the large increase in wireless equipment, information does not seem to come in any quicker than it used to do. In some cases in this exercise it came in very slowly . . . I do feel we must do something to improve it'.[65] Even though one might think that ability to communicate at all in mobile operations rather than speed per se was the main point of wireless, this remark gives a further context for the decision in 1936 of the Jackson Committee to give wireless a lesser role within the infantry than was envisaged in the 1920s.

A series of tank exercises took place in the 1930s, during which the struggle to achieve efficient control by wireless continued. The 1 Brigade, Royal Tank Corps, existed for training purposes under Brigadier Broad between April and September 1931, with MB and MC wireless sets restricted to battalion and company commanders' vehicles because of limited availability. Considerably greater progress in R/T was reported compared with previous years, attributed to greater practice in communications and control due to the concentration on manoeuvre that year. In particular, it was concluded that R/T could be made to work efficiently by Royal Tank Corps operators (as opposed to Royal Signals) if they were sufficiently trained. However, the limited number of sets and the fact that MB and MC sets were too large to fit into light tanks meant that visual signalling by flags and semaphore arms still had to be extensively employed.[66] Messages relayed in such a way were obviously wide open to interception by the enemy, as shown by the fact that the press and other spectators at the exercises possessed a simple card for interpreting the signals.[67] Even when R/T communication did exist, it was often difficult for listeners to hear what was being said above the noise of the tank, though this improved with practice. In reconnaissance detachments, the link back to the originating force was ideally by R/T, but its short range meant that a messenger needed to be sent in a light tank when they were widely separated. This was also the case between patrols and the HQ of the reconnaissance detachment. Since messengers, even in light tanks, were vulnerable, important information needed to be sent in duplicate by different routes.[68]

By the 1934 training period, for which a temporary tank brigade was again formed, some of the new series of wireless sets were available. The report on the training season was written by Hobart, who had replaced Brigadier George Lindsay as commander after a controversial exercise at the end of the season.[69] Several communications problems had occurred and Hobart made a recommendation about how the system should best be changed. His solution demanded the provision of short-range inter-tank sets in all brigade and battalion HQ tanks, something that did not materialize until the No. 19 set was introduced in 1941.[70] A single wireless net was recommended for battalion communications, even though this put considerable strain on the battalion HQ terminal. An R/T range of 10 miles was needed for a tank set, but the MB/MC sets could only communicate 1 mile by R/T; the No. 7 set, 3 miles and the No. 2 set, 5 miles. Pending the arrival of the planned more powerful No. 9 set, it was recommended that the No. 2 and No. 7 sets be adopted and that W/T be used to increase the range. Using Morse was very much a second best option because it was much slower than voice and furthermore necessitated additional training of personnel. Battery charging had also been a problem and a cause of failure; it was recommended that the tank generator be used for charging (though, as described earlier, this was only one of four potential systems, each of which had drawbacks). Experience was gained in the security aspects of wireless, as a result of which, some use of cipher at higher levels and limited use of wireless silence were recommended. Daylight signalling lamps were to be fitted on all tanks, along with a battle aerial that was less liable to damage.[71] Overall, Hobart's recommendations gave a clear plan for improving tank communications.

However, Hobart's report of the 1935 training showed that scarcely any progress had been made in the intervening year. No new wireless sets were available and no daylight signalling lamps had been fitted. Lack of screening of the electronic components of engines caused a great number of difficulties in R/T.[72] In June 1936, Hobart wrote a memorandum on the unpreparedness of the Royal Tank Corps for war, and the War Office admitted that the tank situation was extremely unsatisfactory. As far as wireless was concerned, Hobart noted that while the set decided on was the No. 9, this was not expected in production quantities until 1939, but that the No. 2 and No. 7 sets that were to be used in the meantime had not been forthcoming.[73] At the end of the 1936 training season, just two No. 9 sets were issued, and these were 'a great advance on anything we have had to date'. It was recommended that the No. 7 set should be regarded as obsolescent, and that all tanks be fitted with No. 9 sets before the next season.[74] 200 such sets were needed. Hobart was showing signs of exasperation with the slow rate of progress in other areas as well, 'Year after year the case has been submitted for the provision of a very small short-range set for intercommunication between the tanks of a HQ . . . This year a No. 13 set was issued. It would require a vivid imagination to picture anything less suitable'. There were also problems with communication between tank crew members – voice tubes were in use, but were unsatisfactory, and trials of loudspeakers, internal telephones and combinations with the external wireless had not been successful. A trial of the latter with the new No. 9 set was recommended.[75] At this time, Royal Signals personnel were felt necessary for longer distance communications of 10 miles or so, while a Tank Corps operator was adequate for distances of up to a mile.[76]

When Major General Alan Brooke took over command of the Mobile Division in 1938 after Hobart had been sent to Egypt in the face of a threatened Italian invasion from Cyrenaica, he wrote that the whole technique of wireless control required expanding and improving. At this time, the Infantry Tank Mark I was in production, the turret of which was too small to accommodate a wireless set. However, the larger Mark II was under development, and this was able to house a set. Hobart continued to demand No. 9 sets for the tanks of the second mobile division (later named 7 Armoured Division) that he established in Egypt, and his training report for 1939 shows that he was in possession of 139 sets, but needed an additional 95.[77]

Communications between tanks and infantry remained extremely crude – infantry were supposed to indicate the direction of the enemy to a tank by means of a helmet placed on a rifle, or by hand signals. By 1940, some tanks were fitted with bells on the outside so that infantry could attract the attention of the occupants.[78] The technical difficulty of achieving good communications between the two arms was a major long-term problem that still remained unsolved at the end of the Second World War, but Hobart's preference in the 1930s for all-tank operations may have disguised the severity of the issue at this point.

While the situation in both armoured and infantry communications was unsatisfactory as the Second World War approached, a more positive result held within the Royal Artillery. By 1937, the standard of its wireless communications had improved as a result of new equipment and the signal exercises held within formations and brigades. Full reliance could now be placed on the No. 1 sets between brigade headquarters, battery command posts and observation posts, supplemented, if time permitted, by buried cable.[79] The better performance of communications in the Royal Artillery foreshadowed a general trend during the Second World War and the basic reason for this was that artillery was less subject to rapid movement than the other two arms, allowing line to be laid in many circumstances while, when it did move, its wireless sets could often be carried in vehicles and could therefore be of a more powerful (and heavier) type.

Throughout the 1930s, Royal Signals personnel levels were below establishment – the number that was authorized by the War Office. This was because of a lack of recruitment due to economic and demographic factors and because of high staff turnover.[80] Also, the supply of Royal Signals personnel to units engaged overseas on imperial policing duties had been made a priority, leaving home forces to suffer the full impact of the shortages.

The establishment of the Royal Signals was increased from 5,261 all ranks in 1936 to 6,630 in 1937, a higher proportionate increase than in the rest of the Army.[81] But this did not stop a serious shortage of Signals personnel from occurring in 1938, causing problems with the training of higher commanders and staff. Although efforts were made to rectify the situation, it was said that beneficial results were unlikely to be noticed before the 1940 training season. It had previously been decided that Supplementary Reserve (SR) signallers were to provide communications in the field force for GHQ, L of C and the air component, and some corps and divisions would rely on Territorial Army (TA) signallers.[82] Thus, the recruitment and training of part-time signallers in the pre-war period is an important topic.

The SR was formed in 1924 specifically to boost numbers in, among other parts of the Army, the Royal Signals, for which the existing First Class Army Reserve did not make provisions.[83] Like the TA, it was made up of civilians who trained on an occasional basis, but Supplementary Reservists usually had some technical qualifications. The signallers were mainly recruited from 'Post Office employees and every one . . . is skilled in telephony and telegraphy'.[84] Given this background, they would have been more familiar with line communications than with wireless.

As in the rest of the Army, the reservists suffered from cutbacks and shortages of personnel. The economies of 1931 and 1932 led to camps being cancelled and training grants cut to the bone, though over half the force attended 'voluntary assemblies for training' in 1932 in spite of this. Camps resumed in 1933, but 'the strength of some units already too far below establishment has been still further reduced in camp by improvement in employment. Leave has had to be granted to some men who have just started new jobs'.[85] Photographs of the author's father at the annual camps of the Queen's Royal Regiment (TA) in the 1930s suggest that during the 'voluntary assembly' of 1932, signalling training employed semaphore flags. In 1935, the signalling equipment included Morse signalling lamps and line, and in 1936, the TA was issued with some No. 1 wireless sets so that they could train in the same way as the regular Army.

The doubling of the TA early in 1939 created great strain in the organization and it was necessary to find extra drill halls and headquarters before training could even begin. Overall, it is difficult to escape the conclusion that the sizeable proportion of the BEF that used TA and SR signallers was served by very inexperienced and undertrained personnel at the outbreak of war. They were fortunate in having an eight-month breathing space before active operations began, but signallers in corps HQs and at GHQ were too busy during this period to do more than 'train on the job' under static conditions.

Imperial policing

Between the wars, the British Army was engaged in various operations to maintain peace throughout the Empire and to quell unrest, which provided the opportunity for employing signalling methods in active conditions. One particular sphere of activity was in the Middle East, where Italian expansion during the 1930s required a show of force from Britain to protect its interests and where a rebellion by the Arabs in Palestine occurred in 1936 because of the rapid rise of Jewish immigration. Another completely different set of conditions was encountered by the Indian Army on the North-West Frontier, where in 1936–37, it was involved in pacifying Waziristan, the region centred on the town of Bannu. Both theatres demonstrated the advantages that wireless could bring over and above conventional line and visual signalling, and messengers.

The nature of the operations and the terrain in Palestine and Egypt meant that armoured cars were particularly suitable for use. The 12 Lancers were mechanized from 1928 and all squadrons in Egypt were operating in armoured cars by September 1930. At this point, individual armoured cars were not equipped with wireless, intercommunication being carried out by semaphore or by despatch rider, but squadrons were accompanied by wireless lorries for longer-range communications, which were practised on various expeditions into the desert with considerable success. The 11 Hussars replaced 12 Lancers in Egypt in 1934 and, from 1935 one car per troop was fitted with a wireless set. The subsequent use of wireless during the Arab rebellion in Palestine provided operational experience for the two reconnaissance regiments that was to stand them in good stead and led to rare examples of successful communications in the BEF in May 1940.[86]

The operations in Waziristan were a complete contrast in that any form of mechanized transport was extremely problematic because of the terrain. The modernization of the Indian Army between the wars generally lagged behind the Army in the UK, as a result of budgetary constraints and doubts about the suitability of some equipment for frontier warfare, but the Indian authorities were very keen to update their wireless equipment.[87] In 1931, orders were placed for 48 up-to-date No. 1 wireless sets, so that each infantry brigade in 1, 2 and 3 Indian Divisions could be equipped with four sets (one at divisional HQ and one at each battalion HQ). By 1934, these had arrived and proved to be of great value under active service conditions on the North-West Frontier. It proved to be more difficult to update the old medium wave 'C' sets used by divisional and regional HQs because of local conditions and the great range required in India; it was not until 1939 that trials of long-range No. 3 sets were felt to have given satisfactory results. With the expansion of wireless, compensatory reductions were made in line equipment because of the emphasis placed on economy in the early 1930s. With the introduction of modern equipment, the use of semaphore signalling was reduced in the cavalry and artillery, but many infantrymen were still trained in this method.

A particular issue with wireless sets used on the frontier was transportation. It was often impossible for vehicles to get over the terrain, so that the heavy sets had to be carried by mule or horse. Methods were developed for a No. 1 set to be carried by one animal – the off side load of 77lbs consisted of the set itself and a microphone; the near side load of 77lbs of the two batteries, spare valves and spare aerials; and there was a top load of 5lbs consisting of the main aerial. Sometimes, the components of the set were split between two men when a mule was unable to get up a precipice. Methods of carrying the longer range No. 9 set by pack were also developed, but this required no fewer than five mules to carry a complete station.[88] As described in a later chapter, the lesson that a large number of mules were essential for the operation of the Army in mountainous regions seemed to be forgotten during the planning of the Tunisian campaign in 1943, and had to be learnt again.

The advent of modern wireless equipment was initially warmly welcomed in India because of the known unreliability of line methods in frontier warfare, often due to sabotage.[89] But, wireless was also sometimes found to be unreliable and to suffer from limited capacity. As a result of its experience during the Quetta earthquake emergency of 1935, the Indian Signal Corps realized that lines as well as wireless still remained an essential means of communication, at least for higher command. In this respect, the Indian Army underwent the same learning processes as the Army in Britain.

An example of where communications played a particularly important part was in May 1937, when the Indian Army's Bannu Brigade needed to establish itself during the night on high ground in order to outflank the enemy. Intercommunication between the various portions of the column and its headquarters was to be maintained by LOs and by wireless sets, one set being allotted to the Tochi Scouts who formed the advance guard, one to HQ, one to the rear guard and one to No. 12 Field Artillery Company. The column started at 21:00 hours and had extreme difficulty in proceeding due to the terrain. At 01:10 hours, HQ heard by wireless that the Tochi Scouts had reached the objective, but wireless reports from the rear indicated that the column was very strung out. HQ therefore halted to allow the rest of the column to catch up. Once this had been done, the column moved on and attained its objective in good order. As a result of the outflanking movement, control was re-established over the Sham Plain with very few casualties. Had the column not been equipped with wireless, the operation could not have proceeded so smoothly. However, there was no need to maintain wireless silence for security reasons, given that the tribesmen had no interception sets. Against a first-class enemy, wireless silence would have been essential, illustrating the limited application that lessons from imperial policing activities had on operations in the Second World War.[90]

3

The Phoney War and Dunkirk 1939–40

The performance of communications during the brief period of active operations prior to the evacuation from Dunkirk may fairly be described as unsatisfactory, though it was not as bad as some historians have made out.[1] To a large extent, the problems were the inevitable result of the policies of the previous 20 years described in the last chapter, but it is also the case that the main ways in which communications were conducted during the eight-month-long static period, the 'Phoney War', which preceded the fighting, gave a very inadequate preparation for what was to be required later.

A week after the outbreak of war on 3 September 1939, the first contingent of the BEF landed in Western France and travelled by train to the sector of the Franco–Belgian frontier, near Lille, that it would occupy until May 1940. It was flanked by parts of the French Army to both the north and the south. This contingent consisted of the British Army's General Headquarters (GHQ) and two corps, each comprising two regular Army infantry divisions (1 to 4). Between October 1939 and May 1940, it was joined by one further regular infantry division (the 5), five territorial divisions (42, 44, 48, 50 and 51), and the infantry of three additional territorial divisions (12, 23 and 46). A third corps was formed in April 1940. The 1 Armoured Division did not arrive in France until active operations were already underway, around 20 May.

Little fighting took place during the Phoney War, but the Army was extremely busy with building up its manpower and equipment, and with training and fortifying the front line on the Belgian border, ready for the anticipated German attack. The French and British high commands were also involved with planning an advance into Belgium to take the defensive line forward. Since Belgium still hoped to remain neutral, this could not take place until the Germans started to invade the Low Countries. In fact, it was not even possible for a proper reconnoitre to be made of the proposed new front line until the move forward took place.

Because of the recruitment problems already referred to, the strength of Signals in 1939 was still well below its peace establishment and many of the signallers in the BEF therefore came from the TA and the SR. Within the first contingent of the BEF, only the Signals regiments of I Corps, 1 and 2 Division and 1 Anti-aircraft Brigade Signals were fully trained regular soldiers. Those of II Corps, 3 Division and 4 Division were formed from territorial units and had never completed training or worked with their war staffs. GHQ, L of C and air formation Signals were formed from the SR. During the period before active operations began, these units fortunately had time to practise their duties.

At the point when active operations began in May 1940, the level of train-ing and the degree to which each Signals unit was used to working with its staff varied, largely dependent on how long the formation and unit had been in France. Training in rapid movement was confined to divisional Signals and below; GHQ and corps were too taken up with day-to-day administration dur-ing the static period to allow this, and in any case, it was not anticipated that they would need to move.

On arrival in France, the first task for Signals was to make line connections using the French telephone system. As part of the army staff conversations between the British and the French that had commenced in March 1939, a list of potential telephone circuits had been prepared. The process involved plac-ing a contingent of British signalmen in the main French telephone exchanges, to man the French circuits used by the BEF and the connections to the BEF exchanges. Some initial difficulties were experienced linking to the interna-tional cable system for communication with London, but on the whole, there was good cooperation with the French civil and military authorities. High level communication between the British and French commands was established, but front line communications, the subject of this book, were confined to the national armies.

Telegraph circuits of the French cable system turned out to be far too few for the BEF. This was overcome by superimposing telegraphy on the telephone circuits, using the top or bottom of the audio frequency telephone band for telegraphy, and employing an apparatus known as 'Speech + Simplex' (S+S). There were never enough of these instruments, but they proved invaluable.[2] During the static period, a very large amount of cable was laid by the BEF along its sector of the Franco–Belgian frontier, to connect up its various headquarters and to make up for deficiencies in the French civil telephone network. Hundreds of miles of armoured cable were laid six feet deep to protect against bombing, by employing mechanical diggers and about a thousand men.[3] The operation proved very difficult when the ground became boggy in the autumn, and even more so when it was frozen during the hard winter of 1939–40. This all turned out to be wasted effort since the resulting elaborate system was scarcely used in the actual conflict.

The Jackson Committee recommendations of 1936 had placed strict limitations on the amount of signalling equipment in each division. Moreover, the drive for economy and other defence priorities had meant that the re-equipment programme in the late 1930s only aimed at completing supplies for the first contingent of the field force. The remainder was only equipped to a training scale, the intention being to make up the balance after war broke out. As a result, in September 1939, the two corps and four divisions that formed the first contingent were fully equipped, with the exception of some new multi-channel terminal equipment. But in the Army as a whole, there was a large gap between supply and demand, especially, in the case of signalling equipment, with No. 9 and No. 11 wireless sets.[4] During the Phoney War, it was found that the tasks required of Signals in the BEF far exceeded the highest estimates on which establishments had been based, particularly to the rear of corps headquarters. This was due to the extent of the L of C between the front and its terminals in North-West France, the multiplicity of establishments, the dispersion of major headquarters, and unforeseen channels of communications required by the Air Force, for which Royal Signals were also responsible. Additionally, use of line equipment was somewhat profligate, with less urgent messages telegraphed when they could have been sent by post. These factors led to the number of telephones installed being far in excess of the Jackson limits. The long static period, during which line communication was reliable, also led staff to depend on it, perhaps more than they should have done, leading to problems when active operations broke out.[5]

The magnitude of communication traffic at different levels of headquarters in early 1940 is shown by the following examples:

At GHQ, by the middle of January 1940, 2,280 telegrams and 4,150 DR messages were being passed per day. There were six telephone switchboards, each passing around 500 calls per hour.[6]

At II Corps on 14 January 1940, 3,300 telephone calls were passed through the exchange.[7]

At 1 Division, the average numbers of messages per day in January 1940 were about 300 by telegram and telephone, plus over 400 by DR.

At 3 Infantry Brigade, the average numbers of messages per day in January 1940 were 50 by telegram and telephone, plus 55 by DR.[8]

With this level of activity, it is not surprising that the emphasis was on line rather than wireless links for capacity reasons alone, aside from the security concerns that are discussed below. It is also not surprising that the previously planned amount of equipment proved inadequate, particularly telephone sets and cable, and that many complaints about shortages appeared in the war diaries kept by each formation. However, Brigadier Chenevix-Trench, the SO in C, initially (October 1939) went so far as to recommend a *reduction* in wireless equipment to the Chief of Staff, on the basis that the scale was more than that required for static warfare.[9] His attitude soon changed, partly as a result of the formulation of plans for advancing into Belgium, and partly because of the study in November and December 1939 of the systematic attack by the Germans on Polish communications.[10] The lessons from Poland about the vulnerability of overhead wires to bomb blasts led to their abandonment as a standard medium, and also to concern over the security of civilian cable centres and shallow buried civilian cables laid alongside roads. Policy switched to multi-core cables laid on the ground or preferably buried to a depth of six feet. The Polish experience also showed the importance of having enough wireless sets for emergency use if line failed and the SO in C then recognized that there were insufficient sets in the BEF for this purpose.[11] Alongside this fundamental wireless equipment shortage, more wireless battery charging engines were needed than had been provided because it was found that they wore out through use. Another equipment issue was that LOs needed cars when it became impossible for them to use their motorcycles in icy conditions.[12] The shortfall in the amount of signalling equipment that was now required was partly made up by May 1940, but large gaps remained. For example, the second line territorial divisions (12, 23 and 46) still had no Signals sections at all (as well as many other deficiencies) when they were drawn into the conflict just one week after the start of operations.[13]

In the meantime, strict wireless silence other than for short-range tests was observed throughout the Phoney War for security reasons, a ban that some authors have claimed was 'ordered by the French command'[14] and led to the wireless network being 'practically untested' when action commenced.[15] However, these restrictions were in line with British doctrine and none of the contemporary accounts implies that the British were forced to observe them against their will. At the beginning of the period, a complete ban on wireless transmissions was enforced (even if some sets were used in reception mode for 'listening in to dance music on home and foreign stations . . . by operators during their long stints of maintenance', as reported by Signalman Vollans at one of the brigade headquarters). Vollans also said that wireless training was simulated using line, 'Despite the continuing wireless silence, operator training in the reading and sending of Morse was continued on line instruments. Each morning several Fullerphones would be wired up around the floor of the billet to simulate a group network.'[16]

But wireless began to be used in earnest once it was clear that an advance into Belgium was to be implemented. Listening watch (each of a number of sets sweeping a sector of frequencies) was kept throughout the Phoney War during periods of wireless silence when wireless training was not being carried out, in order to detect any insecurity on the British side, as well as to intercept German messages. The SO in C wrote about the importance of wireless training '. . . by means of protected wireless . . . [which] must be kept warm by constant use'.[17] Protected wireless meant transmitting at low power on special training frequencies, usually in training areas away from the front. It had the disadvantage of not allowing detection of the mutual interference of sets on close frequencies, and the atmospheric problems that might occur on operational frequencies. Nevertheless, it kept operators 'warm'. Even so, the French were concerned that British sets were transmitting at too great a power.[18] By March 1940, 'phone-less days' were taking place. The whole idea of this system was to train people to use other means of communications than L/T, so that in actual warfare, should a line be shelled, the subscriber would already have had experience in finding other means of communications rapidly. This identified problems even if solutions were not always obvious – for example, after one exercise, it was concluded that 'the wireless was not very satisfactory for reasons that were not entirely clear'.[19] Thus, British wireless security was relaxed somewhat from the initial policy of absolute silence at all times, but severe restrictions continued, with instructions sent out to remind recipients of the importance of wireless discipline, and to draw attention to the procedures contained in the Signal Training manuals.[20]

Although it would be incorrect to say that wireless was practically untested in the static period, Signals sections and staff officers were certainly more accustomed to using line. Moreover, since cipher was not needed when using line, at least when Fullerphones were employed, cipher sections had not been exposed to anything like the volume of traffic that would face them during the coming action.

The British always had great and possibly exaggerated respect for the ability of the Germans to intercept wireless messages and to determine their source by direction finding (DF). To prevent detection of headquarters by DF, sets were located no closer than 2,000 yards from headquarters, and to one side looking towards enemy lines. They were then connected by line to the user, a system known as 'remote control'. For example, II Corps had two wireless 'villages', each of four No. 3 sets, placed 2,000 yards to the north and south of its headquarters.[21] Another complex technique to prevent a station disclosing its position was the 'I' procedure, in which a distant third station listened to the transmissions, acknowledged or requested repetitions from the transmitter while the vulnerable station simply listened without transmitting at all. This assumed that the distant station would have the same reception as the vulnerable one, and could only work when there was no need for the vulnerable station to say anything.[22] The visibility of aerials was an additional concern – the No. 3 set, for example, had a 70-foot mast when it was being used over long distances in a static position.

It was not just wireless that posed a security threat – the enemy or the 'Fifth column' could tap into cables, a danger that was mitigated where possible by the use of Fullerphones. Line routes might also be seen from the air and thereby betray the location of headquarters; RAF spotter planes were sent up to see how visible they were, and generally, lines were taken on past a headquarters to disguise its exact location.[23]

Within an infantry division, cable backed up by wireless connected divisional and brigade headquarters and cable then ran down to battalions. Battalions mainly used messengers (for example a runner, DR or LO) to communicate with their companies, who then communicated with platoons by lamp, flag semaphore or runner.[24]

Aside from the testing of communications in the static defensive positions, communications were practised in the mobile training exercises that were ordered for all field formations. In this way, the Signals sections in brigades and divisions had some training under their formation and regimental commanders in mobile operations. But, with higher formations, administrative pressures made such mobile training progressively more difficult to arrange, and in GHQ, impossible. The quality of training varied between divisions. For example, 3 Division was thought by Lieutenant General Alan Brooke, at that time the GOC of II Corps, to be considerably in advance of 4 Division in this respect. The 3 Division's exercises demonstrated the need for a single and cohesive communications base, with the CSO brought in as an integral part of mobile divisional headquarters, as well as the need for more LOs to compensate for the unreliability of W/T and R/T. Lord Gort's GHQ, however, was rehearsed neither in movement nor communications in battle.[25]

It was found that one of the most useful forms of training for the Signals section of an infantry brigade was when they were sent to get experience of true active service conditions on the French front before Metz. This started in December 1939, with approximately a dozen brigades relieving each other at fortnightly intervals before May 1940. The brigades held a section of the Maginot Line, and were engaged in patrols, raids and counter-raids while Signals attempted to draw lessons that would be of use in the coming battles. In case of absolute necessity, wireless as well as field cables was permitted and it was said to have operated satisfactorily even though only a small amount of traffic was carried compared with later demands.[26] Signals gained as much information about wireless as possible within the restrictions imposed, to determine the frequencies that were most suitable for each type of set in the local terrain and weather conditions, how concentrated sets could be without excessive mutual interference, and so on.[27] The 12 Lancers, for example, practised the use of their wirelesses, but did so in the Paris area, well away from the restrictions imposed on the front.[28] Some exercises involved the rapid laying of cable to battle positions and visual signalling.[29] Possible new technical developments and methods of operating were also considered, for example, whether to imitate the use by the Germans of VHF sets and whether to adopt single call sign procedures for security reasons – something that was eventually taken up after Operation CRUSADER in the Western Desert in 1941.[30]

By the beginning of May 1940, strategy in the event of a German attack was clearly established. The Belgians continued to maintain neutrality, and therefore prohibited the Allies from advancing into Belgium before active operations started, or indeed making a thorough inspection of their intended defensive lines. In spite of this, the wish of the Allies to enlist the support of the Belgian Army, the desire of the British to prevent the Germans establishing airfields within easier reach of London, and the desire of the French to keep the fighting away from their industrial areas, all combined to persuade the Allies that they should advance from their defensive positions on the frontier as soon as the German attack on Belgium and Holland took place. 'Plan D' involved an advance up to the River Dyle, where new static defensive lines would be established. It was anticipated that the Belgian Army would be able to hold out long enough (the Chief of Staff of the BEF, Lieutenant General Pownall expected to have 14 days) for this to be achieved.

The advance under Plan D would be controlled by telephone and wireless, and line communications would then be established at the new positions. Use would be made of the underground telephone cable between Lille and Brussels, and signals centres would be established in major telephone exchanges. Additional circuits would be provided by overhead routes and by field construction.[31] The main emphasis remained on line communications, and this appeared logical since the Allies were still anticipating a static defensive battle, but further forward. Emergency wireless backup would be provided in case of breakdown or if it was required to fall back to the River Escaut or to the frontier, but it was anticipated that such movements would be in 'bounds' after each of which, there would be sufficient time to re-establish satisfactory line communications. Certain elements, such as reconnaissance and armour, were expected to rely on wireless, and were meant to be equipped accordingly, even if shortages sometimes got in the way. This was the logic governing the planned structure of communications at the end of the static period.

The evidence from contemporary sources shows that the Royal Signals did not just sit on their hands during the Phoney War. To apply the description 'practically untested' to British wireless systems would be an exaggeration, though it is certainly true that they were not tested in the way that they would ultimately need to be used, in mobile operations at full power. Moreover, GHQ communications were not tested in a mobile operation at all – the vast amount of administration that they had to deal with in the Phoney War did not allow time. Along with the rest of the army, Signals had attempted to learn lessons from Poland, but the key lesson, that events would happen much more quickly than had previously been anticipated, was not properly understood. It is hard to disagree with the summary given by Sergeant Brodie, a signalman at II Corps HQ – 'Most of our communications relied on an elaborate network of cables and were suited to the kind of static warfare that had existed in 1918. It was totally unsuited for a Blitz Krieg [sic] . . .'[32]

Active operations May–June 1940

Active operations began on 10 May, when Plan D was activated in response to the German attack on Holland and Belgium. The BEF crossed the Belgian frontier, breaking wireless silence as it did so, to help control the advance. The main part of the force advanced towards the River Dyle, while three divisions prepared defensive positions further back on the River Escaut in case a withdrawal was required. The BEF had only just established its position on the Dyle when the Germans broke through the French lines to the south, opposite the Ardennes, outflanking the main French and British forces. At the same time, the Belgian Army rapidly caved in under the German attack to the north-east of the British sector. The combination of these two factors meant that it became imperative to retreat, commencing on 16 May. Instead of the planned static battle, with a single eastern-facing front, the Allies found themselves fighting a mobile retreat on two fronts, of which the south-western-facing one was completely unanticipated. There was insufficient time for more than minor counter-offences to be organized, which proved useless against the initiative that the Germans had secured. The British supply lines from North-West France were then severed, causing shortages of all kinds as the BEF and part of the French Army retreated towards Dunkirk, from where most were evacuated before the town was surrendered on 4 June.

In assessing how well communications operated during the battle, it is appropriate to differentiate the period up to 16 May from the later stages. The advance and establishment of defensive lines on the River Dyle were planned beforehand, so that any failure at this stage would reflect particularly badly on the communications system of the British Army, but the retreat after 16 May was unplanned and increasingly chaotic. While the ability to perform well in retreat is a key function of an army and its communications system, the unexpected speed of events made an efficient performance difficult. But despite this, there were many communications successes as well as failures. Above all, the failures that did occur were as a result of, rather than a cause of, the defeat that was inflicted on the BEF.

The greatest source of evidence for this analysis are the daily war diaries kept by every formation and unit so that the Army would be able to learn from its experiences. Those for May 1940 were mostly destroyed prior to evacuation from Dunkirk, but many were reconstructed shortly afterwards as part of the effort to understand and draw lessons from what had happened. This cannot have been an easy task, given the speed of events. Indeed, even keeping a current record was difficult, as Lieutenant General Brooke noted in his personal diary, 'I . . . can hardly remember what happened yesterday. The hours are so crowded and follow so fast on each other that life becomes a blur and fails to cut a groove in our memory'.[33] Details of orders given and exact timings of messages despatched and received have been almost entirely lost. In five formations – I and II Corps and 2, 4 and 48 Divisions – it has been possible to look at the diaries both of the Signals unit and those of their 'clients', the General Staff (GS). With one exception, the same general picture emerges from both sources, but whereas GS diaries were inclined to mention problems, but to be silent about communications when there was no problem, Signals diaries tended to focus on how difficulties were overcome, and to mention periods when everything was working correctly. For example, the GS diary of 48 Division stated that there was no wireless communication on May 25, but did not refer to communications on 26, whereas the Signals diary did not mention the problem on 25, but stated that W/T communications were established to 144 and 145 Brigades on 26th (implying that communications had not been working immediately beforehand).[34] These are entirely understandable human tendencies that need to be carefully considered when trying to arrive at an accurate overall judgement.

The diaries of I Corps show a more serious discrepancy. That of Signals scarcely mentioned any problem in the whole period, whereas the GS diary contains an account of events between 10 and 17 May that is vociferous in its criticism of communications. A possible reason for the disparity is the fact that the CSO of I Corps had not returned from leave at the start of the action, and may therefore have been unaware of the early problems. Interestingly, a different author took over the account of events for the GS diary on 18 May, and proceeded to make no reference to communications, good or bad, until 28 May, when all were agreed that the chaos caused by the retreat into the Dunkirk perimeter made communications extremely difficult. The interpretation of the change in emphasis between the two staff officers is uncertain – it could be that the earlier problems were solved or that the second author was less interested in communications or more accepting of problems.[35] What is clear is that the only way to reach reliable conclusions about the ways in which communications determined the outcome of operations is to examine both kinds of war diary, where it is possible to do so.

Reconnaissance

The organization of reconnaissance (whose function was to provide the Observation stage of the OODA loop) in the BEF impacted on communications and, as it turned out, on its effectiveness as a fighting force. It had been decided before the beginning of active operations to remove reconnaissance units from individual divisions. At the beginning of 1940, some divisions included light armoured cavalry regiments for reconnaissance purposes, but all except one of these (2 Division's 4/7 Dragoon Guards) were withdrawn during March and April and grouped together in 1 and 2 Light Armoured Reconnaissance Brigades, under the control of GHQ. As a result, divisions had no integral recce unit during the fighting in May, conflicting with the idea of a division being a complete fighting formation in itself. It meant that the observation element of the OODA command structure of the division was removed and divisions were consequently dependent on relevant reconnaissance observations being passed on to them by GHQ, placing an additional burden both on the information processing sections of GHQ, and on GHQ, corps and divisional communications. The new arrangements were a failure. The success during training exercises after Dunkirk of those divisions that improvized their own recce units, together with a recommendation of the Bartholomew Committee, led to the formation of the Reconnaissance Corps in 1941.[36]

The 12 Lancers had had considerable fighting experience during its imperial policing activities, had been equipped with wireless since 1930 and had had ten years of experience of controlling operations by this means. It was sent to France on 16 October 1939, operating in armoured cars ahead of the advance into Belgium, with its main mission being to provide GHQ with information on enemy formations and aircraft, the movement of Allied troops and refugees and topographical detail as required. During the battle, it was also used in a mobile fighting capacity. Because of its roving nature, there was no question but that its main means of communication should be by wireless. It was equipped with long-range No. 3 sets, carried on lorries because of their bulk, and No. 11 sets in all its armoured cars. It also carried telephone equipment and a flock of pigeons. The pigeons' home loft was in a house in Lille, where a telephone was installed to pass on any messages received in directly to GHQ. A detachment of 12 Lancers had been trained to cooperate with the RAF in the hope that the latter would be able to help discover where the main German thrust would come. But, in the words of the writer of the war diary, 'no air information whatever was at any time received, either by this means or from the formations we served'.[37]

The 12 Lancers communications worked satisfactorily throughout the conflict, and there was sufficient duplication to overcome any setback. According to the war diary, 'wireless worked without interruption throughout the operations' and 'through the excellence of the wireless which gave perfect communication on the whole front of the regiment, it was possible to bring fire on all tanks seen and to keep all troops advised of the enemy's movements'.[38] For this reason, the pigeons were not needed and were all finally released on 18 May. The good performance was not achieved without some difficulties – a No. 3 set lorry was driven into a bomb crater from which it could not be extracted, but a replacement was available, and on another occasion, two bullets passed through the set in an armoured car, and snapped off the aerial, but still did not put it out of action. Wireless was not confined to the fighting units, but extended to the transport sections as well, which were able to remain in close contact with headquarters throughout.[39] Telephone was sometimes used in combination with wireless, for example, on 22 May when Lieutenant Butler passed the location of enemy lorries by telephone to the CO, who transmitted them by wireless to RSM Fox, enabling him to move to a position from which he could destroy them by fire from his Boyes rifle. Telephone was, however, criticized for being very slow and liable to many interruptions. No references to cipher or code appear in the diaries, so it is not clear to what extent these were used without a problem, or not used.

The 1 Light Armoured Reconnaissance Brigade, which operated using light tanks, had a very different experience. The brigade was formed on 30 March 1940, and in April, was suffering from shortages because its equipment had been diverted to other regiments. At the outbreak of active operations on 10 May, those in the brigade felt that owing to their lack of training, they would only be called upon as a last resort. Nevertheless, they were warned that they might be required at short notice. By 16 May, the brigade was on 30 minutes' notice to move, but as the war diary related, it had no workshop, no maintenance personnel and no means of communications other than DR and liaison officers.[40] Without better communications, it is hard to see how the brigade could have acted in any proper way in a reconnaissance role, or indeed functioned properly as a mobile force. This is illustrated by the fact that a DR had to be sent to a nearby division to bring over any message that might arrive by telephone. The inauspicious start was followed by a series of unfortunate incidents – on 18 May, three tanks were lost to British anti-tank guns; on 19 May, orders were received that were later discovered to be intended only for 12 Lancers; on 21 May, orders were sent via a GHQ motor contact officer, but he got lost; on 23 May, the commanding officer had to go personally to GHQ at 03:00 in the morning to obtain instruction. Eventually, all the vehicles were destroyed and the men were evacuated from Dunkirk.[41]

The Hopkinson Mission was part of 'Phantom', which was the code name of No. 3 British Air Mission, formed in Nov 1939. Its principal role was to furnish the commander of British Air Forces in France (BAFF) with ground information and to supply the same information to GHQ. This was the origin of the later 'Phantom', an information service for the Army, run by the Army. Intensive training was carried out in the static period, particularly in the transmission of information, and since by good fortune, as a report put it, the Hopkinson Mission was not under the jurisdiction of the BEF, the prevalent wireless silence in the static period could be ignored.[42] As with 12 Lancers, the Hopkinson Mission was well trained and maintained efficient communications during active operations according to its reports. 'Flight Lieutenant Zech [was] extraordinarily competent technically and linguistically (using wireless) in finding out from Belgians where to obtain lines and power. Bad operators would have halved the efficiency of the Mission. Had Hopkinson not had about 15 mobile wireless sets, [he] would not have been able to keep in contact with the many fronts about which he sent back news . . . The Type X cipher machine worked admirably save one short breakdown. Had a mechanical expert not been present this would have caused serious delay . . . Three DRs broke their legs, so it was good that we had 10 at the outset'. Not everything was perfect, however. It was felt that 'a more extensive training programme would have been useful [in the] writing of despatches, ciphering and transmission'. This implies that some problems did occur in these areas, but no details are available.[43]

There was thus a clear connection between effectiveness and the length of time recce units had been established and whether they were properly equipped. Within the objectives set for them, 12 Lancers and the Hopkinson Mission seem to have operated well, helped by an efficient communications system, based largely on wireless and well trained operators. By contrast, because of its recent formation and lack of communications and other equipment, 1 Light Armoured Reconnaissance Brigade was unprepared for action. The failure of its communications was, therefore, only to be expected.

But the key problem with all of these reconnaissance units was the level to which they reported – while information often seems to have been passed effectively to GHQ, lower formations received insufficient information. For example, Brooke was observed by GHQ armoured cars as he was travelling between his subordinates, but was never informed that this unit was nearby. He wrote later, 'considering that in the final stages GHQ were out of touch with the situation, I think the best plan would have been to have placed the Armoured Car Regiment directly under my orders at this period'.[44] This suggests that one of the most significant reasons for the slow speed with which the BEF could cycle through the OODA loop was not poor communications, but faulty organization. Divisions *could not* observe because they had no organic recce unit. In his evidence to the Bartholomew Committee after Dunkirk, Major General Mont-gomery stated that a divisional reconnaissance unit was clearly necessary, and the Bartholomew Report duly recommended that divisions should have their own reconnaissance and protective units.[45]

Communications at GHQ

Another problem affecting the efficacy of the BEF's communications was the organization of the GHQ itself. In common with other headquarters, GHQ was initially divided into rear and advanced echelons. However, Lord Gort decided that he needed to be nearer to corps headquarters than was possible with an organization as large as Advanced GHQ, in order to keep in touch with events. He therefore created an additional Command Post, a tactical headquarters comprising himself and a minimum staff, including a Signals section of some 20 men.[46] Although the creation of the Command Post was planned in advance, it caused the SO in C's staff to be split up, and placed an immense strain on Signals personnel.[47] The SO in C was, for the most part, at Advanced GHQ, where he could keep in touch with the main body of the BEF, while his GSO1, Lieutenant Colonel Wade, was at the Command Post, where operational plans were made. According to his biographer, Gort established the Command Post because as well as being commander-in-chief, he was the Army commander and, as such, needed to be near the action. Moreover, he was driven by his char-acter as a fighting soldier by temperament and training. Nonetheless, it was 'an administrative disaster'.[48] In subsequent theatres during the war, the roles of commander-in-chief and Army commander were separated, no doubt in recog-nition of the difficulties faced by Gort at this time.

Both Rear and Advanced GHQ were initially based near to one another at Arras. It had not been intended that they should be mobile, but they were forced to move after Arras became embroiled in the southern German advance. In the early stages of the conflict, Rear GHQ was primarily responsible for com-munication links with the L of C, the War Office in the UK, and the 1 and 7 French Armies, while Advanced GHQ linked with the Hopkinson Mission and Advanced III Corps HQ. The Command Post communicated with Advanced I and II Corps HQs, and with 12 Lancers. Although they had wireless back up, the dominant means of communication between the three parts of GHQ was cable and this meant that the Command Post was effectively tied to the underground international telephone cable, greatly restricting its freedom of movement. On 10 May, it moved into Belgium, but because of the need to stay near to the main telephone cable, it was located initially at Renaix between Lille and Brussels, neither near to main GHQ nor to the fighting troops – effectively the worst of both worlds. It then moved several times as the action unfolded.[49]

The dispersal of GHQ in three echelons caused great difficulties right from the start of active operations. On 15 May, a member of I Corps' staff found that 'lack of good communications with GHQ during the last few days made great difficulties . . . Hours were spent trying to get GHQ [by telephone]. GHQ also had three HQs, Advanced, Rear and Command Post. As often as not after a struggle of an hour or so, communications would be established only to find that the officer or branch required was at one of the other places. It was very exasperating'.[50] The Command Post and Advanced GHQ did not know the movements or intentions of Rear GHQ while the actions around Arras were taking place around 20 May. Difficulty was also caused by the rapid succession of verbal arrangements and counter-arrangements for operations, which were unconfirmed by operational orders. It was often impossible for the SO in C or his representative to know when conferences which he had to attend were being held.[51] When the international cable was bombed on 23 May, reliance had to be placed on DRs, a No. 3 wireless set, and less direct cable links.[52]

Although the corps blamed GHQ for their imperfect communications, there were faults on both sides. The SO in C told the Bartholomew enquiry after Dunkirk that while GHQ never had a complete breakdown of communications with any of the corps under command, there were certainly moments when 'we were not in touch with anybody'.[53] He attributed this, in part, to advanced corps headquarters not going to places where communications were arranged, or not keeping GHQ posted on their movements. He said that this habit started as early as 10–14 May, and persisted until the last days of the campaign. During the retreat, for example, one of the corps headquarters occupied three locations in a 24-hour period; it did not inform GHQ of its whereabouts and the principal means of locating corps headquarters at this stage was by personal recce by an officer of the SO in C's staff. But the fighting itself caused many of the problems, for example, on 17 May, line communications between the Command Post and I and II Corps were disrupted by bombing.[54]

Even when communications were working, the frequently perceived need to use cipher for security reasons led to GHQ cipher personnel being overwhelmed by the volume of traffic, and consequently too many operational messages failed to arrive in time.[55] In some cases, enciphered messages took as much as 36 hours to reach the recipient, and there could be a delay of 3–4 hours before even an 'immediate' message could be dealt with.[56] And the dispersed organization of GHQ meant that even after messages had been deciphered, the information did not necessarily reach the right person. Overall, these factors greatly reduced the tempo at which information cycled round GHQ's OODA loop.

But it was not just the pressure of fighting and ignorance of the location of headquarters that led to problems, since communications with GHQ appear to have been unsatisfactory from the start. The GS Diary of I Corps stated as early as 11 May, during the advance, that its arrangements for communications with GHQ and divisions were 'hopeless. We were depending on civil lines . . . The Corps was extended over 70 miles on three routes and it simply took hours to get through. I spoke to GHQ about the lack of communications being provided by them, as most of our signals resources were being used to get communications going backwards [to GHQ] instead of forwards [to divisions] . . . '.[57] On 12 May, I Corps reported that telephoning to GHQ remained 'hopeless' and continued to be so on 15 May. Delays to GHQ 'may have been due to the exchanges being overworked by civil traffic, refugees making arrangements etc., but we all suspected sabotage. Conversations were cut at critical points time after time. It seemed as though the Bosche were letting us use the lines just enough to make us feel that they could be relied upon and so not force us to alternative lines or to move GHQ up closer, and yet they meant no vital messages to get through'.[58] These suspicions cannot be substantiated and it has been suggested that the actual influence of sabotage by any 'Fifth Column' was probably insignificant. But the British Army suffered considerable damage from the psychological effect and paranoia induced by the phantom menace.[59] During this period, no mention of wireless communications to GHQ was made in the I Corps war diary, even though the communications diagram of GHQ shows No. 3 set links to I Corps. This probably reflects the status of wireless as a backup at this stage, rather than as a primary means of communication.[60]

Towards the end of the retreat, as the BEF converged on Dunkirk, GHQ Signals offices continually moved along with the rest of the Army. By this time, long-range line communication was generally difficult because many existing telephone lines had been cut by bombing, but it was re-established within headquarters when they were stationary for long enough for the laying of army cables to be worthwhile. Wireless was difficult to use while on the move, so most messages were passed by DR, but as soon as movement stopped, it was possible to attempt wireless communications with some success. For example, on 27 May, the Command Post Signals office had to close down its wireless at 13:00 hours when it was forced to move by shellfire, but it re-opened at 15:15, establishing W/T communications with I and II Corps, and with the War Office. However, it was unable to raise III Corps and the Needham Mission.[61]

Movements and organizational changes occurred rapidly as the action progressed, and the communication circuits constantly changed to match new circumstances. A particular challenge was the creation of ad-hoc forces, such as the Needham Mission referred to above, outside the normal army organization. Sometimes, these communicated with the Command Post, and at other times, with Advanced GHQ. While there were doubtless operational reasons for these variations, it is hard to track the changes even in retrospect, and it must have been extremely confusing in the middle of a fighting retreat.[62]

There is no doubt that the basic organization of GHQ was faulty and it is clear that the dispersal of Advanced GHQ into two parts was a major reason for poor communications between elements of the command structure. This, in turn, led to reconnaissance information not being passed on from the recipient in GHQ to the formations that needed to know it, and to inappropriate orders being issued by GHQ because they lacked knowledge of the forward situation. In the terminology of the OODA loop, the problems impaired the ability of Gort and his staff to orientate themselves correctly to the changing situation.

Communications between and within formations

Divisional communications during the advance into Belgium used a mixture of civil telephones and DRs, backed up by wireless, and were generally satisfactory at this stage. Once fighting began, the vulnerability of cable to bombing, shellfire and sabotage became increasingly apparent and there was a constant battle to keep lines open. The situation became even more difficult during the retreat into France and up to Dunkirk, but by using the limited number of wireless sets that was available and by running lines out as soon as they came to a halt, Signals were often able to keep a level of communications open. There is no evidence that TA communications were consistently worse than those of the regular Army, or that those on the unplanned south-western front were particularly worse than those of eastern-facing formations. The overall communications situation was unsatisfactory, and deteriorated as the retreat became increasingly chaotic prior to the evacuation from Dunkirk, but it would be an exaggeration to describe it as disastrous. This account begins by looking in some detail at what happened in I Corps, a pattern that broadly repeated itself in the other corps.

The three divisions initially under the command of I Corps were the regular 1, 2 and the Territorial 48. Lieutenant Colonel Nalder, the OC of 1 Division Signals and future historian of the Royal Signals, wrote a very detailed account of events immediately after returning to the UK.[63] The 1 Division arrived at its location on the River Dyle rapidly, on 10 May, and set up its communications network according to plan, passing new telephone numbers forward by DR and back by telephone. The only problem reported at this stage was a shortage of cable. During the occupation of the Dyle, daily traffic handled by the signals centre was about 600 messages, half by Fullerphone, and the rest by DR. During 1 Division's progressive withdrawal to the River Senne, the River Dendre, the River Escaut and to the frontier, wireless communications were maintained, while line took longer to establish. DRs were extensively used. Some difficulty was experienced with wirelesses transmitting on the wrong frequency because wave meters had lost their calibration in the frequent moves, but this was overcome by a system of test broadcasts using special call signs at pre-arranged times. The 1 Division was involved in the occupation of the Dunkirk perimeter, necessitating a number of ad-hoc arrangements with salvaged equipment, and was finally evacuated on 2 June.[64]

In general, communications in 2 Division were satisfactory in the advance and during the occupation of the Dyle.[65] But cable communications began to fail as soon as the division made contact with the enemy on 14–15 May, with lines being continually cut by bombing, shelling and (or so the division believed) by Fifth Column activity.[66] After the failure of line, wireless came into its own and was used continuously – both No. 9 and No. 11 sets were reported to have worked extremely well. The withdrawal of 2 Division was marked by the same ad-hoc signalling arrangements already noted – when there was a sufficiently long halt, lines were laid, but difficulties were experienced in repairing breaks caused by enemy action. DRs and wireless were employed when lines were out of action. By 24 May, the scarcity of cable and the recognition that operations could no longer be regarded as static meant that wireless became the norm. Wireless worked successfully between 25 and 28 May, but on 29, the sets were smashed to prevent them from falling into enemy hands. Figure 3.1 shows selected verbatim extracts from the war diary kept by Divisional Signals, which give a good idea of the challenges faced by Signals over the period.[67]

After their return to the UK, a detailed war diary was written by 2 Division Signals and this illustrates their movements and activities during the period of active operations. It should be remembered that their judgements on how well communications worked may not necessarily be unbiased.

10 May. Traffic Control Points spaced about 20 miles apart were employed during the advance into Belgium. These used civilian telephone facilities and DRs as a primary means of communication, but each also had a No. 11 (HP) set. The systems were reported to have worked well.

11–12 May. Arrival on River Dyle. Laying of lines within HQ, rearwards to I Corps and forwards to brigades. Wireless was also in use.

13 May. First report of lines being cut by 5 Column. Main Division HQ moved, necessitating extension of lines, all of which were working smoothly.

14 May. First contact with the enemy. Lines to I Corps set alight and destroyed by 5 Column or enemy parachutists.

15 May. Lines laid alongside roads by lorries with no cross-country ability were continually cut by air action, shelling and vehicles while those laid across country usually survived. Wireless consequently came into its own and worked extremely well.

16 May. Division forced to withdraw at very short notice by the serious situation on the right flank. Main Signal office re-established south of Brussels. Lines connected with civilian telephone exchange. Meanwhile, the Divisional commander, Major-General Lloyd, kept in touch using a mobile No. 9 set. In the afternoon, Lloyd collapsed and was replaced temporarily by Brigadier Davidson and then on 19 May by Brigadier Irwin. Having three Divisional commanders within a few days proved somewhat difficult for Signals since they all had very definite, but different, views on communications. During this retirement there was no attempt to control traffic, causing insoluble jams. Fortunately the enemy left them alone at this point. DRs and wireless were the only means of communication, but they worked well.

17 May. Another move ordered, this time by side roads to avoid traffic jams.

18 May. A comparatively quiet day, allowing cable for voice and Morse to be laid to 4 and 5 Infantry Brigades. Tanks of 4/7 Dragoon Guards placed in front of the River Dendre to give warning of enemy approach, communicating to Division HQ on No. 9 sets, with the brigades listening in to get early information. 4/7 Dragoon Guards came into contact with the enemy at 18.00 hours.

19 May. The Division therefore moved off at 01.00 hours. The journey was a nightmare. There was no road discipline and the movement was a shambles. It was fortunate that the enemy did not attack.

Figure 3.1 The experience of 2 Divisional Signals, 10 May–2 June 1940.

20 May. By working unremittingly for 24 hours, line communications were completed, but enemy action caused many breaks. Rear HQ was some 12 miles distant and cable was too scarce and valuable to attempt to lay a line of this length. Consequently communication with Main HQ was by DR only. Supplies of cable were drawn from the I Corps dump, preventing the cable situation from becoming acute. W/T established on the No. 9 set group.

21–22 May. Some 60 miles of cable were laid in this position, but the Division was subjected to heavy artillery fire, which cut cables continually. Line parties made many trips to keep lines through but eventually their two lorries were destroyed and it became impossible to maintain the lines. In the afternoon of 22 May the Division was ordered to retreat again and much valuable cable had to be abandoned.

23 May. The Division had now returned as far as their original positions on the Franco-Belgian frontier. It was possible to use some of the original buried cable system that had been established during the phoney war. The Division's infantry brigades were using W/T and DRs for communications but the Royal Artillery sections laid lines to their batteries. The Division was forced to move again since the German thrust to the south had nearly reached the sea.

24 May. At Neuve Chapelle, with a frontage of 21 miles. This largely precluded the laying of cable and this, together with the fluid nature of the situation, meant that communication was by DR and wireless.

25–26 May. W/T was most successful. Although line parties worked unceasingly, line was never a sure means of communication at this point.

27 May. Still impossible to keep lines through but No. 9 sets worked perfectly with the Divisional commander able to keep in touch by speech with his infantry brigadiers. Information received from battalions that their HQs were surrounded and that escape was impossible by daylight. The No. 11 sets maintained communications but eventually, one by one they failed to answer calls from brigade.

28 May. Retreating towards Dunkirk. Orders were issued by DR but it was very doubtful if they got through as by this time the Division was hopelessly broken up and mixed. However, the No. 9 set with Divisional HQ maintained communications to the three infantry brigades throughout.

29 May. Wireless sets and vehicles were smashed to prevent them being captured. Some sets were salvaged once in Dunkirk and communications re-established to some extent.

30 May–2 June. Wireless communications remained through until evacuation on 2 June, although batteries were running low.

Figure 3.1 (Continued) The experience of 2 Divisional Signals, 10 May–2 June 1940.

Given their lesser experience, it might be imagined that the TA division in I Corps would have had worse communications than the regular divisions. But there is no evidence for this since 48 Division's account accords with that of 1 and 2 Divisions. During the retreat, every use was made of W/T, which was variously described as 'working magnificently', 'most satisfactory', 'working continuously and efficiently' right up to 30 May, when the sets were destroyed and the Division was evacuated.[68]

The experience of II Corps and its divisions shows a similar picture to I Corps. The war diary reported that 'II Corps HQ moved twelve times and on many occasions was split. This made command very difficult and normal communications impossible. The difficulty was largely overcome, however, by means of LOs'.[69] 'II Corps pretty well maintained communications with divisions throughout. There were some hiccoughs. It was possible to get orders through by some means or other'.[70] In fact, during the retreat, the commander of II Corps, Lieutenant General Brooke, acted as his own LO, travelling personally between divisional and brigade headquarters at considerable risk to himself, even though his communications seemed to work sufficiently to confirm his orders in writing 'whenever possible' when he returned to base later. As his personal diaries reveal, Brooke travelled continuously to meet other commanders, right from the start of active operations, seemingly preferring personal contact to the exchange of telephone calls or messages. But this method must have left him out of touch for long periods since there is no evidence that he travelled with a wireless operator, and it must also have been much more time-consuming as well as more dangerous. He presumably felt that the improved exchange of knowledge thereby obtained outweighed the disadvantages. Brooke later wrote that he also regarded travelling as a 'personal reconnaissance', made necessary by the lack of mobile troops directly under his command.[71]

As was the case with GHQ, cipher caused delays at corps headquarters, to the extent that some relaxation in security became essential. A signalman at II Corps headquarters later wrote:

> Wireless was slow because there was a two hour delay through the cipher office and the teleprinter to GHQ broke down – as usual there were no spare parts. We started sending "phonograms" over the telephone lines by reading out groups of cipher numbers. Very tedious and time consuming. CSO agreed innocuous signals could be sent in plain language, and soon this extended for some messages to be transmitted in clear by wireless.[72]

In 3 Division, there was particular emphasis on cable and LO rather than wireless for security reasons, and indeed complete wireless silence was ordered on 20 May, with staff ordered to withdraw sets from the infantry brigades 'to make sure'.[73] This decision presumably reflected the concerns of the GOC (Major General Montgomery), later expressed to the Bartholomew Committee, that German DF would use wireless transmissions to get an accurate fix on the Division's location. Perhaps as a corollary, 3 Division frequently reported shortages of cable and interference on civil telephone lines. Wireless was still silent on 22 May, but was operating again on 27 May, though 'little used'. During the 'manoeuvre that saved the field force' that night, in which 3 Division moved to cover the gap caused by the withdrawal of the Belgian Army, the Signals diary stated that because the range was too great for W/T and the movement too rapid for lines to be used, DRs once more provided the only real link.[74]

It is clear that infantry formation headquarters had problems in communicating on the move at this time. It had been intended that they would be mainly reliant on line, but this was impossible when moving, and even wireless was difficult with contemporary technology. As Signalman Vollans, who was based at a brigade HQ, explained:

> It was never easy to maintain regular contact with out-stations when a group was on the move. In the jolting and vibration of a speeding vehicle accurate adjustment of the dial readings was a problem. Signals could be weak or distorted, and call signs missed because of interference.[75]

Additionally, the No. 3 set with which headquarters mostly communicated with one another had a greatly reduced range on the move while using a roof aerial.[76] Signals offices, therefore, required stability to function efficiently even by wireless, and it is scarcely surprising that in a situation when all the communicating parties were continuously moving, periods of non-contact occurred. Headquarters communications systems in general, and particularly those of GHQ, were designed primarily for a static situation, so that they struggled in the fluid fighting retreat. This does not, however, mean that the systems never worked; as soon as Signals offices were stationary, they rushed line parties out and set up longer aerials to increase the efficiency of their wireless sets. It took time for connections to be made (between one and three hours appears typical), but after that, the offices were 'open for business'. But because of bombing and shelling, maintenance of line communications was a constant struggle even when static.[77] Cut cables sometimes prevented supporting artillery from responding effectively to calls for help from the infantry, a problem exacerbated when wireless links proved unreliable due to lack of practice in the Phoney War or the inadequate range of wireless sets.[78] There was a shortage of DRs and they faced considerable problems – in particular, the blocking of roads by refugees and inaccurate maps made finding anyone extremely difficult.[79] However, communications did not collapse nor does it appear that wireless was 'useless' – a more temperate judgement is required.

OOD → A: Delivery of Orders

It is impossible to make an accurate assessment from surviving records of the proportion of orders that succeeded in reaching their destinations in the final phase of the OOD → A loop. Failure was clearly prevalent and a number of examples are given in this section, but as already explained, this does not imply that failure was the norm. Battalion orders often failed to get through because lines had been cut. For example, on 22 May, the headquarters of the 5 Battalion Northamptonshire Regiment had no means of passing the order to withdraw to its companies from their positions on the Escaut, though they eventually withdrew of their own accord.[80] Similarly, on 16 May, No. 7 Platoon of the 7 Battalion Royal Norfolk Regiment received no orders to withdraw until an LO eventually got through several hours later.[81] The failure of DRs to deliver their messages was a frequent cause of difficulty. For example, on 28 May, the 2 Battalion Northamptonshire Regiment sent two DRs to 11 Brigade headquarters to warn them to withdraw, but they both failed to reach their destination; in the end, an LO got through in a Bren Gun Carrier. Messengers could also be far too slow – No. 3 Company 1 Battalion Grenadier Guards were overwhelmed on 20 May when its mortar cover ceased firing too early, and it had no rapid means of communication with its artillery to instruct them to continue firing.[82] The lack of wireless links between battalion and company HQs made it very difficult for battalion commanders to understand the situation when lines were broken, and it was therefore impossible for them to exercise effective control. The predicament of the 1st Battalion Coldstream Guards on 21 May on the Escaut provides a good example of this – the situation was so vague that they had no idea about the best action to take. The visiting brigade commander was equally in the dark and left it to the discretion of the battalion CO to choose a means of restoring the position.[83] The use of Verey lights was one way of communicating rapidly, providing the form of the signal had been agreed in advance. Even then, problems could occur, as for example, when the enemy by chance used the same signal (two green Verey lights), causing a platoon to withdraw erroneously.[84]

Problems were not confined to lower commands. The GOC of 4 Division was unable to communicate with his rear guard on 17 May, when the DR failed to reach them.[85] Also on 17 May, three copies of an order from I Corps to 5 Division were sent, two by separate DRs and one by a Motor Contact Officer. None of them reached the division before it moved.[86] Again on 17 May, I Corps sent a DR to II Corps, but the DR lost his way and was seriously delayed, rendering the information out of date. It took the sending of two liaison officers before the CO could clarify the situation. Direct contact between the corps was not re-established until the following day, and then, it was by telephone rather than wireless. On 26 May, Brooke was asked by the commander of I Corps Heavy Artillery 'whether I should like the support of Corps artillery. I thought at first he was joking and asked him whether I Corps had no use for his services. He informed me that apparently not since he was receiving no orders from them.'[87]

The three most common comments on the communication of orders that are contained in regimental histories and war diaries are the failure of lines because they were cut by shellfire and bombing, the failure of DRs to get through, but paradoxically, the success rather than the failure of wireless communications (although failures are, of course, also reported). This could be an indication of the relative reliability of the three main methods of communication, but it is more likely to be a product of the expectations that existed. In the Phoney War, communications were primarily by line and messenger, both of which were reliable under quieter circumstances. When these methods broke down in active warfare, it was a shock, and therefore noteworthy. Conversely, wireless was little used in the Phoney War; so the fact that it could continue working when the other methods failed came as a pleasant surprise, and was therefore remarked upon.

The BEF was sent to France in 1939 to conduct a static defensive battle, in which infantry communications were primarily based on line down to battalion headquarters and messengers below that. Wireless backup was provided for the infantry, but there were insufficient sets to take the place of line during mobile operations. Contrary to the assertions by some historians, considerable wireless training did, in fact, take place during the Phoney War, even though the number of sets was too small and there were restrictions on their usage. The concerns about security and the imposition of wireless silence on some occasions were very much part of British doctrine and were not imposed by the French. Moreover, subsequent highly critical accounts of the performance of communications during the battle itself have been found to be unjustified. Certainly, breakdowns occurred on many occasions during the retreat towards Dunkirk, but communications often worked satisfactorily as well. Given the chaos, it is not surprising that problems occurred, and it has been concluded that most of the problems in signalling were as a result of the defeat of the British Army, and not a cause of the defeat.

4

1940–43: Home Forces: The Army in the UK

Following its defeat in France, the British Army was primarily involved in one active theatre in Europe and Africa – the Western Desert – where a series of battles were fought by Eighth Army against the Italians and the Germans, culminating in the decisive victory at Alamein in November 1942. But also of great importance was the build-up and training of the forces at home, which grew from the elements of the BEF that were evacuated from Dunkirk to a greatly expanded UK-based Army. From these forces were formed the First Army, which invaded Tunisia in late 1942 and the 21 Army Group that invaded North-West Europe in 1944. The development of communications systems in the Western Desert and in the Home Forces proceeded in parallel during 1940–43.

The aftermath of Dunkirk

After Dunkirk, it was recognized that the tempo of German mobile warfare was much faster than had been anticipated, and that British communications systems would therefore have to make much more extensive use of wireless in the future. This implied more and better equipment, more training in how and when to use it and continuous practice. Given the loss of equipment at Dunkirk and the expansion of the Army, Home Forces faced considerable problems in implementing the revised policy, particularly since they faced the threat of imminent invasion. Fortunately, no invasion took place, allowing time for a build-up of equipment and personnel, individual training and numerous unit and formation training exercises. Between 1940 and 1943, there were considerable advances in wireless technology, most notably the arrival of mobile sets for use below infantry battalion headquarters, equipment that had been completely absent in France and Flanders. There were also many other important developments in C3 systems, for example, to facilitate the transfer of units and formations from one command to another, for communications between artillery, armour and infantry, and for communications with the air force and navy. Many of the important changes involved developments of procedure and manning levels as much as of principle–doctrine in its widest sense encompassing the totality of the command and communications operating system. Perhaps it was because of a failure to recognize the importance of disseminating this broader understanding of communications doctrine that different practices arose between the Eighth Army and Home Forces.

Shortly after the BEF returned from Dunkirk, the Bartholomew Committee was formed to consider the lessons of the operations and to 'suggest modifications in organisations, training and equipment which should be made to meet the problems with which the British army will be faced in the event of an attempted invasion of this country'. Reports were submitted to the Bartholomew Committee by Royal Signals and others, and the Committee interviewed a large number of officers from the BEF.[1]

The main conclusion of the Bartholomew Committee was that future battles would be much more mobile than had been anticipated before 1940. It felt that the BEF 'did not make the best use of wireless', due to a lack of training and practice because of wireless restrictions in the static period, an ingrained habit of wireless silence for security reasons, and fear of DF. While it recognized that communications organization and equipment was inadequate at the Army and corps levels, 'in front of corps, the teaching of the Training Manuals and equipment is satisfactory for both mobile and static warfare'. The implication was that there was sufficient wireless equipment at divisional and lower levels, but that it was not used enough. As shown in the previous chapter, it would have been more accurate to say that the BEF had not been adequately equipped with wireless because of the doctrine laid down by the Jackson Committee in 1936, and that wireless restrictions had exacerbated the shortages of equipment.

The Bartholomew Committee recommended that greater use should be made of wireless at all times, that restrictions should be minimized and that once contact with the enemy had been made, wireless should be used to the maximum. The history of the BEF indicates that there were two barriers to making greater use of wireless, the first being the rule on wireless silence and the second being the shortage of sets and operators. The Bartholomew Committee gave firm recommendations on the former, but its attitude to the latter issue could be described as somewhat ostrich-like – the position of the Committee was that equipment was adequate, but insufficiently used, and increasing the supply was not recommended in the Bartholomew Report. Perhaps the Committee felt that since restoring equipment quantities even to their establishment levels was so problematic at this time, there was no point in demanding more, but indicating the desirable direction of travel might have been useful. Furthermore the performance of communications equipment was felt by the Committee to have been mainly satisfactory, which can hardly be said to be the case even if the technology for improvement was lacking at the time. Though it is possible to be critical of the Bartholomew findings in relation to communications, it must be said that the main thrust of the recommendations was undoubtedly correct, and moreover, the speed with which the committee came to conclusions was remarkable – for example, the Committee's agenda on 15 June 1940, only two weeks after the evacuation from Dunkirk, included three detailed proposals for the relaxation of restrictions on the use of wireless.[2]

Dealing with the security aspect of wireless, the SO in C of Home Forces, Brigadier Chenevix-Trench, maintained in his evidence to the Committee that fear of DF was much exaggerated, and that risks were negligible below corps headquarters. His rationale was that it was impossible for the enemy to know which wireless sets were worth trying to locate because there were so many, but his view was not shared by Major General Bernard Montgomery, who stated that German DF was very effective. The Committee recommended that precautions against enemy DF needed to be taken, including the use of remote control to operate sets positioned away from headquarters, periodic moves of sets, and the digging in of sets for protection. The other wireless security issue was interception. The greater the activity, the harder it was for the enemy to know what was worth trying to intercept, and this applied especially to R/T, which required an interpreter. For short-term tactical messages and forward of corps, cipher was too slow and unnecessary – a simple delaying code was sufficient. It was noted that the Germans had largely transmitted in clear, and that their messages had been intercepted without difficulty. The value of this information was disputed between different witnesses, however. To accompany the extended use of wireless, Chenevix-Trench recommended an enhanced system of policing wireless discipline to reduce risks, involving both the finding of illicit wireless sets and policing the operating methods of authorized sets.

While the Committee judged the Signals organization in front of corps to have been satisfactory, this was not the case behind corps. The Committee criticized the Signals organization of GHQ rather than Gort's decision to divide it into three sections, even though this had arguably caused many of the problems. Chenevix-Trench was not overtly made a scapegoat for the failures, but he was invalided out of the Army in early 1941 (he lived until 1974) and according to Lieutenant Colonel Wade, who had been his G1 in France, the news of this retirement was 'conveyed to him in an inexcusably tactless way'.[3] Perhaps this apportionment of blame stemmed from a reluctance to criticize Gort shortly after he had extricated the BEF from Dunkirk against all probability. Moreover, the Committee felt that Gort had been given an impossible task in being responsible for liaising with the War Office and allies as well as having executive command of the BEF, and perhaps thought that this was the reason why he had divided GHQ into three sections. It recommended that the executive function should, in future, be given to a mobile Army headquarters, under GHQ, while GHQ Signals, being tied to international cables, was not suitable for mobile operations. The establishment in the Middle East of a regional commander, who dealt with London, with Army commanders reporting to him, was in line with this recommendation. However, the splitting of headquarters remained a matter of debate. In North Africa, Italy and North-West Europe, Montgomery and others regularly established a tactical headquarters in much the same way as Gort, but by that time, resources had grown sufficiently to deal with the additional strain.

The Bartholomew Committee considered command and control doctrine. Verbal orders at conferences had been normal, and written confirmation had been a matter of opportunity – divisions had usually managed to confirm theirs, but brigades had seldom done so. The insistence of *FSR* that verbal orders must be confirmed in writing was re-affirmed and there was no recommended change to the style of command. In evidence to the Committee, the Quartermaster General of the BEF, Lieutenant General Lindsell, had advocated greater freedom for subordinate commanders to act on their own initiative, but he had been a lone voice in favour of a more flexible, mission command, style of system. The Committee discussed the problem of striking a happy mean between over-rigid control and 'passing the baby', and concluded that *FSR* was 'not far wrong'. They quoted the statement in *FSR* that 'the actual method of attaining the objective will be given in sufficient detail to ensure coordination of effort, but so as not to interfere with the initiative of subordinate commanders', and believed that this met Lindsell's criticisms. Unfortunately, the method of application of *FSR* took little account of the subtle wording, and restrictive control remained the dominant system in practice. The relative demands on communications of different command styles was not discussed, in particular, the fact that mission command would have eliminated the need for many of the messages passing between subordinates and their commanders was not mentioned. The limited carrying capacity of wireless had been recognized, but the emphasis was placed on reducing the length of orders, not on a system to reduce their numbers.

The main thrust of the Bartholomew recommendations on communications was immediately encapsulated in a Training Memorandum issued by the SO in C on 18 July 1940.[4] This emphasized the importance of wireless and stated that the policy of limiting wireless training for security reasons had not produced the required standard of operation. Future training would be unrestricted as regards time, and security would be preserved by employing as many stations as possible simultaneously, sending as much traffic as possible and practising various other means of deception to confuse enemy interception and DF services.

Much equipment had been lost and considerable casualties had occurred among signallers in France and Flanders. Although an additional 275,000 men joined the Army in June, July and August 1940, the demands for personnel from several other arms meant that Signals establishments in each formation were restricted, so that in order to allow increases in wireless personnel, reductions in line construction establishments had to be accepted, even though this prejudiced the satisfactory operation of line communications. If wireless was intended to replace line, this trade off was reasonable, but ever since the 1920s, Signals officers had believed that wireless and line were complementary modes of communication, each suited to different conditions. They believed that the organization should be able to provide adequate levels of both, when required. It was not until the beginning of 1943 that the cuts were restored and Signals establishments were brought up to an adequate level. In the meantime, there were substantial recruitment and training tasks to be carried out. The production of wireless sets could not be increased overnight because of limited skilled labour and manufacturing facilities in the British electronics industry. Lend-lease from the United States did not have an immediate impact on wireless supplies and it was not until 1942 that production facilities allowed a really substantial increase in sets, as shown in Table 4.1. The production of telephones is shown for comparison, indicating that line communications continued to be very important in spite of the cuts in the manpower dedicated to them. Meanwhile, the low production levels of wireless sets led to serious shortages.

Table 4.1 Production of war office signal equipment[5]

Year	Wireless sets	Telephones
1936–39	4,000	36,000
1940	20,000	58,000
1941	26,000	100,000
1942	101,000	113,000
1943	193,000	136,000
1944	144,000	111,000

Home Forces 1940–43

The Bartholomew Committee recommendations marked just the start of the development of C3 doctrine, which continued to evolve in the period up to the end of 1943. There were two particularly active phases. Immediately after Dunkirk, the Army concentrated on rebuilding and reorganizing its forces and preparing to counter-invasion, and it was not until 1941 that a revised communications doctrine was fully developed. Once equipment was built up during 1942, the revised doctrine could be tried out in practice and there was increasing feedback from active overseas theatres. Doctrine (more accurately, the version of doctrine propounded by the War Office, since it turned out that Eighth Army had gone its own way in some respects) underwent substantial revision during the first half of 1943. At the end of this process, comprehensive systems of line, wireless and messenger communications had been established, suited to different stages of mobile warfare, with appropriate variations to accommodate the special needs of infantry, artillery and armour. They had been tested in the many Home Forces training exercises that took place and were disseminated in a variety of War Office publications.

It had been decided early in the war that doctrine would be laid down in *Military Training Pamphlets* (*MTP*) that would be revised from time to time, not by renewing General Staff Manuals or *FSR*. Doctrine was also disseminated in other War Office publications – *Army Training Memoranda* (*ATM*), *Army Training Instruction Pamphlets* (*ATIP*), the *Field Service Pocketbook* (*FSP*), and in the case of communications specifically, by the SO in C's and other CSOs' training instructions. *Notes from Theatres of War* and *Current Reports from Overseas* served to share the lessons from actual experience in active theatres.

This section examines overall communications and security policy, followed by issues specific to and between the infantry, artillery and armour. Tracking the labyrinthine twists and turns of policy development over the period would be tedious for the reader and is not felt to be worthwhile; therefore, only the end result as it applied to Home Forces and First Army in early 1943 is described. In its overall attitude to wireless and line communications, Army doctrine effectively underwent a circular tour between 1935 and 1943. It started and ended by treating the two means on their merits, advocating one or the other or both, depending on the circumstances. The Jackson Committee's recommendations for the primacy of line communications in the infantry was an aberration, if an understandable one, given the circumstances of 1936.

Communications policy distinguished between three phases in battle, namely Offensive, Defence and Withdrawal, each of which were described in the *Military Training Pamphlets Numbers 2, 3 and 4* of 1943. Importantly, these integrated communications into the body of the text, whereas earlier publications had contained a Signals section as if it was peripheral to the main issues. In the Offensive phase, wireless should be regarded as the primary means throughout the division; cable should be used during preparatory stages, and taken as far forward as possible, but wireless should be the main means in the attack itself. In the Defence phase, the emphasis was also on wireless, which might become the principal means in the latter stages of the defensive battle, but a good line system should be provided whenever time permitted for traffic carrying and security reasons. In the Withdrawal phase, too much reliance should not be placed on line and wireless should be the main method. Aside from wireless and line, DRs and runners formed a very important part of the communications system and visual methods and pigeons were also held in reserve.

The role of carrier pigeons as a subsidiary means of communication through-out the war deserves some attention. They were not particularly reliable, but were a method of last resort, to be used when all else was unavailable, undesirable for security reasons or had failed. As far as the Army was con-cerned, a particular disadvantage of pigeons in mobile warfare was the need to establish lofts in fixed locations, connected to headquarters by telephone or wireless. To overcome this difficulty, mobile lofts were used, but they were far from ideal – it took two to three months to train the birds and they needed 48 hours to settle to a new locality when the mobile loft was moved. Home Forces training exercises did not show a positive picture – it was said that the speed of movement and state of training of birds in a mobile role detracted from their full value. In spite of this, a limited number of pigeons continued to be used until the end of the war. Thirty two pigeons were awarded the

Dickin Medal for outstanding service in the Second World War, generally for delivering messages when no other method was available. For example, two pigeons won the medal in September 1944, *William of Orange* for delivering a message during Operation MARKET GARDEN and *Scotch Lass* for bringing 38 microphotographs across the North Sea from Holland, despite injury. An example of when pigeons were used as the method of last resort occurred during the third attack on Cassino in March 1944. Two officers, each with a pigeon stuffed in his battledress, crawled at night through enemy lines to reach a unit that had been cut off and whose wireless batteries had run out. The plan was for a heavy artillery barrage to be laid all around the position, leaving a safe lane through which the troops could pass back to safety, but the unit needed to be informed of this. Once the officers had communicated the plan to the stranded men, the pigeons were released carrying a message that the plan had been understood and that the barrage could begin. After perching on a rock perilously close to enemy lines for some minutes, presumably to recover from their ordeal, the pigeons took off again and delivered the message successfully. The barrage commenced and the unit made good its escape.[6]

Overall communications doctrine was modified to meet the special circumstances of the infantry, artillery and armour, but common to all three arms was the Achilles heel of security. The insecurity of communications remained a problem throughout the war and could only be mitigated, but never totally solved. While precautions had to be taken with DRs (who could get lost or be captured or killed), and line (which could be overheard or tapped into), by far the biggest problem was with wireless.

As we have seen, the principal security precaution for wireless at the start of the war was wireless silence – in other words, not using it when in contact with the enemy. Secondary methods were cipher for W/T, restrictions and code for R/T, and periodic changes of frequency and call signs. By 1943, that order of priority was changed by moving wireless silence to third place rather than the first, and adding the rider that 'no fixed rules can be given since the importance of secrecy must be weighed against the need for control and information'. But the habit of imposing silence died hard. It caused problems, for example, in the major Home Forces training exercise SPARTAN in April 1943, after which the C-in-C wrote, 'wireless silence is a great handicap to communications . . . [it] should only be imposed as part of a general deception plan to cover strategic moves. Once contact has been gained, the imposition of silence during mobile operations will seldom be justified'.[7]

Great attention was paid to other means of ensuring that the enemy gained no useful information from wireless traffic. The periodic changing of frequencies and call signs improved security, but there was a real danger that these efforts to deceive the enemy might also result in confusion among British forces – for this reason, at a conference in December 1941, it was decided that changing call signs only and not frequencies would be acceptable, provided they were changed every 48 hours.[8] The British Army used both 'single' and 'double' call signs during the war. To explain, the stations in a wireless net needed call signs to identify themselves to the other stations. At the start of the war, double call signs were used in which the commander would identify himself when calling someone in his formation – 'Hello RNB, RNA calling', to which RNB would reply, 'Hello RNA, RNB answering'. A listening enemy would soon be able to form an idea of how many elements there were in the formation. Trials of a more secure single call sign system, already used by the Germans, were carried out by Home Forces in November 1940, and were introduced in the Western Desert on 15 October 1941. Under this system, a commander wishing to call a subordinate would use the subordinate's call sign but not his own – 'Hello RNB, RNB calling' to which RNB replied, 'Hello RNB, RNB answering'. If the subordinate wished to call the commander, he would say, 'Hello RNB, RNB calling' to which the commander would reply, 'Hello RNB, RNB answering'. Only when the commander wished to call the whole group did he use his own call sign. This system looks extraordinary at first glance, but it has to be remembered that each party on a given wireless net knew whether he was the commander or the subordinate, and so it did work. When properly used, it was effective in helping to maintain security, but it was initially confusing and was not always adhered to by inexperienced British formations.

Another undesirable side-effect of ensuring wireless security was the difficulty that formations experienced in contacting one another unless arrangements had been made in advance. Formations in the BEF had frequently been transferred from one higher command to another at short notice, but neither the higher nor the lower formations knew each other's call sign or frequency at that particular time. Similar problems existed in making contact with lateral formations (those on the same level in the command structure) when they had different higher commands. Even if the required information was obtained, an unexpected wireless station coming in on a net was treated as suspicious, probably an enemy intruder. One way of overcoming the problem was to send a DR to physically carry the information between formations, but if the distances were large or the enemy lay between them, other means had to be found. This gave rise to the 'watching wave' or 'guard set' procedure, whereby all formations knew a wavelength and code signs that they could employ when required. It was necessary for each formation to allocate an operator and set to listen continuously on the wavelength in case anyone tried to make contact.

Infantry

In the BEF, infantry communications had been more primitive than those of other arms, and consequently, they now showed the biggest changes. The Signals establishment in an infantry division rose by 51 per cent from 491 in 1938 to 743 in 1945, compared with a 20 per cent increase, from 629 to 753, in an armoured division.[9] The amount of wireless equipment was increased dramatically and the doctrine was changed accordingly.

Following the Bartholomew recommendations, a major reorganization of the infantry division was carried out in 1941. It was argued that centralized control of supporting arms would often be impossible in mobile operations, a belief implying that long distance communications could not work satisfactorily. Fighting should therefore be carried out by groups of all arms. A divisional reconnaissance regiment was established to take the place of the former divisional cavalry regiment, including scout platoons of armoured reconnaissance vehicles and mounted infantry. However, the implications for Signals of these changes were not made explicit, and indeed it was said that for Royal Signals, 'no tactical changes are involved'.[10]

At a conference in April 1941, Major General Phillips, who had taken over as SO in C from Chenevix-Trench, said that the reorganization 'had dismissed divisional signals in five words'. He went on to say that Divisional Signals must be able to provide communications in mobile operations, and that this implied more reliance on wireless and less on line. He had therefore applied for an increase in the establishment as well as for a greater number of more powerful sets.[11] A considerable increase in establishment numbers was granted (leaving Royal Signals with a manpower deficit compared with the new establishment of nearly 20,000 men at the end of the year).[12] Nevertheless, the requisite increase in the numbers of wireless operators was only possible by sacrificing a cable laying detachment. By August 1941, the SO in C believed that the increased wireless resources were now 'sufficient for Signals to be reasonably sure of meeting a tactical change' without a re-allocation of sets between sections. In the infantry brigade, it permitted permanent wireless groups, including links to all batteries and any part of the reconnaissance battalion operating in advance of the brigade. It took some time before all these sets were provided, but it was then found that equipment and manning levels were still inadequate. This unsatisfactory situation remained until the Godwin-Austen Committee of 1943, set up to review and standardize communication procedures after the Tunisian campaign, made recommendations to resolve it by a further increase in the Divisional Signals establishment.[13]

Infantry communication in the BEF below battalion headquarters had mainly been by orderly, because there were too few wireless sets and those that were available were, in any case, too heavy to be readily portable – two men could not carry the essential components of a No. 1 or No. 11 set for more than 1,000 yards. However, more easily portable sets were being developed – trials of the No. 8 set took place in the summer of 1939, leading to the development of the No. 18 set (a picture of which appears on the cover of this book).[14] The initial allocation was six No. 18 sets per battalion, but numbers continued to increase so that by 1944, 31 No. 38 sets (a development of the No. 18) were authorized for an infantry battalion.[15] Although considerable advances were made in infantry wireless, it was not as successful in overall terms as wireless in the Armoured Corps and artillery. One factor in this was that the infantry tended to show insufficient interest in wireless, leading 'inevitably to a lack of skill'.[16] This lack of interest may be attributed partly to the conservatism of infantry officers allied with their heritage of using line and runners. Another reason is that, as described in more detail in later chapters, infantry portable sets often failed for a variety of reasons, some technical and some due to poor operation. Lack of confidence led to lack of use, which in turn compounded the likelihood of failure.

Infantry and tanks needed to communicate with one another to co ordinate action, and to enable infantry to warn tanks of dangers such as concealed anti-tank guns and minefields which, because of their limited view, they might not see for themselves. Making a merit out of the absence of any other means, a training manual of 1939 maintained that simple visual signals were 'preferable to any device or apparatus', but because of his limited visibility, the system could only work when the tank commander made himself highly vulnerable by standing up in the turret.[17] By February 1940, tanks were being fitted with a bell for infantry to attract the attention of the occupants, still requiring the tank commander to stand up in the turret. Later on, telephones were installed on the outside of tanks to enable communication to take place when infantrymen were close enough, for example taking cover in a slit trench, sometimes a location of an infantry company headquarters.[18] These methods were obviously inadequate for longer distance inter-arm communications.

In the absence of a technological solution, emphasis was put on a 'common doctrine' so that armour and infantry front line troops would be able to anticipate the other's requirements without the need for conversation. This could only be attained by training together. In addition, the commander of the supporting tank battalion could accompany the infantry brigadier, so that orders could be co ordinated. Such an arrangement could also have the advantage that front line infantry could make use of the superior communications of the Royal Armoured Corps for transmitting information back to their commander. Although initially specified in detail, the methods by which infantry and tanks should work together were written in looser terms by May 1943, 'in spite of the natural desire to have every detail cut and dried for training purposes, the diverse conditions under which battles may be fought necessitate a wide variation in the exact methods to be employed'.[19] Another reason for being vague was that no satisfactory technological system existed, and as a result, major problems recurred with infantry and infantry–tank communications in Italy and North-West Europe later in the war.

Artillery

Great strides were made with the communications systems of artillery, starting from a manifestly inadequate level. Communication in artillery regiments at the beginning of the war used despatch riders. There were six wireless sets at headquarters, but within each battery, there was no wireless communication. Once the regiment had been deployed, a training document of April 1939 said that the commander could no longer exercise control except of his reserve, and that the main use of his wireless sets was to transmit additional reconnaissance information to higher command. It continued with rather vague advice, 'It may therefore be sound to establish observation posts with wireless communication and advantageous if such posts can be near selected battery or troop HQs. No definite system can be laid down and the commander must use his wireless sets as he thinks fit'.[20] This was a far cry from the highly organized and effective communications systems later achieved by Royal Artillery.

By April 1941, the issue of wireless sets had increased dramatically. In the new organization, each two-troop battery was to be equipped with seven No. 11 sets, three of which were long-range high-powered (HP) sets carried in armoured observation post (OP) vehicles, formalizing the suggestion made in 1939. To avoid placing too much reliance on telephone and line, artillery needed to train in using wireless more, especially W/T since R/T was more liable to jamming. Good wireless discipline was needed since there was unlikely to be more than one frequency allocated per battery.[21] The effect of efficient wireless in armoured OP vehicles was to increase the importance of directing fire by observation and to increase liaison between artillery and supported troops when not physically close. Armoured OPs could keep the advance under close observation and report back to the guns using wireless. In addition, a No. 18 set was added to each armoured OP so that it could communicate with the infantry net, which by October 1941, included sets at each battalion and company headquarters. In summary, the benefits of the system were that all OPs knew what was going on, fire plans could be put quickly into operation, small artillery fire plans could be largely controlled by observation and infantry had to deal with only one, control, OP.[22]

There were still limitations to the wireless resources of higher levels of command in the Royal Artillery. Those at a divisional level were insufficient in May 1941 to provide communications for the Commander Royal Artillery (CRA) during the approach march, but this was remedied when the Signals establishment was increased in August 1941 so that it was possible to provide the CRA with wireless communications at all times.[23] Even then, the normal scale of artillery communications imposed limitations, and additional resources sometimes had to be provided. As soon as it was clear that an attack would be mounted under corps control, it was essential that commanders made an additional allotment of communications resources (wireless sets and cables) to the artillery. Without this help, they 'would not be able to guarantee that switching of massed artillery fire that is proving of such decisive importance'.[24] By the end of the war, it was felt that the arrangements for wireless resources were sufficient for the CRA to control artillery under conditions of mobility and disrupted line communications.[25]

Armour

Because it had always been accepted that tank communications would primarily be R/T, there was no comparable change in communications doctrine in armoured forces to that in the infantry. But it was realized that line communications as well as wireless were needed, for use when formations were 'in harbour', in training and refitting areas, and when planning operations.[26] Wireless sets themselves were improved, with the No. 9 set being replaced from 1941 by the No. 19 set, which incorporated a 'B' short-range inter-tank set for use within squadrons as well as the normal 'A' set for communicating with higher command. Although wireless for all inter-tank communications was the objective, crews were still being trained in the use of flag systems in December 1941 in case wireless was not available or broke down.[27] The No. 19 set also included an intercom amplifier for communication between the tank crew. This represented a considerable advance over the primitive methods available in 1939 when 'the commander moved off by kicking the driver in the back, steered by prodding his shoulders, and halted by pulling his hair'.[28]

From 1941, each armoured divisional headquarters was supplied with an unarmoured Royal Signals lorry carrying a No. 12 set for communication with higher command over longer distances. The No. 12 set had a W/T range of 25 miles on the move and 60 miles when stationary, compared with 15 miles on the move for the No. 19 set. Headquarters also had sets that rebroadcast all traffic on the command set to receiving sets in the other armoured command vehicles, so that everyone immediately knew what was happening.[29]

The rear link at tank regimental headquarters communicated with brigade headquarters on the brigade net. Below that there were two options – either all other sets in the regiment could be on one regimental net, or separate frequencies could be allotted to each squadron, with the rear link tanks in each squadron linked to the regimental net. The former gave the commander direct and instant control over the whole regiment, but limited the use of wireless within squadrons and was more demanding of accurate netting. The latter gave squadron commanders individual control, made it easier to net, but increased the length of time to transmit orders from top to bottom.[30] Commanders remained free to choose between the two options; largely out of habit, the Royal Tank Regiment was accustomed to use the former, single frequency system, while most cavalry regiments used the other method.[31]

In the same way that infantry brigades were supported by Army tank battalions, armoured divisions came to include motor battalions consisting of vehicle-borne support troops providing reconnaissance and assaulting power. The reconnaissance element was provided by scout platoons. From small beginnings, these had expanded by the end of 1942 so that each platoon had a headquarters and three sections of armoured carriers. There was a wireless set at the platoon headquarters and in each section commander's carrier. The platoon commander controlled by wireless, DR or flag signals, while the section commander controlled by flag signals or personal visits. This limited the dispersion of carriers within a section to no more than 200 yards. The assaulting element was provided by motor platoons, the headquarters of each having a wireless set. By January 1944, the reconnaissance element had developed further into an effective force of four officers and some 60 other ranks.[32]

Signals training 1940–43

Home Forces were in a somewhat similar position to the BEF during the Phoney War of 1939–40, as they waited to be involved in real fighting. Some volunteered for or were sent abroad to active theatres, but the majority spent the best part of four years in training, leading to a feeling that the war was 'dragging on' and that they 'might never be needed'.[33] Meanwhile, training exercises practised troops for the eventual invasion of North-West Europe and helped to formulate the communications doctrine that has already been described. It was during these training exercises, especially in the larger scale ones, that Signals were able to assess the adequacy and distribution of their manning levels and the manner in which their systems operated in totality.

Between 1939 and 1942, Royal Signals expanded from 34,000 (of which only 10,000 were regular soldiers) to about 150,000 of all ranks. Some of this increase was due to the transfer of cipher duties from Intelligence to Signals, some to an increase in the Signals establishment of formations and the filling of those establishments (many units were below establishment in 1939) and some due to the increase in the number of formations. Only males were recruited initially, Royal Signals being classified as one of the fighting arms, but it became increasingly difficult to find the quality of male recruit needed for the more skilled jobs. In late 1941, for example, the SO in C complained that some of the recruits passed to Royal Signals by the COs of other units were medically unfit.[34] To alleviate the situation, women personnel from the Auxiliary Territorial Service (ATS) were recruited from 1943 to take over the major part of the War Office and Command systems in the UK, and were subsequently sent to work on L of C communications in active theatres. Eventually, there were some 165,000 of all ranks involved in signalling, of whom 15,000 were women.[35]

Royal Signals itself expanded as a proportion of the total Army from 4.1 per cent in September 1939 to 5.1 per cent in February 1945. In active theatres, the increase was more dramatic, rising from 3.2 per cent in the BEF to 6.2 per cent in the Middle East prior to Alamein. The proportion depended on the state of operations. It was higher when launching and establishing a force, then lower when operations began, rising again as the L of C increased, and rising considerably as fighting troops moved on, reducing the total number of troops, but leaving behind a considerable number of Royal Signals personnel to staff the semi-permanent communications.[36]

The great majority of men in Royal Signals were 'tradesmen', soldiers who were trained in particular technical skills, and who were paid up to 25 per cent more than ordinary soldiers. The more skilled trades such as lineman-mechanic were paid more than, for example, a lineman, who was only paid slightly more than a normal other-ranker. Table 4.2 shows which grade of tradesman was given to each function in Royal Signals, the number of such functions on the Home Forces establishment in October 1943, and whether there was a surplus or a deficit of men in each function. It was generally easier to fill less skilled occupations, such as driver mechanics, than more highly skilled trades, such as electricians, resulting in a surplus of the former but a deficit of the latter.

Different trades required different abilities, but in general, signallers needed to be more technically able than average soldiers. Ex-Post Office employees and those who had already been trained in the TA, Home Guard or Boys Brigade were often posted to Royal Signals because of their existing skills, and some account was taken of the preference that recruits expressed when they were asked what type of Army occupation they preferred. Motivations for wishing to become a tradesman in Signals included the extra pay that trade qualification brought and the use that their skill might have after the war. The Army believed that it could not obtain sufficient skilled labour for its needs, but a committee set up in 1941 under Sir William Beveridge countered, on the basis of interviews conducted with soldiers, that the Army did not make proper use of the talent that it already possessed. The committee said that if the Army carried out a proper assessment of its personnel and allocated men who already had relevant experience in civilian life to appropriate occupations, most of its shortages would be solved. This suggestion was

Table 4.2 Trades, Grades and numbers in Home Forces Royal Signals, October 1943[37]

Trade	Tradesman Grade (A highest, D lowest)	Home Forces Basic Ceiling	% Surplus (+) or Deficiency (−)
Operator Wireless and Line	B	10859	+2%
Lineman	C	9444	0%
Despatch Rider	D	4632	+3%
Operator Keyboard and Line	B	3365	−15%
Electrician	A	2621	−21%
Driver Mechanic	D	2299	+60%
Signalman Group D	D	1881	−4%
Instrument Mechanic	A	1875	−16%
Operator Special	B	1679	+1%
Operator Switchboard Telephone	D	1274	+8%
Clerk (General Duties)	C	1231	+11%
Vehicle Mechanic	A	1097	+24%
Lineman Mechanic	A	1093	−5%
Driver Operator*	C	655	*
Loftman (Pigeons)	D	590	−9%
Draughtsman	C	265	−2%
Storeman Technical*	C	85	*

* newly established trades at this time.

controversial to say the least, and the report was only published in February 1942, after Cabinet approval.[38] As a result, a General Service Selection Scheme was set up in 1942, whereby a new recruit was enlisted in the first instance into a General Service Corps, and only allocated to an occupation after his six weeks' basic training on the basis of various tests and an interview by a Personnel Selection Officer.[39]

Individual training

After their basic Army training, other ranks in the UK destined for the Royal Signals went to the Signal training centres, which were enlarged and increased in number from one to three at the outbreak of war. Even so, the UK centres were unable to cope with the number of recruits, some of whom were therefore sent to training centres in the Middle East and India. Depending on their trade, the training for other ranks in Signals lasted around six months during the war compared with nine months in the late 1930s.[40] Approximately 18 weeks of technical training were spent at a training centre, the exact time depending on whether the weekly course modules were passed first time or needed to be repeated. As men were trained, they were placed in 'holding battalions', where they were formed into sections of various types (light wireless sections, line construction sections, despatch rider sections, etc.) for later transfer to their operational units.[41]

The recollections of three soldiers serve to illustrate the selection and training of signalmen at this time.[42] At the start of Signalman Newland's basic training in 1943, he undertook a personal selection test consisting of written English and mathematics papers as well as practical tests to determine his level of manual dexterity and ability to solve practical problems. As a result of a good performance, he was selected to be posted to Royal Signals rather than to a general infantry unit, with his main training as an Electrician Signals taking place at Catterick. Signalman Smith also trained as a wireless operator at Catterick, which according to him, was 'a God forsaken place where apart from acres of Army huts and buildings, there was nothing but miles and miles of moors'. According to Newland (who was only aged 18 at the time, as his comments perhaps indicate), 'old regular officers . . . were frequently placed in charge of training units, being too old for active service. They sometimes ended up in overall charge of technical training, which they did not understand . . . These old officers often had little concept how to motivate us and did not seem to appreciate that we would never have volunteered for the peacetime army'. The administrative staff was generally made up of non-technical regular soldiers, but some of the NCO instructors were wartime conscripts, making use of their civilian knowledge.

Over a period of 16 weeks, Newland learnt to repair army radio transmitters and receivers, telephone equipment, including small exchanges and battery chargers. The course comprised weekly modules on different subjects, at the end of each of which there was a test that had to be passed before the following module was taken. Failure meant retaking the module and if it was still failed, it was likely that the recruit would be transferred to a less demanding (and less well paid) Signals trade. Newland failed one weekly module, on the No. 19 set, but passed it the next time and also just passed the overall examination at the end of the course. Smith's training as a wireless operator took about six months, a major task being the learning of the Morse code. Receiving Morse was taught using a Creed Automatic machine, which could be set to send at a given number of words per minute, increasing over the period of the course. Sending Morse was taught using inter connected Fullerphones. Signalman Metson undertook a driving and vehicle repair course in order to qualify as a driver mechanic in the Royal Signals.

The technical training of officers of Royal Signals, which lasted longer than that of any other officer group in the wartime Army, was carried out at the School of Signals. Those destined to become officers in Royal Signals needed to have above average technical ability as well as leadership skills. It seems likely that the class prejudices in selecting potential officers that operated in other parts of the Army also operated in Signals, and this may have resulted in some good officer material not being put forward by their commanding officers.[43] Those recommended for officer training undertook a 12-week initial technical course before being transferred to an Officer Cadet Training Unit for nine months, where they learnt more about technical matters and were taught general subjects, including tactics, arms training, law and organization.[44]

Officer and NCO signalling instructors for other arms, responsible for training regimental signallers, were trained at the School of Signals. The increasing demand for wireless training meant that a considerable amount of time had to be devoted to this subject while others on the syllabus had to be dropped. The peacetime regimental signalling instructors' course lasted for three months, but had to be reduced to two months during the war to speed up the training process.[45] Other ranks who volunteered as regimental signallers after their initial six weeks' training, were given a selection test. Provided they passed, they underwent a three months' signals course given by regimental instructors and were then tested by Royal Signals personnel. The failure rate was high (75 per cent in one account), but if they showed promise, they could retake the course. They then joined the regimental signals platoon.[46] The standard of operating in these platoons tended to be lower than in Royal Signals itself, for example, in the speed with which they could send Morse.[47] A lower level of signals training was given to some other men in the form of a short course.[48]

The predominance and wide dispersion of wireless in Royal Armoured Corps communications meant that there was a particularly large training task to be carried out there, both for new troops and for regiments that were converted from infantry to armour. In each converted regiment, four officers and 12 other ranks were selected as wireless instructors and underwent a 12-week course. Officers spent two weeks on wireless training while other ranks who were selected as tank wireless operators took a 10-week course, eight weeks spent on wireless and two on gunnery (wireless operators in tanks doubling as loaders).[49]

Unit and formation exercises

Although it would have been ideal for individual signallers' training to be perfected prior to their involvement in formation exercises, this was often not possible in practice, and these exercises frequently exposed individuals' inadequacies. The nature and objectives of unit and formation exercises were dependent to a considerable extent on the war situation. In the period following Dunkirk, unit and formation exercises were primarily 'anti-invasion' exercises, but as the threat of invasion diminished after Germany invaded Russia, normal field exercises became more common. In XII Corps for example, four full-scale exercises were planned for early 1941, two defensive and two practising the normal field role of corps and divisions.[50] As the prospect grew of offensive action in North Africa and France, exercises to practice amphibious operations took place. While smaller-scale exercises involved infantry, armour or artillery only, larger ones involved all three teeth arms together and the RAF.

Each formation took part in a very large number of training exercises of different scales and types. In 1942, for example, the CSO of II Corps listed 14 different exercises in his war diary. These ranged in scale from practising the movement of armoured vehicles, to practising divisional HQs and troops in the establishment of line and wireless communications, to large-scale complete army exercises.[51] A gradual improvement in signals performance occurred so that, by March 1943, the SO in C was able to congratulate Chief Signal Officers on the standard of communications and to write that while some imperfections remained, great progress had been made in the past year.[52] Training exercises showed where improvements were needed in the areas of command and communications equipment, operating systems, manning levels and individual signallers' performance. As these lessons were absorbed, and especially as more and better equipment became available, the performance of communications systems improved.

An overriding difficulty in all exercises was the challenge of making them realistic, and this applied to communications as much as to other aspects – for example, too much reliance might be placed on GPO telephone lines that would not be available in a real-life situation and on DRs who were more likely to get through to their destination in exercises than in real war.[53] Up to the end of 1941, at least, it was also vital not to neglect the operational imperatives of protecting the UK against invasion. Thus, some equipment could not be removed from permanent signal offices for the sake of exercises, and resources had to be borrowed from other formations, leading to an additional lack of realism.[54]

Immediately after Dunkirk, there was considerable variation in how much equipment was held by different formations, and in some cases, there was too little for them to train at all. It took a long time for the required amount of equipment to be supplied and shortages continued to be felt even after supplies of equipment had increased considerably. A continuing pattern right up to the end of the war was that as equipment levels increased, the possibilities for communication also rose, and the demands for equipment went up even more. Training exercises tested the quality as well as the quantity of equipment and the way the sets were operated, showing where equipment and practices needed improvement.[55]

The campaign in France and Flanders in 1940 and the experience of the high tempo of operations that the German Army was able to sustain did not persuade the British to abandon their commitment to restrictive command methods, but it did persuade them that their communications systems needed to be radically overhauled. By 1943, improvements had taken place in all aspects of communications and these enabled commanders to exert considerably better control over the mobile battle. Many of the lessons from training exercises contributed to the War Office documents that recorded the evolution of communications doctrine. There remained a constant need for practice and improvement in the work done by individual signallers and signalling units and in the performance of equipment. However, real operational experience in Tunisia exposed the shortages in manpower that had not been evident from training exercises at home as well as a disparity between the operating systems of Home Forces and those of Eighth Army that had been developed in the Western Desert.

The Western Desert 1939–42

Some deficiencies and potential improvements were evident from the performance of communications during the earliest operations in the Middle East, but there was little opportunity to implement any changes at this point. Thereafter, command and communications systems evolved in the light of each battle so that the systems in place at the victory of Second Alamein in November 1942 were on a completely different scale and far more elaborate than at the start of the process, and proved successful in that battle.

In the first half of 1939, because of the deteriorating political situation in the Middle East, its importance as a source of oil and its position on the route to India, a new Middle Eastern Command was established in Cairo, with General Wavell as Commander-in-Chief. He had responsibility not only for Egypt and the Western Desert, but for East Africa and the area north towards the Caucasus, a potential line of attack against the oil fields of Iraq. Only the events in the Western Desert, where the bulk of military activity in 1940–42 took place, are described here. The British added a mobile division, later renamed 7 Armoured Division, to their small Egyptian garrison in 1939 and brought in 4 Indian Infantry Division. 1940 saw the arrival of Australian and New Zealand divisions, and a South African division arrived in 1941, all remaining independent in terms of discipline, training and administration, and reporting to their own governments as well as to the British Commander-in-Chief. Since 'Free French' and Greek forces also arrived, the British Army became a very disparate force, with complicated additional command and control issues. It was not until the threat of an invasion of Great Britain had receded at the end of 1941 that substantial additional British troops were sent to the Western Desert.

The first major military operation, known as Operation COMPASS, December 1940–February 1941, was a comprehensive victory over the Italians. But as soon as the German Army arrived in North Africa to reinforce the Italians, the British suffered a series of reverses. They were beaten back from the advanced positions in Cyrenaica that they had achieved after COMPASS during March and April 1941, and the garrison at Tobruk was invested. The attempted counter-attacks, Operation BREVITY, in May 1941, and Operation BATTLEAXE, during June 1941, were failures. In November 1941, the British launched a major offensive, Operation CRUSADER, but although this may be classed as a British victory, it was less than decisive and was followed by a severe defeat at Gazala in May–June 1942. The subsequent rapid German advance was resisted at First Alamein in July 1942 and at Alam Halfa in August–September 1942. By this time, the British Army was at last receiving plentiful supplies of men and equipment while the Germans and Italians went short as a result of the war in Russia and because of the success of British naval and air attacks on their extended supply lines. The British victory at Second Alamein, November 1942, was decisive and led to the retreat of the Axis forces back towards Tunisia.

The British communications doctrine established in the straitened circumstances of the mid-1930s rightly gave primacy to wireless in armoured divisions, but allowed for little or no line in forward areas in active operations – it was, in fact, the converse of the doctrine for infantry. In the same way that the experience of France and Flanders in 1940 led to demands for a much greater provision of wireless within infantry divisions, the experience of desert warfare in 1941 taught that armoured divisions needed line as well as wireless for efficient and secure communications. In both cases, the end result was a doctrine encompassing both methods, so that one could take over from the other as circumstances dictated. Only when sufficient resources became available during 1942 did it become possible to provide equipment and trained personnel to make this doctrine a reality. These developments went together with an increasingly integrated use of armour, infantry and artillery, so that armoured divisions came to incorporate both armoured and mobile infantry brigades, forcing their signals doctrines to converge.

The vast distances in the Western Desert caused particular problems for communications. The range of telephone over field cable was sometimes insufficient to allow line communication even between static higher headquarters, necessitating the use of wireless with its attendant security issues and reception difficulties, or the use of messengers, which imposed delays. The range of wireless varied considerably, depending on circumstances – on the move, using ground wave, it was often insufficient, though it could be immense when stationary using sky wave. The skip distance could make it difficult to communicate at a range of 40–60 miles, distances that often needed to be covered. Moreover, the open desert terrain meant that single battles sometimes stretched over hundreds of square miles, so that armoured and highly mobile forces predominated and could exercise their ability to manoeuvre to the full. Command systems were challenged to keep pace with events, and the ability of commanders to receive and absorb information about what was happening and to react appropriately was stretched and often exceeded. As a result, Field Marshal Rommel, the German commander, wrote, 'Reconnaissance reports must reach the commander in the shortest possible time; he must take his decisions immediately and put them into effect as fast as he can. Speed of reaction decides the battle. Commanders of motorised forces must therefore operate as near as possible to their troops and must have the closest possible signal communication with them . . . I tried all possible methods of . . . communication with the fighting troops and concluded that a headquarters near the front . . . gives the best results'.[1] The British came to the same conclusions, though it took some time to implement them.

The failures and successes of communications influenced the overall performance of the British Army, but there were many other factors involved. This meant that success or partial success in battle could be achieved with imperfect communications, while failure could occur after communications systems had been improved. They were only the medium by which the different elements of the OODA loop were linked, and however good the connections might have been, they could not make up for basic faults in reconnaissance, the understanding that commanders obtained from that reconnaissance, their decision-making ability and the ability of the army to carry out their orders.

The build-up of forces in 1939 and 1940

As part of the establishment of Middle Eastern Command, Brigadier R. E. Barker was appointed SO in C at the end of 1939 with the task of building up a communications system to serve both the Army and RAF in the entire theatre (Palestine, Syria, Iraq and the Sudan as well as Egypt, and later, the Western Desert). He remained in overall charge of Signals until he was relieved by Brigadier W. R. C. Penney in November 1941.

The 7 Armoured Division (7AD) Signals started training in the Middle East in October 1939. By the end of 1939, its strength was 11 officers and 344 men, close to the desired peacetime manning levels (or 'establishment'), but some 270 short of its war establishment, the main shortfalls being in wireless and line operators, drivers and electricians. It took until November 1940, six months after the declaration of war by Italy, for its manpower to approach war strength, just in time for the launch of COMPASS.[2] Equipment was also built up over this period, though all signal equipment remained in short supply right through to mid-1942.[3] In March 1940, 7AD took part in a full-scale exercise with 4 Indian Division (4ID) during which 20 No. 9 sets, four No. 3 sets and DRs were used for communications, but no line was used at all. DRs were still operating on motorcycles at this point – it was later recognized that motorcycles were too difficult and dangerous to ride in desert sand, and they were largely replaced by four-wheeled vehicles. After Italy declared war in May, wireless silence was imposed in forward areas except where wireless was specifically authorized, necessitating the use of dummy aerials in training exercises. Lines were laid between units, but these required considerable maintenance – one line party, for example, took four days to repair a long link damaged by bombing.[4] Even the permanent poled line between 7AD and the headquarters of Western Desert Force (the forerunner of Eighth Army) was very inadequate at the end of June 1940, not just because of bombing, but because it could not cope with the signals traffic that was passing along it. Maintenance of sets, battery supply and charging caused difficulties – a continuing theme in desert warfare. Under active wartime conditions, 7AD's communications systems increased in complexity, in conjunction with increasing material and personnel resources.

During July 1940, Armoured Command Vehicles (ACVs) were introduced to 7AD, the headquarters consisting of a number of such vehicles housing the commander, his staff, Intelligence and Signals. These were effectively mobile offices all linked together by line when stationary, and by wireless when on the move. They enabled the headquarters to keep pace with the rest of the division in order to shorten communication links, while giving some protection from enemy fire. Early ACVs were found to be too cramped and were replaced in time by larger six-wheeled armoured lorries. The number of ACVs increased and they became increasingly sophisticated. In May 1942, for example, there were five ACVs at 7AD's advanced headquarters.[5]

By July 1940, the performance of Royal Signals' wireless and line operators in 7AD was judged to have improved with experience, but the SO in C was nevertheless critical – 'I find that [Royal Signals officers], particularly non-regular officers, are extremely vague as to what rules exist with regards to signal organisation, procedure and traffic . . . Officers must be conversant with *and understand FSR* Volume II Chapter II, the *FSP* Pamphlet 2 and *STM* I, V and All

Arms'. The regimental signallers in 7AD were too slow, unable to read more than eight words of Morse per minute compared with about 25 words per minute by a good Royal Signals operator.[6]

The Signals unit of 4ID arrived from Bombay in October 1939. By the end of October, it comprised 13 officers and 389 other ranks, divided equally between British and Indians. Many Indian other ranks carried out the same signals trades as their British counterparts (wireless and line operating, for example), but others had lower grade occupations, such as private servants and sweepers. Although some did not speak or understand English, all Indian signallers were taught the Roman alphabet and were able to send Morse messages that had been written out for them. There were occasions, however, for example at Gazala, when language caused problems between Indian and British formations. As in 7AD, 4ID's wireless and line equipment was built up, and though extensive cable networks were laid, there was more emphasis on wireless than there had been in an infantry division in the BEF in May 1940. This was necessary because of the distances involved in likely operations and the need to cooperate with the mobile 7AD. Manpower in 4ID Signals remained static until December 1940 and then increased to some 550 by June 1941.[7] As in 7AD, wireless silence was imposed during October and November 1940, and this meant that wireless operators were somewhat out of practice when COMPASS was launched in December. Nevertheless, compared with the situation before, the two divisions in the Western Desert Force had received a large amount of training prior to COMPASS, both individually and working with one another.

Italian forces launched an attack with seven divisions across the Egyptian frontier on 13 September. The British withdrew before them without becoming seriously engaged, and the Italians halted to build up a supply line some 70 miles into Egypt, forming a string of fortified encampments and remaining in this position until the start of COMPASS in December. The British intercepted Italian Morse and R/T signals, noting speech down phonetically. They also used wireless for intercepting the messages of their own patrols – for instance, by listening in to the internal frequency of 11 Hussars on 8 August, the headquarters of 7AD became aware of a large-scale movement of enemy aircraft and was able to arrange for the RAF to attack them, destroying 15 out of 27 aircraft.[8] The system by which headquarters listened to the internal wireless messages of forward British troops later became known as 'J', and this example shows that 'J' methods were used more than a year before the break out from Tobruk in November 1941, the origin of 'J' according to some official histories.[9] 'J' was effectively a means of speeding up the O → ODA link in the higher command system and obviated the need for reconnaissance troops to decide what was and was not worth reporting – commanders themselves could listen in to the observations and decide what was interesting. The Germans employed a similar system to listen to their own troops as well as to their opponents.

The defeat of the Italian Army, December 1940–February 1941

The Italians still showed no sign of resuming their offensive in early December 1940, and Wavell decided that the Western Desert Force had achieved a sufficient strength and level of training to carry out Operation COMPASS. Perhaps influenced by his experience as a Signals officer during the First World War, the Army commander, Lieutenant General Richard O'Connor, ensured that British security was tight – verbal rather than written orders were issued to a small number of senior officers, while more junior commanders and troops were kept in ignorance, and wireless silence was observed as the troops moved into position. During the operation itself, orders were mainly given by R/T.[10] The British forces were greatly outnumbered by the Italians but inflicted a decisive defeat. They then proceeded westwards and destroyed the retreating Italian force at Beda Fomm. The operation showed the effectiveness of a small well-trained mobile force, moving with high tempo against a larger, static and unprepared enemy, whose reconnaissance did not alert them to the imminent attack. At the end of the operation, however, the British forces were in an exhausted condition. Moreover, the difficulty of maintaining command and control over a large battlefield had been made very clear, and had shown wireless communications over large distances to be unreliable.

Although Wavell's despatch on the operation praised the 'admirable work' done by Royal Signals and did not mention any areas for improvement, there were many problems with communications.[11] Wireless was often unsatisfactory, due to lack of operators, unreliable sets, flat batteries and changes in the frequencies used by one formation not being known about by others. Some of the problems may have been exacerbated by the lack of live wireless usage for security reasons in the lead up to the action, while others were simply due to ignorance and bad operation. For example, one formation had difficulty using the frequency allocated to it and decided to use another's frequency instead.

This prevented the Army commander from communicating with both of them. Fortunately, he was able to visit some formations personally at crucial moments during the first part of the operation, involving a great deal of time because of the large distances involved.[12] By these means, it was just possible for O'Connor to maintain control despite the signalling problems, helped by the small size of the British forces in relation to later battles. However, as distances increased still further, he was no longer able to do so. Major General Creagh, the commander of 7AD, personally made the decision to proceed to Beda Fomm where the Italians were finally cornered, because he was out of touch with O'Connor.[13] The fact that Creagh later made it clear that he would have consulted O'Connor, had he been able to do so, illustrates the restrictive nature of the British command system, though it also demonstrates that some commanders did use their initiative when required.

At the start of operations, 4ID had laid cable back to Army HQ, but as the division moved forward rapidly, line communications became erratic and wireless was generally the only feasible means of communication. However, it was found difficult to co ordinate artillery batteries by R/T due to insufficient and unreliable sets. Fewer wireless problems occurred within 7AD than in 4ID, but even though the fighting portion of 7AD was generally well supplied, support functions such as the engineers, repair workshops and Service Corps lacked the sets needed to communicate with forward troops. It was clear that all parts of the Army needed a large increase in the number of wireless sets.

The issue of where a commander should place himself was a continuing dilemma, just as it had been for Gort in the BEF. Major General Beresford Peirce, the divisional commander of 4ID, occupied a very forward position and was able to maintain control of his brigades with a single wireless set. On the other hand, the commander of 7 Armoured Brigade found that he became out of touch with his rear link back to division when he was on the move in order to keep up with the front line. Afterwards, he reflected that he would have been better able to co ordinate his forces if he had remained stationary, away from the action, with a short-range No. 14 wireless set (in addition to his main No. 9 set) connecting him to his rear link.[14]

Wireless battery charging was a particular difficulty and continued to be an intractable problem over the next two years. Wireless in many tanks was designed to work off the main tank battery, charged by the engine. Since tanks were stationary for long periods, the wireless ran this battery down. In other types of tank and in infantry formations, it had been planned that batteries would be charged at headquarters and taken forward, but this system did not work over the extended distances in the desert, and there were too few charging engines (petrol-driven generators) for them to be taken forward for decentralized use.

'J' was used by 7AD to overhear 4ID's communications with its brigades, giving valuable information that was not received through normal channels until many hours later. The British were not the only ones listening to their transmissions – a captured Italian Signals officer stated that interception during the battle provided valuable information from messages sent in clear.[15] However, the wireless silence prior to COMPASS was effective in ensuring surprise, and the Italians were so disorientated during the battle that they could not take advantage of the intelligence that they obtained.

In summary, the British experienced many communication problems, but they were not sufficiently severe to prejudice the overall success of the operations because of a variety of more serious failures in the Italian Army. On the British side, several lessons about communications were learnt, but the lack of resources either to replace or increase their equipment, and the way in which formations were shuttled around the Middle East, meant that progress in the immediate future was impossible.

Developments in command and communications, March 1941–September 1942

After its initial success against the Italians, the British Army suffered a series of defeats, causing it to re-evaluate all aspects of its operation, including the command and communication system, which performed unsatisfactorily on many occasions. This examination did not go so far as to question the restrictive, top-down, command structure, but many other aspects were revised and the communications system evolved considerably over the 18-month period. The problems with communications during COMPASS reinforced the conclusions that the Bartholomew Committee had drawn after Dunkirk – it was essential that all formations were provided with wireless so that they could cooperate with one another in mobile operations. The doctrine was clear even if the limited supply of sets prevented its full implementation for some time. After CRUSADER, there were enough sets to provide headquarters with two independent wireless systems and the benefits of this policy were made very apparent after two command vehicles were destroyed in the attack on 7AD headquarters at Gazala in May 1942.[16]

The emphasis on wireless rather than line began to change during 1942. One reason for this was the increasing prevalence of mines as a means of slowing tempo, allowing line communications to become more effective again. Even in armoured divisions, line communication assumed ever-growing importance. But Rommel was adept at restoring mobility to the battlefield in spite of minefield defences and, for much of the time, wireless still had to be relied upon. Line and wireless were thus complementary means of communication, as Royal Signals had always maintained since the 1920s. It was only in the autumn of 1942 that sufficient equipment was available for this obvious doctrine fully to be put into effect. Meanwhile, equipment levels improved and were reinforced by improvements in technology. But the supply and training of operators continued to be a challenge; not only did each formation require additional operators, but the number of formations in Eighth Army continued to increase.

Prior to BATTLEAXE (June 1941), neither of the two formations involved was able to train sufficiently – 7AD had only just been reformed and re-equipped, and 4ID had only recently returned from the Sudan. The commander of 7AD said that his formation had still been somewhat disorganized at the start, having been brought forward piecemeal as and when equipment became available, and the 7AD Signals war diaries for May and early June 1941 do not give the impression of a smooth running operation. Wireless sets were proving unreliable due to age (some dating back to 1937), and shortages meant that some tanks lacked sets altogether. Battery-charging engines were unreliable because sand damaged their bearings. Operators were inexperienced – out of 32 operators in one troop, no more than 10 were considered to be competent.[17] 4ID Signals also suffered from shortages in equipment in BATTLEAXE, notably wireless batteries, charging sets and telephone cable, and these were particularly acute in artillery units.[18] All of these problems contributed to the defeat.

After the unsatisfactory conclusion of CRUSADER (November 1941), considerable efforts were made to identify what had gone wrong with communications. Training had not been adequate and there had been numerous problems with wireless equipment. There was a lack of sets at the start of operations, and too many different types of set, not all of which could operate in the same frequency range. There were also shortages in wireless spares, in batteries, distilled water and acid and in charging sets. Breakdowns and heavy losses in action made the situation worse. Apart from providing a larger number of compatible sets, it was recommended that recovery and salvage facilities be improved, and that Signals stores be brought further forward to facilitate re-equipment. From a technical standpoint, there was a need to improve the performance of long-range sets and direction-finding aerials to help supply sections to locate their fighting troops in the dark. Remote control, whereby an officer could be connected by telephone wire to a wireless set some distance away, was deemed essential and was needed on all types of sets. On a more positive note, the skip distance problem was overcome for the first time by using an intermediary when two parties were unable to communicate directly, leading to a system of interception and re-broadcast on medium wave from Malta. It was recommended that this system of intermediaries should be extended.[19]

Partly as a consequence of the lack of time for training, there were several instances in CRUSADER of operators working on incorrect frequencies, making it difficult for other formations to make contact. Better wave meters were needed and it was recommended that a single fixed frequency (the 'watching wave') should be broadcast on an Army basis to assist in the calibration process. Divisions had provided their own rear links, so that the signallers belonging to the division were responsible for communicating with unknown operators at corps, rather than corps signallers being attached to the division. When problems occurred, parochial loyalties had led to mutual accusations of blame, and a more cooperative attitude was called for. The shortage of manpower was highlighted, with more signals operators and drivers needed. Many other improvements and recommendations were made after CRUSADER to alleviate minor problems, but the cumulative effect was considerable. The arrival of Penney, the new energetic SO in C, the additional staff that were authorized by Lieutenant General Auchinleck, now the Commander-in-Chief, and the increased material resources that were becoming available enabled good progress on these improvements to be made during the early months of 1942.[20]

The communications failures at Gazala (May–June 1942) were mainly the consequence of other failures in the Army's systems as opposed to being the cause of those failures in the first place. The overrunning of the headquarters of 7AD on 27 May, for example, was due to faulty interpretation of reconnaissance reports, rather than the mechanics of signalling. This particular incident is worth exploring in depth since it illustrates the realities of the decisions facing commanders and the role of communications in the OODA loop. There had been debate among British commanders about whether Rommel would focus his main attack in the centre of the Gazala line with a feint to the south, or whether his main attack would be a southerly outflanking movement. Accordingly, British armour was split between the middle and south, with the intention of moving it appropriately when the direction of the attack became clear. Using information from Ultra (information provided by Bletchley Park after some Enigma codes were broken), Auchinleck had correctly predicted the likely date of the German attack. He also expressed the strong view that the main attack would be in the middle of the line. Senior British commanders knew that he had access to a secret source of reliable information (though they did not know its precise origin), and gave his views particular credence as a result. Evidence from TACR (air reconnaissance) on the evening of 26 May, and from 7AD's armoured cars overnight, that a considerable Axis force was moving south, was not acted on in time because of this. The war diaries of 7AD indicate that communications were working correctly – 'wireless worked well all day and during the night – reports coming in from [armoured cars] the whole time'.[21] It was the misinterpretation of the information received that was responsible for 7AD headquarters being unprepared for the 'surprise' attack. In the terminology of the OODA loop, the observation stage and communications between observation and orientation were satisfactory, but the orientation itself turned out to be incorrect.

The divisional armoured car reports were also heard at Corps – Michael Carver was GSO2 of XXX Corps and listened all the time to 7 Motor Brigade's forward control net to the armoured cars, as well as to 7 AD's, another example of the 'J' system. He contacted 7AD headquarters to check that they had heard the reports and to press them to take evasive action. Two armoured command vehicles were destroyed in the attack on 7AD headquarters, with several officers including Major General Messervy, the divisional commander, taken prisoner. But some of the reforms in signalling that had been made after CRUSADER then came into their own so that communications were still possible from the vehicle used by the Division's intelligence officers. This, however, was a mobile interception station and its operators were unaccustomed to transmitting, and consequently had difficulty tuning the transmission side of their No. 9 sets to the correct frequencies, in order to tell other formations what had occurred. Moreover, the officer in charge, Captain Vaux, was worried that the Germans had probably obtained the codebooks and ciphers from the destroyed ACVs, and felt restricted in what information he could transmit. Because of this, two LOs were sent to Corps, of whom one succeeded in getting through.

The situation following the overrunning of 7AD Headquarters became chaotic. Brigades were temporarily placed under the command of other divisions, causing considerable signalling difficulties as they were all using different R/T codes and none knew the others' call signs. Signals security evaporated with information on the frequencies of wireless nets being transmitted in clear because nearly every cipher and code had been captured. The commander of 7AD Signals visited Corps headquarters personally to obtain extra codes and call signs to try to sort out the confusion. This state of affairs occurred frequently throughout the Gazala battle, according to an after-action report. Formations and units were joining and leaving the command of 7AD daily, and in some cases almost hourly so that, to the detriment of signal security, a very wide circulation of divisional frequencies and codes had to be made. But even so, units arrived without the required information because of the difficulty of getting it to them in time.[22]

In spite of the problems, the benefits of new equipment were becoming apparent at this time – 1 Armoured Division was said by its CSO to be fortunate in possessing the No. 19 wireless set, which he felt had several advantages compared with the older No. 9 set used by 7AD. With its speed and clarity, it enabled the division to control all its operational components on one R/T group of up to 20 stations (compared with about five groups in 7AD). The simplification and wider dissemination of information had great benefits. Line was also used much more at Gazala than in CRUSADER, particularly at night. The combination of line and wireless meant that communications in the Division were claimed to be 'uniformly good', in spite of worries about batteries and a lower standard of training among new recruits.[23]

Throughout 1941 and the first half of 1942, the control of front line infantry remained dependent on line communications to connect companies to battalion headquarters when they were static, and on runners and DRs when they were on the move. This meant that the coordination of attacks between infantry, artillery and armour was hard to achieve, and that difficulties arose when unexpected events occurred. The problem was exacerbated by the restrictive command system of the British Army, which believed in setting a plan and adhering to it unless permission to change it was obtained from above. The speed at which the front line could react was therefore greatly reduced by slow communications. While the concept of mobility had certainly penetrated infantry formations, they still lacked the communications equipment needed for fully mobile operations. At Gazala, for example, instructions were given that 'all units will ensure that routes between company and battalion HQs are marked so that runners can find their way in the dark', and 'each unit will maintain a board at their HQ showing the distance and bearing to other HQs'.[24] In 3 Indian Motor Brigade, runners did 'splendid work. . . under very difficult circumstances'.[25] The need for a front line infantry wireless set had been recognized in the 1930s, and the No. 18 set, specifically designed to connect battalion to company headquarters, had entered service in November 1940. It was not until the late summer of 1942, however, that there were sufficient supplies and operators in the Western Desert to extend wireless links down to individual companies of infantry and motor battalions.

Command structure

Army headquarters in BATTLEAXE was at Sidi Barrani, the furthest forward base from which tactical reconnaissance aircraft could operate and from which sure communications with the RAF fighter base at Maaten Baggush could be maintained. But Sidi Barrani was 60 miles from the battlefield, beyond the range of ground wave wireless and equal to the minimum skip distance for sky wave communications under favourable conditions. The location of the Army headquarters was thus an unsatisfactory compromise, and in the event, it led to the GOC, Beresford-Pierce, being out of touch with what was happening to his two divisions. It impeded both the efficient command of the Army and the efficient dissemination of reconnaissance information from the Army to its divisions.[26]

Similar difficulties were caused during CRUSADER by Lieutenant General Cunningham's decision to establish Eighth Army's forward headquarters at Maddalena, near RAF headquarters, but 80 miles from the fighting at Sidi Rezegh, and over 60 miles from the two corps headquarters. Bearing in mind the experience in BATTLEAXE, three special 'army commander' long-range wireless sets were issued to Army and corps headquarters in the hope that R/T communications could be maintained. Cunningham claimed afterwards that they had worked, but he also said that R/T was not enough, because of security issues and because of the fallibility of the sets. From his daily handwritten account, it is clear that Cunningham did not rely on R/T, but spent much of his time at one or other of the corps headquarters, which he reached by aeroplane in 20 minutes. While at XXX Corps headquarters on 20 November, communications with his own Army headquarters were sometimes 'most sketchy', and while at XIII Corps headquarters on 23 November, he was not in touch with XXX Corps. These visits enabled him to be in close touch with part of the action, but at the cost of losing sight of the whole picture.[27] Even when Cunningham was at his own headquarters on 24 November, the commander of XIII Corps, Major General Godwin-Austen, sent him a letter rather than speaking on R/T, with the first part written at 09:00 and the second part at 12:45, when events had rendered the first part out of date, after which it was delivered by aeroplane.[28] The net result was that commanders and formations were too slow in reacting to the high tempo of the German counter-attacks. Following CRUSADER, Signals recommended that they should be consulted about the choice of locations for headquarters to ensure that communication issues were taken into account.

The lessons of BATTLEAXE and CRUSADER were apparently not learnt in this respect since exactly the same problems occurred at Gazala. The GOC of Eighth Army, Lieutenant General Ritchie, located himself at Gambut, close to RAF headquarters, but some 60 miles east of the fighting, presumably because this helped inter-service liaison and guarded against the possibility of Army headquarters from being overrun by the enemy (which had led to the capture of O'Connor in 1941). But, as a result, he only learnt of the wreck of 7AD on the morning of 28 May, 24 hours after the event.[29] This contributed to his slow reaction to events in the battle and provided another example of the unfortunate consequences of trying to run a fast-moving battle from afar. Even worse delays occurred when Auchinleck started to give Ritchie operational orders from Cairo. Several instances occurred of Auchinleck doing this when he was not up-to-date with the situation on the ground, resulting in uncertainty in the command system.[30] Effectively, Auchinleck had placed himself in the Eighth Army OODA loop, but had not ensured that the observation stage was feeding into his Cairo headquarters; it might be possible to run a battle from a distance of hundreds of miles with today's technology, but it most certainly was not in 1942, when being even 60 miles from events caused problems.

Learning from experience, Auchinleck himself established a tactical headquarters for Eighth Army on Ruweisat ridge before First Alamein (July 1942), in the middle of the defensive line, rather than basing himself close to RAF headquarters, which was some 40 miles behind. This reduced the reliance on line or wireless communications between the Army, corps and divisional commanders (though, as it happened, proximity did not seem to aid understanding and cohesion between Auchinleck and his subordinates). Moreover, being so close to the battle made the orientation stage of his OODA loop much easier; he could instinctively feel the demands of the battle. The earlier argument that proximity to the RAF was necessary to facilitate air support did not prove to be the case at First Alamein, where the RAF was very effective. The air and land efforts were uncoordinated, but the effect was complementary, helped by clear battle lines between the British and Axis armies in contrast to the mixing up of forces that had occurred in many previous encounters.

After Auchinleck had been dismissed, Montgomery, the new Army commander, immediately moved his main headquarters back to more pleasant surroundings at Burg el Arab, close to RAF headquarters, but in a similar way to Auchinleck, he also established a small forward tactical headquarters for Eighth Army with good communications, so that it could keep up with a mobile battle. The establishment of a third, tactical, headquarters became common for higher formations in the period before Second Alamein, and proved to be a solution to the problem of how commanders could keep in touch with events while retaining the large staff needed to run a restrictive command system.[31] In doing this, the British had, in fact, come to the same conclusion as Rommel – that proximity to the battle was essential for a commander. It was the system that had been adopted by Gort in the BEF with negative consequences, but the quantity and efficiency of communications equipment were now sufficient to make it work.

Because he felt that the performance of the British armoured divisions had been unsatisfactory in CRUSADER, Auchinleck decided that, in future, they should contain less armour and more mobile infantry, like a German Panzer division – one armoured brigade and one motor brigade group would form a more balanced force. However, it took a year to implement this organization.[32] Brigades were allocated their own artillery, engineers and Signals sections, becoming self-contained brigade groups. This development was controversial. Its advantages were that it increased flexibility and reduced the communications task between the different elements – for instance, the CSO of 7AD wrote that the decision to make brigade Signals independent of divisional headquarters at Gazala had facilitated the frequent changes in command structure that took place. But it impeded central control and could allow the relatively small formations to be picked off one by one by the enemy. After Gazala, in recognition of these disadvantages, Auchinleck removed command of artillery from brigade level, and placed it under central command to facilitate the organization of mass gunfire. Even though the gun batteries were dispersed at First Alamein, they were under the central direction of the CRA of XXX Corps, and achieved heavy and effective concentrations of fire on key targets, incidentally proving that their intercommunications worked.[33] When Alexander and Montgomery took over in August 1942, the division, rather than the brigade group, was firmly re-established as the main tactical unit.[34]

The British plan for CRUSADER relied on flexibility, assuming that their TACR would be able to track the movements of the enemy, communicate this to the commanders on the ground and that they would then be able to manoeuvre the enemy into a position where a direct trial of strength would take place. But the plan did not work. TACR was unable to provide enough information because the weather was bad, it was difficult to distinguish friend from foe, and relatively few reconnaissance aircraft were available. The British armour failed to organize a concerted attack in strength, and once again suffered heavy casualties from the German and Italian anti-tank guns. Breakdowns in both line and wireless communications within and between the different formations frequently occurred, and there was no systematic transfer of information from the front line to enable commanders to understand what was happening within their own sector, let alone communicate this so that the Army commander could assess the overall position. Units had no time or adequate means to report back in the whirlwind of action that was taking place; the LO system was embryonic, and although 'J' was used to coordinate the break-out from Tobruk, its use was not widespread at this stage.[35]

To remedy these problems after CRUSADER, it was recommended that mobile interception sections should be increased in number, along with mobile DF sections. In addition to listening to enemy transmissions and locating the position of enemy units, the latter were systematically to carry out the 'J' system of listening to the transmissions of British forward units.[36] Unfortunately, resources were insufficient to allow an increase in 'J' before Gazala, and the lack of rapid feedback of information to all corps and army headquarters was a contributor to that defeat.

Security issues

The insecurity of wireless transmissions was a continual threat and was the subject of a great deal of attention. Security was sometimes too slack, leading to the compromise of a number of operations, and sometimes it was made so tight that efficient coordination of forces became very difficult. By the end of the period, prior to Second Alamein, sufficient lessons had been learnt for a sensible and generally secure system to be operated. Even so, the experience of the pursuit after Second Alamein showed that damaging breaches of security could still occur.

The commencements of BREVITY and BATTLEAXE did not surprise the Germans – analysis of British wireless traffic enabled them to predict the timing of the attacks. On the first and second days of the three-day BATTLEAXE operation, Rommel obtained a good picture of British strength and positions from captured documents and wireless intercepts, enabling him to optimize his attacks on the following days. The extent to which British wireless was intercepted was shown by a message from a German commander to his units – 'It is intolerable that I should receive more speedy information about our own troops from intercepted enemy traffic than from your reports'.[37] Attempts were made by the British to put interception into practice themselves, but these 'failed owing to shortage of [interception] sets'.[38]

It was not that the British were unaware of the dangers of interception – Creagh wrote afterwards that he was able to say little on R/T to Beresford Peirce and that he spoke in Hindustani to the commander of 4ID, one of the reasons for this being that codes had been compromised early in the action.[39] However, commanders did not appear to realize how much a short conversation could reveal, nor that the Germans used captured Indian soldiers to translate Hindustani and to interpret other 'guarded messages'. Enciphered W/T messages were more secure, but they were slow, particularly when routine messages held up urgent operational communications.[40] The security of communications plainly needed to be improved in several respects.

Between the end of BATTLEAXE and the start of CRUSADER, the most important development in Signals was the introduction of the more secure single call sign system in October 1941 and the simultaneous introduction of a new army call sign book, both of which necessitated training and provoked initial resistance.[41] The new system proved satisfactory during CRUSADER and helped to avoid alerting the enemy to the impending attack. Learning from earlier security breaches, considerable efforts were made prior to CRUSADER to keep the enemy unclear about British intentions. Discussion of the operation was limited to very few senior officers, and the only written documents were the minutes of their periodical conferences, which were sent by name to those attending.[42] Work on defensive positions was carried out at night to avoid observation by the enemy and a lengthy wireless silence was imposed. Rommel acknowledged afterwards that the latter was effective, '[The enemy's] concealment of his preparations was excellent. The wireless silence . . . prevented our interception service from detecting his approach march'.[43] However, it caused British operators to become out of practice, and this meant that communications were very shaky at the start of the battle.[44] Since wireless silence could in itself have indicated an imminent offensive (though the German evidence suggests that this was not, in fact, the case), it was later recommended that a constant level of wireless traffic should in future be maintained. The use of code and cipher in CRUSADER showed an improvement compared with BATTLEAXE, but many leaks occurred due to bad or inexperienced operators, or officers being careless when using R/T. Delays in ciphering sometimes forced transmissions to be in clear – more cipher staff were needed. No large changes in security practice were recommended afterwards, however, just the need to abide by existing rules.[45]

Sophisticated deception measures were also taken before CRUSADER. For example, by organizing a gradually increasing amount of W/T traffic to and from dummy tank regiments at Jarabub in the south, the Germans were deceived into believing that an attack would come from that direction. The operation was covered by Britain's most thorough and sophisticated effort at deception since 1939, but this did not in itself lead to success, since although the deception made it more difficult for the Germans to understand what was happening, the defensive actions that they took were appropriate to the true situation.[46]

Trucks were mounted with tank-like superstructures made of wood and canvas to deceive air reconnaissance planes (left hand picture in Figure 5.1). Wireless posts were set up nearby to transmit false messages to complete the deception of enemy intelligence. Another complimentary form of deception was to disguise tanks as trucks (right hand picture).

In the more defined defensive positions at Gazala, which included the greater use of minefields to slow down the pace of an enemy attack, cable was widely used, helping to increase security.[47] But as soon as the German attack took place, wireless was extensively used. Under the extreme circumstances following the overrunning of 7AD headquarters early in the battle, wireless security collapsed,

Figure 5.1 Dummy tanks and dummy trucks in the Western Desert. Picture obtained from the Imperial War Museum.

reiterating that, whatever precautions were taken, defeat caused immense problems in communications.[48]

Signals initially believed that wireless security at Gazala had generally been good. However, they were wrong, as they were shocked to discover from the records of a German intercept section captured on 10 July 1942.[49] The Germans had been able to form a clear picture of the size and disposition of British formations, while the interception of requests for additional supplies on rear links had enabled forthcoming operations to be anticipated. Most of the information was based on plain language R/T and W/T messages. Additionally, the placing of R/T codes in a plain language context had allowed some codes to be broken, and some low-grade syllabic cipher messages had been deciphered, perhaps from captured keys. There was no evidence of the breaking of high- or medium-grade cipher, however. The British countermeasures in response to these revelations were fairly weak, perhaps in recognition of the inevitability of some insecurity when wireless was used. It was ruled that W/T and R/T messages should be kept to a minimum and plain language wireless messages were absolutely forbidden if line existed. The issue of comprehensive lists of call signs and code names was to be restricted. An increase in W/T traffic on 'Q' (supply) links before operations should be avoided by the use of lines, or if line was not available, by messengers.[50] The capture of the German intercept section re-emphasized the relative security of line communications, providing a further impetus to use line whenever possible. This and the discovery of the identity of Rommel's 'Good Source' (the US military attaché in Cairo whose despatches to Washington had been deciphered by the Germans, furnishing them with much useful information about British intentions) undoubtedly limited the efficiency of German intelligence.[51]

But the Germans continued to have success in intercepting and making use of wireless traffic, particularly when the British felt that there was no time to use cipher – on 10 November 1942, for example, messages were sent by W/T in clear in order to reduce congestion in the Eighth Army cipher office.[52] The problem was that cipher could sometimes impose delays on command systems, which could be more damaging than possible interception by the enemy. In an effort to accelerate the OODA loop at Eighth Army headquarters, the time taken to process enciphered messages was monitored – on 23 July 1942, for example, the maximum delay was just under two hours, and this was caused by the exceptional circumstances of seven priority messages being received together at the same time.[53]

The effect of communications on the performance of the British Army between March 1941 and September 1942

There were several reasons for the defeat by the Germans of the British forces at the end of COMPASS in early 1941 – the strength of force required to hold on to Cyrenaica had been underestimated; the forces employed were inexperienced; lack of air reconnaissance meant that the strength of the enemy forces was not appreciated early enough; the British tanks were inferior to those of the Germans; and finally, there were many failures in communications. During the German advance, the single greatest setback for the British was the destruction of much of 2 Armoured Division, and in spite of other mitigating factors, poor wireless communications played a considerable part in its defeat.[54] After the enemy had broken through, the headquarters of 2 Armoured Division was never in touch with the whole force under its command because of a breakdown of signal communications. This was due to the loss of wireless command vehicles and lack of opportunities for charging batteries and because the skip distance of sky wave caused wireless to fade.[55]

The performance of communications during BREVITY was also unsatisfactory, with interception giving the enemy warning of the impending attack and delays in the transmission of messages between WDF and its formations contributing to the failure. Similarly, communications problems played a substantial role in the failure of BATTLEAXE. Wavell attributed this failure to three main causes – the enemy was clearly ready for the attack and had prepared a counter-attack; the enemy had much greater tank strength in the forward areas than expected; and 7AD had been hastily reformed and had not settled down.[56] The first reason was certainly because of German interception of British wireless communications and the lack of deception measures to disguise the British advance. That the British should have known so quickly about the interception of their messages by the Germans is attributed to field intelligence rather than 'Ultra'.[57] The second reason for failure was also due to insecurity in British communications, coupled with a failure of air reconnaissance. With regard to the third reason given by Wavell, the hasty commitment of 7AD to battle meant that the flawed tactic of employing two armoured brigades with different types of tank (cruisers and the much slower 'I' tanks) had not been practised. As a result of BATTLEAXE, 7AD was subsequently entirely equipped with cruiser tanks in CRUSADER. Aside from the factors mentioned by Wavell, the communications problems caused by the remote positioning of Army headquarters were an additional cause of failure. Overall, problems with communications were a major contributor to the failure at BATTLEAXE. However, another fundamental problem was that the British did not appreciate the superiority of Axis tactics in armoured warfare, and in particular, how the German tanks had withdrawn behind the 88mm guns, luring the British tanks onto them. They did not, therefore, make a fundamental change in their own tactics prior to CRUSADER, contributing to that operation's patchy success.

After CRUSADER, senior Signals officers claimed that communications had worked well, but at the same time, they recommended several improvements, effectively admitting that problems occurred. Indeed, the war diaries of 4 Armoured Brigade of 7AD catalogued a series of communication failures after the fierce fighting in November.[58] There was clearly a political need to maintain a public face of success, while at the same time, trying to put right the faults that they knew had occurred. Similarly, Major General Messervy, the GOC of 4ID, praised Signals. But another report from 4ID mentioned communications problems when its command was passed to Eighth Army from XIII Corps during the confusion following Rommel's 'dash to the wire' and the difficulties that different elements of the New Zealand Division had in communicating with one another.[59] 4ID also had communications problems during the pursuit of the retreating Axis forces because of the very large distances involved.

The fact that both positive and negative opinions were being voiced at the time may be one reason why contradictory overall judgements have been made by some authors on the performance of Signals in CRUSADER – 'wireless communication between units and HQs was so faulty as to create something near chaos';[60] 'signal communications were. . . a disappointment';[61] but 'CRUSADER was a technical success for British Signals'.[62] The particularly dense fog of battle in CRUSADER has been blamed on poor signalling between front and rear, whereas it was at least partly because the front did not really understand what was going on, and was therefore incapable of even attempting to pass back the relevant information. CRUSADER was a British victory, but it was achieved at a very high cost and was not nearly as decisive as had been hoped. Sub-optimal communications were partly responsible for this less than satisfactory performance.

With the exception of the faulty wireless security referred to above, the technical operation of wireless and line signalling proceeded much more smoothly at Gazala than in CRUSADER. An after-action report stated that while

CRUSADER had involved continuous movement and latterly a rapid extension of the L of C, the Gazala campaign had been one of static periods, withdrawal and shortening of the L of C. Consequently, charging of batteries, maintenance of equipment and delivery of replacement equipment had not presented the same difficulties. The static nature of the battle (relative to CRUSADER) meant that line could be used more extensively, bringing its attendant advantages of increased security, and consequently, the ability to use plain language on many occasions.[63] Considerable improvements in the communication system between the Army and RAF also allowed air power to be used more effectively, though the length of time senior commanders took to make decisions limited the benefit.

Overall, communications were better at Gazala than they had been in CRUSADER and the evidence suggests that they were not responsible for this defeat of Eighth Army, which was due to other factors. In the first place, the starting position of the British forces at Gazala was unsuitable for defence, stemming as it did from the desire to launch an attack on the Axis forces at the earliest possible moment. However, the biggest failure was in command in its widest sense. Reconnaissance information on Rommel's initial moves was misinterpreted, as it was when he was fighting his way westwards out of the 'Cauldron'. This showed again that provision of information was only the start of the process – commanders required insight to interpret the information correctly in the Orientation phase of the OODA loop, and talent to exploit it. Unfortunately, at Gazala, British commanders appeared lacking in both the latter attributes, possibly, in the case of Ritchie, because the bulk of his experience was as a staff officer rather than as a fighting commander in the field. According to Carver, who was present at the headquarters of XXX Corps, the failure of higher command extended beyond the confines of the OODA loop; he accused some of the commanders of obstructing one another in the interests of their own formations while not being adequately controlled by Ritchie, in whom they had little confidence.[64]

In view of the chaos caused by the defeat, the rapid retreat and the loss of equipment, it was probably inevitable that communications would not perform well as the British fell back on the Alamein line. The flight from Tobruk and the somewhat disorganized stand at Mersa Matruh were marked by various communications failures at Army, corps and lower formation levels. The main reasons for the further defeat at Mersa Matruh were the completely inadequate size and disposition of the British forces and the rapidity of Rommel's attack, exacerbated by a lack of cooperation and communication between Auchinleck (who had just dismissed Ritchie and appointed himself as Army commander), and his two corps commanders. This was partly attributable to a failure of wireless, it being practically impossible to maintain line communications in those circumstances. Furthermore, many of the troops had only recently been rushed in from other locations in the Middle East; their signallers were barely trained on hastily issued equipment and were certainly unused to cooperating with the other formations alongside which they found themselves.[65]

Second Alamein, October–November 1942, and the pursuit into Cyrenaica

Montgomery insisted on waiting for the build-up of his forces to be completed before he attacked, and Second Alamein was not launched until the full moon on 23 October, by which time, the British had received a huge increase in equipment and men. The communications plan for Second Alamein encompassed both wireless and line in forward areas with its principles based on contemporary doctrine – '. . . when movement is rapid, wireless becomes the primary means, but line communication must be established whenever possible. For the deliberate attack, when time is available, line communications are essential. To protect these lines against damage by enemy shell fire or bombing and, moreover, by our own armoured vehicles, resort must be made to burying, and the buried section must be in continuation of the permanent line layout. The latter must be pushed as far forward as possible . . . Duplicate lines by alternate routes must be provided, and special attention paid to artillery communications'.[66] Channels of communication were duplicated and re-duplicated so that failures could be overcome by switching to another route. This policy was the result of commanders thinking previous experience through to its logical conclusion, rather than inventing an entirely new system. It flowed inevitably from the fundamentals of wireless technology and the limitations of available equipment.

A highly elaborate system of lines was laid in advance in each sector of the Alamein line, with a main artery connecting three telephone exchanges – one at the starting line of the intended advance, one at an intermediate 'dispersal area' and one at the forward edge of the British minefields. Lines were then run from each exchange to Traffic Control Points (TCPs) on the intended tracks through the minefields. Spare positions were left on each exchange board to allow for last minute requests for lines to military police posts, Royal Engineer detachments and administration units. As the approach progressed, the columns could connect to the nearest TCP to establish communications.[67] Once the slow advance began into the enemy minefields, Signals personnel followed, laying surface lines. This system made it possible to maintain wireless silence to avoid alerting the enemy to the impending attack, as well as making use of the greater reliability of wire and the speed gained by not having to employ codes or ciphers. The large number of lines in forward areas meant that there had to be an increase in the number of line laying detachments in the four armoured and three infantry divisions; total manpower had to remain the same, however, so the line sections at corps had to be reduced accordingly.[68]

The theory of laying lines up to and through minefields sounded simple enough, but it was a good deal more difficult and dangerous in practice. Corporal Barron of AK Line Laying Section of the 5 Brigade of 2 New Zealand Division gave a graphic account of extending his brigade telephone line forwards:

> Sheridan, Simpson and myself started off from brigade HQ, keeping the 23rd Battalion in sight until we struck a bad patch of shelling where Simpson was wounded by a shell which also cut our line right at the [line] layer. We sent Simpson walking back and Sheridan and I carried on . . .
>
> It was very bright moonlight by this time and when we came to the first enemy minefield we could plainly see the odd mine. I spoke to the [Brigade Major] at brigade on the line and he told me to push on . . . I had a walk across the field and the Engineers said they wouldn't be long [clearing the gap] . . . Anyway, we carried on, then stopped to put a new coil of wire on [the layer] and Sheridan pointed to something nearly under the back wheel and asked me what it was. One look was enough for me to recognize a French type mine. Then when we had a good look we saw we were about sixty yards or so into a minefield . . .
>
> When daylight came we took our line through the field but couldn't hook up to 22 as their CO wasn't there and no one else would say where they wanted the phone. CO did eventually turn up and after about an hour decided where he was going to have his headquarters . . .
>
> Every time I spoke to the [Brigade Major] or the Brigadier they wanted a report on the fighting. Told them every time there was nothing doing on our front but a lot of small arms [fire] to the right. When I say nothing I mean there was only an occasional flare up for a moment or two . . . .
>
> [Mine] was the first vehicle after the Engineers' two 3-tonners [to pass through the minefield gap] and it was only a matter of twenty minutes after that

that I told the [Brigade Major] I was past the 23rd final objective ... My line was only cut twice but of course while we were laying we couldn't keep on speaking to the [Brigade Major]. I think he did tell us to ring him every ten minutes or so and perhaps I did let him wait a good long time sometimes as I couldn't see much use in ringing when there was nothing to report and when there was he didn't take any notice of what I told him.

It was a very easy night for us that night; all the luck was with me. That line of ours seemed to have a charmed life as it wasn't because of any shortage of enemy shelling that it didn't get cut more often ...

For the manner in which he laid the brigade line close up behind 23 Battalion in its advance towards its objective, Corporal Barron received an immediate award of the Military Medal. The citation specifically mentioned his exemplary coolness under fire and standard of leadership, which enabled him to carry out his difficult task with success, as well as his initiative in passing back valuable information to the headquarters of 5 Brigade during the attack.[69]

The increase in resources had finally allowed the extension, using No. 18 sets, of wireless down to company level in some infantry brigades. These sets had been used by 5 New Zealand Brigade in their disastrous attack on Ruweisat ridge on 15 July during First Alamein, but their batteries had run down very quickly and, because telephone lines were severed, communications had once again relied on runners.[70] While some battalions welcomed the introduction of the set, others were less enthusiastic, believing it to be more trouble than it was worth, a particular problem being the shortage of light 'battle batteries', that allowed the set to be used by one man. In their absence, the set was operated by two men, as shown on the cover of this book, creating a bigger target for enemy snipers and disconnecting if the men moved in different directions in the heat of battle. A large number of battle batteries was promised for Second Alamein, and it was intended that the set should be extensively used when line communications were unavailable.[71]

The CSO called for training programmes on the set to be put in place and for all brigade signal officers to be enthusiastic about it, and to ensure its efficient use.[72] In practice, batteries and spare valves for the No. 18 set were not as readily available in Second Alamein as had been hoped and the power and robustness of the set were suspect. As a result, battalions sometimes became out of touch with their sub-units so that runners and LOs had to be relied upon once again.[73] Difficulties were prevalent with the No. 18 set at Second Alamein, but it nevertheless marked a major advance in infantry communications.

Since suddenly imposing total wireless silence before an operation could alert the enemy, regular periods of wireless silence were imposed from the beginning of October so that the enemy became accustomed to them. During these periods, communication was exclusively by line. Conversely, there were also periods when line was not used at all so that wireless operators became accustomed to being under pressure and could keep in practice. In addition to security measures, the British mounted an elaborate deception plan to persuade the enemy that the attack would not take place until the November moon and that when it came, the main thrust would be from the southern, rather than northern, end of the line.[74]

The provision of information to commanders was greatly improved. Army and RAF intelligence services (known as 'Y') were expanded; these assembled information about enemy positions and intentions through a variety of sources, such as air reconnaissance, wireless interception and interrogation of prisoners. In October 1942, the 'J' service was expanded with the objective of monitoring all British W/T links forward of corps headquarters.[75] The resource allocated to 'J' involved some 20 receiving sets, a staff of about 50 and a large number of vehicles, but this resource was only sufficient to monitor selected W/T nets when particular units were involved in key stages of a battle. 'J' proved valuable in Second Alamein – for example, by collating all the individual transmissions of front line troops, it indicated when the Axis troops started to retreat after operation SUPERCHARGE at the beginning of November 1942, well before even the German commanders knew that they were beaten.[76] A typical 'J' patrol went forward in a scout car containing an operator of a receiving wireless, a coder and an operator of a wireless transmitter, as well as a driver and an NCO. The receiving set was tuned to the wireless net of the targeted forward troops, and the operator noted down any items of interest such as the attainment of operational objectives. He passed these to the coder for decoding as necessary and encryption into the 'J' service's cipher, in which they were then transmitted back to the 'J' squadron's headquarters, usually located adjacent to corps or Army main headquarters. It was here that the information was deciphered, collated and passed to the corps or Army commander, often several hours before he might have received it through normal means.[77] The importance of passing back information by normal means was also emphasized before the battle, and brigade and artillery commanders were instructed to appoint an officer to be responsible for doing so.[78] The top-down approach to command was stronger than ever at Second Alamein.

The battle did not proceed completely as planned. Fierce resistance by the Axis forces, combined with the difficulty of penetrating the minefields, meant that progress was hard to achieve. Various changes to the battle plan took place before the weight of numbers and air superiority finally enabled the British to break through by 4 November. The Axis forces then staged a fighting retreat. The British pursuit was too slow to cut them off, and they escaped across Libya and eventually into Tunisia.

The attacks on the minefields were planned to commence with a large-scale creeping artillery barrage, which was largely co ordinated by line communications, though backed up by wireless. Infantry battalions advanced behind the barrage to form bridgeheads. Sappers cleared gaps through which supporting tanks passed, followed by other infantry battalions, which 'exploited forwards'. In a training rehearsal in 5 Indian Brigade, two line laying parties followed the advance battalions in jeeps, while brigade headquarters used a No. 18 set to 'J' into the battalion forward groups to obtain information on the progress of the attack.[79] It was only after the infantry had broken through that armoured divisions could follow and attempt to destroy the enemy. After the battle, it was reported that the links down to infantry battalions using No. 19 sets generally worked well when brigades could not use line communications, but it was recommended that they should be carried in armoured vehicles rather than in vulnerable soft-skinned lorries. Below battalion headquarters, however, the No. 18 sets were sometimes found to be insufficiently powerful and robust and needed to be augmented by runners.[80]

An illustration of front line infantry communications in action is provided by an account of the attack on Miteiriya Ridge by the 21 Battalion of 2 New Zealand Division. The attack was launched at night and required careful navigation by compass at a company level; the direction was checked by battalion headquarters through its inter-company wireless links, using direction finding techniques. Once the companies had reached their objectives, they reported by wireless to battalion headquarters, 'A' Company needing to use 'B' Company's wireless to do so because their own was out of action. At 03:00 on 24 October, the success signal flares were put up. The battalion then used wireless and sent runners to brigade headquarters to pass on this information, the runners being used as insurance in case the wireless signal did not get through. The battalion signal platoon was employed during the attack to keep in touch with the linked sub-units and, once the objective had been reached, in keeping inter-battalion communications open by repairing lines broken by shellfire and checking company wireless sets. It also laid telephone lines back to battalion headquarters. This system of wireless and line appeared to work satisfactorily.[81]

The 7 Armoured Division began the battle in the south as part of XIII Corps, aiming to move through the 'January' and 'February' minefields. It succeeded in crossing January, but was then caught between the two minefields, and commanders decided that it would be too costly to proceed further. During this phase, there was some uncertainty about how far the advance had reached, but this seems to have been because front line commanders could not tell how far they had got, owing to the absence of geographical features, rather than failure to communicate the information. The rear Signals of 7AD recorded that 'all channels of communication (were) working well', though 7AD main Signals found that they were unable to maintain lines because of heavy shelling. With progress halted in the south, 7AD was ordered to move northwards through the minefields into Army reserve, keeping a period of wireless silence to hide their presence in the northern sector. Lines were laid from 7AD headquarters to its brigades at every move, making use of the exchanges that had been set up beforehand.[82]

At the beginning of November, the British finally broke through the minefields and started to pursue the Germans as they retreated. After the minefields had been crossed and movement became more rapid, communications switched primarily to wireless and difficulties were immediately encountered, as evidenced by such comments in 7AD Signals' war diaries as – 'Wireless communications difficult on the move due to distance, interference, atmospherics, dampness, electrical storms . . .'; 'Corps R/T forward [wireless] group all chaotical [sic] due to lack of discipline mainly and bad netting.'; '. . . intermittent difficulties due to interference and atmospherics'.[83] The distances between formations in the pursuit were often enormous – for example, on 19 November, the main headquarters of Eighth Army was 42 miles from its rear HQ, 90 miles from X Corps headquarters, 300 miles from XIII Corps headquarters, and 170 miles from 10 Armoured Division. It was the intermediate distances between the ground and sky wave that gave most problems due to skip distances – X Corps reported difficulty in working distances between 60 and 120 miles, both on R/T and W/T, particularly at night, and 10 Armoured Division could not get in wireless contact with corps or Army headquarters when they were 40 miles away.[84] They lacked a sufficiently powerful set for operating R/T on ground wave at a 100-mile range, which would have overcome the problem. Security problems occurred, particularly on administrative wireless links, warning the enemy and giving them time to escape.[85] Other problems included battery charging and cipher bottlenecks. The issues were scarcely new, but as the review of operations later commented, 'The fact that few new lessons came to light does not mean that old ones need not be repeated'.[86]

Signals officers attributed the problems with wireless during the pursuit to several causes. Apart from technical limitations, users were often at fault – for example, if R/T failed because of range, inexperienced users believed that communications had broken down, rather than switching to W/T. Few staff officers had adequate knowledge of how wireless worked. Interference between the nets of formations fighting close to one another was often due to a lack of wireless discipline, when operators departed from their allotted frequencies, but frequency congestion due to the large number of nets was a fact of life, and an unavoidable cause of interference. As in previous operations, changes in the command structure occurred with bewildering rapidity, causing the usual associated communication difficulties – it was subsequently recommended that all formations should, in future, know the main frequencies of all other formations so that communications could be re-established when such changes happened. In addition, the regular changes in the frequencies used by individual nets gave rise to confusion; although they were introduced for security reasons, it was concluded afterwards that they were undesirable since they were unlikely to deceive the enemy for long, and were detrimental to communications.[87]

The failure of the pursuit to cut off and destroy the remaining Axis forces has been variously attributed to petrol shortages, rain, traffic congestion, booby traps, fear that Rommel might stage another 'bounce back', and lack of determination.[88] Problems with wireless communications have also been blamed.[89] However, there is a view that cutting off the Axis forces was virtually impossible, 'Since 1941 neither army had ever succeeded in cutting off the other in the desert in a pursuit – the laws of logistics simply would not allow it'.[90] The case against wireless communications is therefore unclear, but it seems reasonable to conclude that the chance of completely destroying the Axis army immediately after Alamein, even if it was slight, was not helped by communications failures.

To conclude, poor communications were an important cause of the defeat in Operation BATTLEAXE and of the unsatisfactory progress of Operation CRUSADER. However, the serious defeat at Gazala followed the pattern of Dunkirk, in that defeat caused the communications failures rather than the other way round. These events led the British to change the way they fought battles and the way communications operated, while at the same time, large quantities of equipment were at last becoming available. The subsequent victory at Second Alamein was assisted by these improvements in communications systems, but equally, the failure to destroy the Axis forces afterwards was, in part, due to problems with wireless. Much progress had therefore been made, but communications systems were still imperfect.

Operation TORCH and Tunisia 1942–43

The invasion of French North Africa and an advance eastwards, coupled with the advance of Montgomery's Eighth Army westwards after Alamein, was intended to clear North Africa of Axis forces as well as diverting German resources from Russia, where the majority of the German Army was fully engaged. Under the overall command of the General Eisenhower, the Anglo-American TORCH landings took place on 8 November 1942 in Casablanca, Oran and Algiers, with the British First Army (under Lieutenant General Anderson) only being involved in Algiers. This landing encountered very little resistance from the Vichy French. The location of the landings, particularly whether there should be a landing in Tunisia, had been the subject of considerable debate between Britain and the United States. Among other factors, there was uncertainty over the reaction of the French, and the fear that a failure to land in Tunisia would allow an Axis force to be built up there. The latter was counterbalanced by concerns that a landing in Tunisia would be at the mercy of Axis air power based in Sicily. In the event, German and Italian troops occupied Tunis and nearby airfields extremely rapidly, before the British and US forces were able to advance to prevent them from doing so. First Army, along with the US II Corps and Free French troops, advanced into Tunisia during November and December, but became bogged down across a wide front, and made little overall progress until they were reinforced by Eighth Army at the end of April 1943. Meanwhile, Eighth Army pursued Rommel's army right across Libya and into Tunisia, but failed ever to entrap it. The two British armies, US II Corps and the Free French came under the command of 18 Army Group under General Alexander in February. By April 1943, the Allied forces were considerably more powerful than the depleted Axis force, whose supply lines had been seriously disrupted by the RAF and the Royal Navy, and who were effectively surrounded. Victory eventually came on 13 May 1943, resulting in over 200,000 Axis prisoners of war, and allowing the invasion of Sicily to go ahead in July.

Operation TORCH was the first large-scale amphibious invasion in the Second World War. The performance of communications during the operation was inconsistent – many inadequacies were exposed, but there were some successes. It provided very useful training for future, more strongly opposed, landings during the invasions of Sicily, Italy and North-West Europe. First Army had had no previous operational experience, and there were many areas where the training it had received as part of Home Forces proved insufficient. Troops needed the detailed orders of the British restrictive command system, even though this increased the demands on communications. Furthermore, the mountainous terrain in Tunisia meant that the problems of communication for First Army were considerable, in some ways different from those that had been faced by Eighth Army in the Western Desert, and more akin to what would later be encountered in Sicily and Italy. Communication difficulties contributed to the overall failure of First Army to make headway against the Axis forces between November 1942 and April 1943. They also continued to affect Eighth Army, despite all its experience and as it approached the Tunisian theatre, signals security issues contributed to the failure to trap the Deutsches Afrikakorps before it joined up with the other Axis forces.

Communications practice turned out to be inconsistent in the British Army. Some relevant communications lessons that had been learnt in the Western Desert, and had been incorporated in War Office documents such as *Notes from the Theatres of War*, seem to have been missed, misunderstood or ignored by First Army. As a result, many practices, particularly as regards security and the usage of line as opposed to wireless, differed between First and Eighth Armies, causing several problems after they joined together in April 1943. These led the War Office to form the Godwin-Austen Committee, the purpose of which was to define a common communications system for the whole of the British Army in Europe. In summary, communications had a considerable impact on the campaigns of late 1942 and the first half of 1943 and the lessons learnt during this period helped set a new direction for the future.

Operation TORCH

TORCH was the culmination of a long period of study, training and trial runs for amphibious operations. The landings did not pass off smoothly, showing that amphibious assaults were fraught with difficulty and that the Allies had a lot to learn. Fortunately, the colonial French Army put up a generally half-hearted resistance to the landings in Algeria, so that no major disaster occurred.

Six reports on the Signals requirements of combined operations were issued between December 1941 and May 1942, which covered command and control, equipment, security and Anglo-American cooperation. It was decided that a key element in the control of operations should be the provision of specially equipped headquarters ships, on which would be concentrated senior commanders, extensive naval and military communications equipment and a means of communicating with air support. Although there was an element of risk in concentrating so much in one vessel, this was the only way of ensuring close cooperation and communication between all the elements in the force. Despite the fact that ships were in short supply, HMS *Bulolo*, an armed merchant cruiser, was obtained by Combined Operations Headquarters, and was converted during 1942. It was not available for the Dieppe raid of August 1942, but played a key part in TORCH. *Bulolo* carried approximately 20 wireless sets, as well as line terminals for connection in harbour. The wireless used by the assault troops themselves needed to be light, portable and waterproof. Since wireless silence was essential to achieve surprise, no transmissions were allowed anywhere near the point of attack and because of fear of disclosure of an unusual force, the ban was later extended even to the point of embarkation, for example in the UK.[1] Sets therefore needed to be netted some time before disembarkation, and it was found that the best way of achieving this in a reliable way was through the use of crystal control.

In place of a variable frequency tuner, crystal sets had a separate, specially manufactured silicate crystal for each desired frequency. This limited the number of available frequencies on each set (to three pre-determined frequencies in the case of the No. 46 set, for example) any of which could be selected at will. Before use, the desired frequencies for each set were decided upon and appropriate crystals were installed. So long as the crystals were accurately made (and this was not always the case with manufacturing problems sometimes causing a crystal to receive and transmit a frequency different from its nominal value), there was no need for further tuning and all sets were automatically netted. By contrast, variable frequency sets, which had tuning dials enabling them to operate on any frequency within a certain range, could easily slip off frequency over time, so that different sets in a network might not be able to communicate until adjustments had been made.

During 1942, various small raids on the French and Norwegian coasts were carried out, culminating in the Dieppe Raid by Canadian troops in August.

Dieppe was a controversial operation that ended in failure with considerable loss of life. Communications problems played their part in the failure. Signals security was woeful – a captured letter from a German intelligence officer stated that 'the messages taken [during the Dieppe operation] – over 150 and all in clear – were wonderful and of outstanding importance to our command'.[2] Further amphibious training exercises after Dieppe showed that communications problems had not been solved before Operation TORCH was launched.[3]

Combined Operations doctrine was expressed in a series of War Office pamphlets, which emphasized the need for wireless security and summarized the concept and workings of Beach Signal Units.[4] The latter were combined naval and Royal Signals units, normally located some 100 yards from the fore-shore, which acted as signal centres in the early stages of the assault, providing communications between formation headquarters ashore, the beaches on which the troops were landing, and the ships. Because they were normally set up very early in the operation, all of their equipment was initially carried by hand or on handcarts. As more formations and headquarters were landed, the structure of communications changed and became more complex; the diagram below shows the position when the Main Beach Signal Office (MBSO) acted as a brigade signals centre.

The command structure during TORCH was not a model of simplicity, complicated by the need to present the landings as an American operation because of anti-British feeling among the Vichy French following Dunkirk and the sinking of part of the French fleet in 1940 by the Royal Navy. For this reason, 78 Division, the first British formation to land at Algiers, was initially under the command of 34 US Division, and the Divisional Signals officer of the latter was in command of communications, which comprised a mixture of British Army, Royal Navy and American Army sections.[5] Given that there were many differences in outlook and procedure between British and United States signal organizations, this increased the difficulty of an already highly challenging operation. After the landing had been completed, Major General Evelegh resumed command of 78 Division and Divisional Signals were reorganized into normal tactical groups. V Corps later took over command of 78 Division and 6 Armoured Division, and finally First Army assumed command of the British forces which, in the initial stages, were scarcely bigger than a normal full division. There were thus a large number of senior Signals officers in relation to the number of signallers and signals equipment, but none of them had experienced active conditions in the Western Desert. In fact, neither the CSO of First Army (Brigadier Thursby-Pelham) nor that of V Corps (Brigadier Willway) had seen active service

Wireless Function of a Main Beach Signal Office (MBSO)
When acting as the Signal Centre for Brigade Headquarters
(Brigade HQ is ashore before its Signals Section)

Three Battalion HQs, each with a 46 set and a 22 set

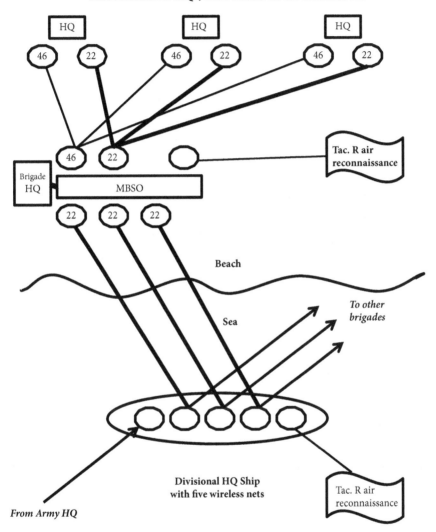

Figure 6.1 Function of a Beach Signal Office.[6]

since the First World War. It was not until February 1943, when Major General Penney, the SO in C of the Middle East, was transferred to be CSO of 18 Army Group that First Army Signals came under the command of an officer with experience of fighting in the Western Desert.

The performance of communications during the TORCH landings at Algiers was inconsistent and, on the whole, unsatisfactory – Brigadier Scott, the senior British Signals officer in Allied Force Headquarters (AFHQ), wrote that 'almost all formations have reported that signal communications in the early stages of the operation were inadequate'.[7] There were three sectors in the landings. Within 'A' sector, which was entirely composed of British troops, the 17 Platoon of 1 Battalion East Surrey Regiment was deposited over a mile from where they should have landed, and lost a large amount of equipment. The platoon commander later wrote, 'Thank God our landing was unopposed. We had landed, but in some disarray and on the wrong beach'. Nevertheless, he made contact with company headquarters by wireless, and the platoon eventually began the march towards Algiers.[8] No major problem was reported at this point, but the dry sandy soil considerably reduced the range of wireless sets, and it was not until they moved inland from the beach that matters improved.[9] 'B' and 'C' sectors consisted of US and British Commando units. In 'B' sector, landing craft became widely dispersed, and some battalions were spread over 15 miles of the coast, with damaged communications equipment. It took considerable time for the units to gather themselves together again, and it was extremely fortunate that there was practically no opposition.[10] No. 6 Commando found that their wireless range was reduced and that interference from static and other stations was very noticeable. The battle batteries on their portable sets ran down more quickly than expected, but even so, all their sets except one were working at the end of the operation, and the opinion of their war diarist was that the signal section had worked 'magnificently'.[11]

Various communication lessons were drawn from the landings. It was recognized that the specially designed headquarters ships were essential; HMS *Bulolo* and HMS *Largs*, its equivalent at Oran, 'proved their value beyond doubt'.[12] Verdicts on exactly how successful *Bulolo* had been were less clear. While one account stated that communications to and from the vessel had been very satisfactory, another said that there had been appreciable delays because its systems had been completely inundated by the volume of army, navy, air force and political signals traffic.[13] The latter report said that the workload had been anticipated, but whereas it had been expected that pressure would slacken quickly, in fact, *Bulolo* had been the sole link with the outside world for nearly a week. The recommendation was that, in future, shore stations capable of handling military and air communications should be set up soon after landing.

The function of the Beach Signal Unit in acting as a link between formation headquarters on shore and headquarters still afloat was not satisfactory – Beach

Signal Units had not had sufficient time to get working before headquarters landed, and it was sometimes difficult for commanders to find them. More time was needed for them to set up, and in the meantime, headquarters needed to be landed together with their own portable wireless sets. Greater priority needed to be given to disembarking signals detachments from ships, and far more signals equipment needed to be landed in the assault and immediate aftermath than had been allowed for in TORCH. This lack of equipment was because there had been a continual struggle between Signals and other arms for space on board ship during the planning stage of TORCH. According to Brigadier Scott, 'time and again, the decision was in favour of fighting troops and Signals were dramatically cut ... [commanders and staff] won't provide adequate signals and then they say that [Signals] have failed'.[14] Signals were not the only ones to complain, however; the Brigadier Royal Artillery (BRA), First Army wrote that 'throughout the bidding for shipping space in London everything was ruthlessly cut and cut again until many of us began to wonder whether units would ever function at all'.[15] The recommendation by V Corps that in future landings, each wireless set and its personnel should be duplicated 'irrespective of the War Establishment' needs to be set in this context.[16] A much larger scale of operation would be needed before duplication was a possibility.

As far as equipment was concerned, the crystal control of the No. 46 set was praised, and it was felt that it should be fitted to all wireless sets used in the assault phase. A small, light receiving set was needed by all assaulting formations to keep them in touch with events. Lorry Command Vehicles (LCVs) were difficult to stow on board ship and to off-load (one was dropped on the quay at Bone, destroying all the signals equipment that it contained); four-wheel drive jeeps would have been extremely useful as well as or instead of these.[17]

However, the difficulties with communications in TORCH were peripheral to the main problem facing the Allies. An armistice between the Allies and the French was signed on 10 November, but by this time, the Germans and Italians had already moved forces into eastern Tunisia and on the same date, RAF reconnaissance reported that 120 German aircraft had arrived at Tunis airport.[18] Because of the priority given to fighting units, no useful quantity of British signals equipment was landed at Algiers, 400 miles from Tunis, until 12 November and even by 14 November, 78 Division's Signals vehicles had still not been unloaded.[19] Having landed so far away, the Allies were not in a position to prevent the establishment of an Axis force in eastern Tunisia. The French forces in Tunis, who might have put up useful resistance, vacillated and did not act decisively, one way or the other. The combination of these factors meant that

there was no chance of an Allied 'walk over' in Tunisia, which was the most opti-
mistic of the possibilities considered beforehand.[20] The Allies were condemned
to fight a campaign; the question is whether communication failures contributed
to the length of time that it took.

First Army operations November 1942 to April 1943

The Allies began their advance eastwards from Algiers on 13 November 1942,
as soon as sufficient units had disembarked from the ships, and less than a week
after the first landings. Higher formation headquarters remained in Algiers as
equipment continued to arrive and to be unloaded. The advancing forces then
encountered resistance from Axis forces, and a stalemate ensued, which lasted
until the middle of January.[21] Difficulties in communications occurred at both
higher and lower levels, which were a factor in the inability of the British to
produce a concentrated attack. Problems of line communications occurred to
some extent because insufficient attention had been given to lessons gained by
the Eighth Army in the Western Desert, but wireless problems were mainly due
to the weather, the terrain and to inexperience among operators.

Communications by wireless and line had been planned between First Army
advanced headquarters, the First Army command post, 78 Division, and lower
formations. However, as soon as the advance started, First Army headquarters
at Algiers became cut off because of the distances involved and the speed with
which forward formations were advancing. To overcome these problems, Lieutenant General Anderson, the GOC of First Army, moved his command post
forward to Philippeville, but even here, communications were poor.[22] Army
headquarters later moved forward to Constantine and remained here for most
of the campaign, but Constantine was about 200 miles from V Corps and this
distance caused continuing difficulties.[23] Wireless was problematic – for instance
W/T functioned between 78 Division back to First Army and forward to 36
Brigade at 07:00 on 19 November, but failed at 09:00 when night frequencies
were replaced by day ones. The 78 Division Signals reported continual problems of wireless failure due to the terrain and atmospheric conditions throughout the rest of November and December. Nor were line communications an
adequate substitute; army line could not keep up, civil lines were often non-
existent or in a bad state of repair, and in any case, insecure. Both types of
line failed through bomb damage. These problems caused delays in transferring
orders – on 23 November, for example, the divisional commander contacted 36

Brigade by using a civil line to a railway station, from where DRs carried the mes-sages to brigade headquarters.[24] It was certainly inevitable that army lines would find it difficult to keep up with the rapid advance, but it was also true that neither sufficient supplies of line nor sufficient line laying sections had been provided. One of the recommendations of Godwin-Austen in the summer of 1943 as a result of these experiences was that an additional cable detachment should be added to the War Office establishment of Divisional Signals, but it appears that this had already occurred in Eighth Army by the end of 1942.[25] If the War Office knew of this de facto change in Eighth Army establishments before TORCH, they should perhaps have allowed for it in the planning, but given the all-round shortages of manpower, it still might not have materialized.

There is no doubt that the mountainous, wooded country of Tunisia was a major cause of problems in First Army. Fighting in the mountains required a large number of infantrymen and played havoc with communications, as evidenced by a report of the experiences of 36 Infantry Brigade, taken from the diaries of Major J. K. Windeatt, the Brigade Major.[26] It shows very clearly some of the reasons for First Army's slow progress during this period and also illustrates the many difficulties with communications. Windeatt was respon-sible to the commanding officer for the running of the brigade headquarters, including the issuing of orders, processing of situation reports from battalions and to divisional headquarters, communications and intelligence matters. For communications, the Brigade Major was assisted by two Royal Signals officers and their detachments. Normally, three subaltern LOs were attached to the headquarters, one from each battalion, who travelled personally to their battal-ions when wireless communications were bad or failed, as frequently happened in Tunisia.

The brigade was involved in an action commencing on 26 March 1943 under the command of 46 Division. The plan was to outflank the enemy by advancing across difficult terrain; 46 Brigade was to capture the first line of hills through which 138 Brigade was to pass, supported by tanks from North Irish Horse. According to Windeatt, 'if ever troops were incorrectly launched into battle, ours will be this time'. This was because the divisional commander did not have a grip on the situation and the plan seemed to ignore the 'Q side' (logistics) of the planning.

Brigade headquarters moved to a mine building for the battle – 'a shocking place as a very bad track is the only way of reaching it . . . so everything will have to be man-handled'. Wireless communications were very bad. 'Couldn't do any-thing with the 19 set, interference terrific. Sent a bloke half-way up the hill at the back with a 46 set . . . Brigade Signal Officer is having the hell of a time'. By dawn of 28 March, the Buffs had not reached all their objectives, owing to the country rather than enemy action. The tanks with the Buffs could not get very far up the hill and mistakenly shot up the Buffs themselves; it was obvious that the plan for putting tanks over the hills would not work. The Buffs got to their objective later in the day in spite of encountering very dense undergrowth about six feet high, quite impassable in places. 'The 46 set saved the communication situation, as without it [HQ] couldn't have kept in touch with anyone. The 19 set was still hopeless [because it was screened by the hills]'.

After the capture of the hills, brigade headquarters moved forward on 29 March to another mine building in the woods. 'The country here is an absolute bugger, very thickly wooded, cork oaks, and where there aren't woods, there is thick undergrowth . . . and looks its worst in this rain . . . No wireless works to anyone except the Argylls. The rain and the trees are wicked for R/T'. They were also at the mercy of enemy aircraft, based nearby on permanent airfields not affected by the rain. Windeatt went forward with the command wireless truck to join his brigadier.

> What a disastrous trip. We set off with a wary eye on the sky and bailed out several times though our bit of road was not shot up. What a sight this road is; dead horses and mules and God knows how many of our written off vehicles along it . . . our truck passed out with a petrol stoppage, so we were stuck until Geoffrey Hagger our Brigade Signal Officer came back . . . to give us a tow. We'd just got underway when almost 6 ME's or FW 190's came down out of the sun. They were on to us before there was time to do much. The first bastard got Geoffrey with his MGs before he could reach the ditch . . . I had just reached the ditch when a 250 kilo bomb arrived in it about 20 yards beyond me . . . Never have I made myself so small . . . After what seemed a hell of a long time probably a minute or two they cleared off . . . The jeep was full of bullet holes . . . but the wireless still worked. I got on the air but couldn't get Brigade HQ for some time, during which there was another visitation from the air . . . No more bombs this time, just machine gunning . . . Got on the air again and got the Argylls who were asking for artillery fire. None of the Gunners wireless was working, they have been useless all along, not a patch on our 138 Field Regiment or any of 78 Division gunners for that matter . . . Got onto [HQ] where [the Assistant Brigade Signal Officer] was holding the fort. Told him to get division to put the guns down and also to ask for some fighter cover. Both arrived in due course.

It was found that wireless signals were screened in hilly country in an erratic and unpredictable manner; but First Army eventually learnt that the difficulty could be overcome by re-siting the sets, using different aerials, using greater power or using relay stations.[27] These issues were not just a result of First Army's initial inexperience in a battle situation, since Eighth Army's experienced 4 Indian Division had the same difficulties later in the campaign, and subsequently its 51 Division found that wireless in hilly terrain in Sicily was similarly problematic.[28] Difficulties with static interference in the winter in Tunisia had been anticipated in the planning stages of the operation, but the need to carry sets up hillsides (by man or mule) had not been thought of beforehand, even though it had been common practice before the war in India on the North-West Frontier.[29] The problems with the hilly country might have been better anticipated by the planners of TORCH, but cannot be blamed on lack of attention to the lessons learnt by Eighth Army.

Figure 6.2 Wireless carried by mule in Tunisia. Picture obtained from the Imperial War Museum.

As a result of the problems of wireless and line, commanders struggled to coordinate the attacks even of wholly British troops, let alone of the US troops who were also involved. Problems with front line infantry communications were also considerable, and commanders in 78 Division maintained that 'not enough time was allowed for planning attacks. Unless every soldier knows his part in the operation, chances of success are limited'.[30] No comment could better encapsulate the way in which British restrictive command systems, requiring detailed orders before soldiers knew what to do, could slow things down. However, mission command would have required a high standard of training, and, according to Brigadier Scott, this was 'completely lacking among the troops which did the initial landings in TORCH'.[31] A restrictive command system was probably inescapable because of this fact. 'Constant changes' took place in the formations under command, which greatly inhibited the maintenance of communications efficiency – 'an old lesson that needs re-emphasis'.[32] No direct evidence has been found of attacks failing as a result of all of these difficulties, but it is obvious that continually failing communications cannot have enhanced the chances of rapid success.

After-action reports by senior Signals officers discussed the perennial question of when to use line versus wireless, the need for more wireless training, an improved signals supply system, more line and wireless equipment, improved security and better command vehicles. They believed that advanced formation headquarters should be kept as much forward as consistent with adequate line communications and rear headquarters needed to be sited within a reasonable distance of them.[33]

At the end of the Tunisian campaign, in an endeavour to discover the lessons that had been learnt by lower formations, a questionnaire about communications was issued by the British Military Training Directorate. Most of the questions were suggested by Penney, the CSO of 18 Army Group, and in some instances, could fairly be described as leading or even accusative, for example, 'On how many occasions in the very suitable country of N. Africa have you made use of visual (lamp)?' Even if it may have distorted the answers obtained, his style of question makes it possible to tell in detail how Penney thought front line signals should have operated. In the infantry, company commanders themselves as well as their signallers should have been using No. 18 and No. 38 sets to communicate both with battalion and supporting artillery, and when the commander was away, the Company Sergeant Major should take over the set from him. Lamp should have been used. Lightweight assault cable was needed so that line communications could be extended forwards as troops advanced, but was currently unavailable, so that forward communications had made little progress since the First World War. Motor battalions employed No. 11 and No. 19 sets. Artillery used No. 18 sets to communicate with infantry, No. 19 sets to communicate with armour, and No. 21 sets for longer ranges. Artillery needed to be competent with W/T as well as R/T, and there was an opportunity for them to use lamp as well. Armour used No. 19 sets.

Although opinions varied, the consensus was that the No. 18 set was satisfactory, but the No. 38 set was insufficiently robust, insufficiently rainproof, suffered from frequency drift and restricted the movement of the user. The way to improve forward infantry communications was to improve the reliability of the No. 38 set (or to replace it with US-style 'Walkie-Talkies') and to provide more of them to allow for casualties, as well as to provide assault cable. The latter would also be useful for artillery observation posts. Regimental signals officers were satisfactory, but some signallers needed more training before coming to the front line. The artillery No. 21 set had insufficient range and did not perform well at night. The No.19 set was first class, as was the No. 12 set. Battery charging seemed to be less of a problem than in earlier campaigns.[34] Lamp had not been used, but it might have been due to Penney's influence that visual signalling by lamp and semaphore was later extensively used in Sicily and Italy on occasions when wireless was unreliable because of the terrain.[35]

The 1 Parachute Brigade was involved in various operations soon after TORCH. Special methods of communication were required, which worked adequately, if imperfectly, in these early operations. The 3 Parachute Battalion was dropped near Bone a few days after the TORCH landings, but faulty navigation meant that they ended up scattered over a wide area. Once again, it was fortunate that there was no opposition. Army No. 22 and Admiralty No. 65 wireless sets, charging engines and handcarts for transporting them were also dropped, enabling communications over distances in excess of 300 miles in favourable conditions using W/T. One set of wireless containers was mistakenly not dropped, necessitating a return flight the next day. Communications were slowed down by inefficient cipher systems as an after-action report made clear – 'a grievous heartburn was the result of watching the Battalion cipher personnel at work. There was no system for them and when wireless was working R5 [excellently], it was completely neutralised by this section'. But in spite of this, communications were judged to have worked well overall.[36] The 2 Parachute Battalion was dropped south-west of Tunis on 29 November in an operation

costing a large number of casualties. Its commander was in touch with brigade headquarters by wireless on 1 December and was informed that the main attack on Tunis had been postponed. Communication within the battalion was less sophisticated – on 2 December, he signalled to his men to retreat from a very tight spot using his hunting horn.[37] Later in the campaign, parachute troops were generally used in a conventional infantry role, arguably a wasteful way of employing highly and expensively trained troops that caused much dissatisfaction among its personnel.

Once the initial Allied assault had petered out, the period until the middle of January 1943 was described by a contemporary First Army document as 'stabilization of front: minor activity', following which the period up to the end of March was one of 'enemy offensive action' against the British, American and French sectors of the very wide front.[38] The War Office evidently realized that there were problems with communications in First Army, since an officer was sent out from England to investigate the situation at the end of January 1943.[39] Shortly after Penney was appointed to be CSO in February 1943, he instructed a staff officer to conduct a review of Signals security. The resulting tour of formations between 18 and 22 February revealed that First Army was not using the same single call sign procedure as Eighth Army and that this was both detrimental to security and confusing. Since the instruction to Home Forces in July 1942 was to use an identical system to that of Eighth Army, this is somewhat surprising, but records certainly show that a fundamentally different procedure was in use in some parts at least of First Army.[40] There is evidence that the correct single call sign procedure had been completely misunderstood by some recipients, so it is possible that operators had devised their own more obvious, but less secure, system.[41] In any case, Penney immediately issued instructions for First Army to adopt Eighth Army's system.[42]

For much of the campaign, First Army had insufficient cipher personnel to deal with secret line messages and wireless traffic, but when the revised single call sign system was introduced, cipher establishments were also increased and cipher delays had reduced by the end of the campaign.[43] Penney claimed in April that 'the standard of operating has increased to a remarkable degree' and attributed this to training on the job. He recommended more realistic training by Home Forces.[44] But improvements in signalling in First Army were not universal, one reason being that new, inexperienced formations were continually arriving from the UK. The 1 Division arrived in early March, and suffered shortages of line supplies during April. On 29 April, the Division's Signals diary reported that 'the need for wireless security is only gradually being appreciated by the staff'. The 4 Division arrived at the end of March, and a four-day monitoring of wireless channels in April identified numerous security breaches.[45] A fairer assessment of the extent to which communications in First Army were improving is given by studying 78 Division, which had been in action from the beginning of November, but the record is not very convincing. Considerable problems were still being experienced in 78 Division with line communications in April, and the continuing need to carry wireless sets by mule pack over the mountainous terrain also led to difficulties.[46] A Canadian officer attached to 78 Division Signals in March 1943 reported numerous problems with the supply of wireless equipment. Replacement sets arrived without batteries or other essential parts; batteries arrived uncharged; spare parts for the wrong type of set were sent; and half as many wireless vehicles arrived as the sets they were to carry.[47] The system of supply using ordnance depots was evidently faulty, and this led Godwin-Austen later to recommend that supply should be through dedicated Signal Parks. The performance of Signals in First Army did improve somewhat between November and April, but its communications were still problematic.

Security issues in Eighth Army after Second Alamein, January–April 1943

Eighth Army communications doctrine in the first half of 1943 held that both line and wireless should be extensively used in both armoured and infantry formations. The higher information capacity of line compared with wireless was one reason for the emphasis on this medium, with security being another important driving force. It is therefore noteworthy that substantial faults in the security of Eighth Army's communications occurred. In defensive positions, armoured formations laid lines to connect each brigade headquarters with its recce section, with each of its regiments, with its artillery and with divisional headquarters. In advances, the emphasis was on wireless, but line was maintained as long as possible until the advance started. During halts of more than 48 hours, lines were laid as for the defensive position, while for shorter halts, a less extensive line layout was adopted.[48] A generally similar approach was adopted by infantry divisions. In a mobile period, before contact was made with the enemy, wireless alone was relied upon. Once contact was gained, a skeleton line system was laid, but 'commanders had every confidence in the wireless . . . as they had mostly been using these links for 18 months'. In a set battle, the infantry division laid out a full line system whose principles included duplicate direct lines to brigades and artillery regiments, and extensive lateral lines between brigades and battalions. They found it more difficult to make a perfect line layout in the mountains than in the desert, but Eighth Army Signals believed that 'by changing methods appropriately . . . good line communications [can be achieved]'.[49]

During its pursuit of the Germans across Libya and into Tunisia, the main communications problem experienced by Eighth Army was in the area of security. For instance, the wireless net between Eighth Army, First Army and 18 Army Group was closed down on 3 March 1943 following a breach of security. And prior to the attack on the Mareth line later in March, German field intelligence, 'in what it considered to be its most important achievement', had obtained advance information of the plans.[50] The source of this information may have been the capture on 14 March of a British reconnaissance patrol with papers and maps indicating where 154 Brigade had been ordered to move. On 15 and 16 March, German intelligence reported 'an unusual radio silence', and intercepted messages stating that call signs would be changed on 17 March, and that zero hour would be 01:30 hours.[51] These breaches of security may have made the direct attack on the Mareth line more difficult, and it appears that insecure communications were to blame.

Another problem at Mareth was the discovery of New Zealand Corps' 'left hook' before it was put into effect. This discovery cannot have been a surprise to the Germans, since Rommel had warned of the probability of an outflanking movement for some time.[52] An early warning was provided by the capture of a British reconnaissance party north-west of the Mareth line on 25 January, and it appears that German air reconnaissance made the actual discovery.[53] It does not seem that communications failures can be blamed for this problem, nor was the discovery particularly serious, since it merely confirmed what had been expected. The German General von Armin was on the alert and immediately ordered a rapid retreat from Mareth. According to the British official history, the main damage was done by bad staff work, which meant that 4 Indian Division was blocked by 1 Armoured Division, and the Axis forces were given 12 extra hours in which to escape.[54] In fact, the Germans had continually avoided being trapped ever since Alamein; it seems unlikely that this time would have been any different, however secure British communications had been.

Security breaches continued later in March – on 25 March, it was found that various codes had been compromised by 50 Division and heavy losses of signal equipment had occurred in its 151 Brigade; perhaps as a result of this, a new commander for 50 Divisional Signals was summoned by CSO Eighth Army the following day, who arrived on 5 April. On 29 March, a liaison officer was captured while taking a cipher table to the French 'Force L' and it was assumed that this cipher had been compromised.[55] Due to the volume of traffic, cipher delays occurred, and these may have tempted operators to send messages in clear, compromising security.[56] Moreover, the large number of wireless sets – and their direct use by commanders rather than by trained signals operators – meant that a larger number of officers needed to be fully aware of security procedures, increasing the likelihood of lapses.[57] The 4 Indian Division and 50 Division were said to be very lucrative sources of this kind of information. The Germans also found valuable clues about what was likely to happen from the habit of imposing wireless silence when 'some 3000 daily cipher messages would drop to 50 twenty four hours before an attack'.[58] Clearly, the SO in C's proposal of early 1942, that such alerts should be avoided by maintaining a steady flow of wireless traffic, was not implemented consistently by Eighth Army. These were the reasons why, in spite of the warning given when two German 'Y' sections were overran in 1942, a replacement German section had little difficulty in tracking Eighth Army moves and intentions in the pursuit across Libya and into Tunisia.[59]

Penney's verdict at the end of the campaign was that Signals security in Eighth Army was better than in First Army, because it had a proper signals element dedicated to checking security and had had more training and practice. However, greater attention to security was still needed in both armies.[60] Insecure signals were, of course, by no means the only or even the main source of Axis intelligence information; air and ground reconnaissance, captured soldiers and documents and agents were also very important. It may also be noted that compared with the vast amount of high level information about Axis intentions available to the Allies through Ultra, the Axis was relatively poorly provided.[61]

The meeting of First and Eighth Armies, March–May 1943

As Eighth Army drew closer to First Army in Tunisia, congestion in the airwaves became an increasing problem. Most army sets used the frequency range between 1.8 and 7.5 Megahertz, and it was desirable to leave at least 10 Kilocycles between nets to avoid mutual interference.[62] Thus, fewer than 600 independent frequencies were available. First and Eighth Armies needed approximately 500 frequencies each, and there were also requirements from the RAF, US II Corps, the Free French (and the enemy). Some overlap was bound to occur. At a conference on 5 March 1943, it was decided to allocate unduplicated frequencies to key headquarters in each army. There would be overlap in the remaining frequencies, but this could be dealt with by judicious allocation of the same frequency only to geographically separated nets, and by careful control of the power at which they transmitted.[63] These measures seemed to have been effective, since reports of mutual interference in Tunisia were infrequent. They were repeated on many subsequent occasions.

However, First and Eighth armies differed in their basic philosophy of how line and wireless should be used, with IX Corps providing a specific example of the problem. This formation, which commanded the armoured divisions of First Army as well as some infantry divisions, only came together on 25 March 1943, and fought three actions in April and early May. In the first of these, it was commanded by Lieutenant General Crocker, with 34 US Division under command as well as 6 Armoured Division (6AD) and 128 Brigade Group, showing that the separation of US from British formations had still not been completely achieved. In the second, Crocker had 1 Armoured Division (1AD) (ex-Eighth Army), 6AD and 46 Division under command. On 27 April, the GOC of 1AD, Major General Briggs, temporarily replaced Crocker, who had been wounded during the demonstration of a projector infantry anti-tank (PIAT) weapon. Three days later, Lieutenant General Horrocks arrived from Eighth Army to take over, with 4ID, 7AD, 6AD and 4 Division under command, of which the first two were ex-Eighth Army formations. The bewildering changes of commanders and formations cannot have made the job of Corps Signals very easy, particularly since the latter were, in any case, very inexperienced. Probably stemming from his background as an officer in the Royal Tank Corps, Crocker believed in 'extreme mobility' and had directed that his tactical headquarters should be able to control the battle from LCVs in motion. As a result, the Corps operated primarily on R/T, quite at odds with the Eighth Army doctrine described above and also with that practised by V Corps. In reality, it was found that the time spent in motion by the LCVs was negligible compared with the time spent stationary, and reliance on R/T caused 'great difficulties' in early April. These difficulties may have resulted in the oblique comment by the CSO that 'full implications must be taken into account before wireless silence is ordered', since in the absence of line, wireless silence would have restricted communications to messengers or to face-to-face meetings. The problems, together with the arrival of the new

commanders from Eighth Army (Briggs and Horrocks) caused tactical headquarters communications to be changed primarily to line and cipher W/T. 'The
organisation of 1AD was fixed, while that of 6AD underwent changes'. In other
words, there was a rapid realignment of armoured communications to the pattern established over the previous two or more years by Eighth Army. Nor were

Figure 6.3 The telephone exchange at Main Eighth Army headquarters, 4 March 1944.
Picture obtained from the Imperial War Museum.

differences in communications doctrine restricted to armoured formations. In IX Corps, 'the disinclination of the [infantry divisional] staff to use R/T led in some cases to lines being laid on an unusual pattern'.[64]

The CSO of the infantry-dominated V Corps also referred to wide differences in outlook on the type of communications required in different situations – 'the chief issue is between lines and wireless'. About 95 per cent of communications in V Corps had been by line, showing which opinion had been predominant, even if this was partially justifiable by the 'semi-static conditions which prevailed for approximately 5 out of the 6 months of the campaign'. At battalion level, infantry did appear to have espoused the doctrine of line in defence and wireless in attack, at any rate, in theory, as shown by the operational orders in the Grenadier Guards and Hampshire regiments; so it seems that the disparity lay more at divisional and corps levels.[65] What was more alarming in the V Corps report was that the remaining 5 per cent of communications caused R/T resources to be heavily strained, while W/T nets seldom used their full capacity. It seems questionable whether V Corps could have coped with a more mobile battle.[66] This situation, armoured formations primarily on R/T alongside a line-dominated infantry, shows that the doctrine espoused by the Jackson Committee of 1936 because of shortages of equipment, was still being felt in 1943, even though the battle experience of the BEF and the Eighth Army had clearly shown it to be erroneous.

The differences that had existed between First and Eighth Army communications were summarized in a note by Penney to General Alexander on 14 June 1943, forming the background to the Godwin-Austen Committee. Penney drew attention to the independent, divergent and uncoordinated signal developments in North Africa and the Western Desert, which had caused considerable difficulties and confusion when formations from the two regions were mixed. He wrote that some were a function of the different conditions and terrain, but many were unnecessary, and he listed 12 examples. These covered the usage of wireless and line, wireless procedures including security requirements, the organization of 'Y' services, and the number of wireless networks and the manpower to deal with them. He wrote that action to achieve standardization must be taken by the War Office, which alone knew the overall factors of supply and demand and which alone could make final decisions.[67]

Why had First Army adopted such different policies from those of Eighth Army, which had evolved from the experience of over two years of continuous operations? It does not seem that Eighth Army was unwilling to pass on its thinking. Its experience had been communicated in a series of *Notes from the Theatre of War*, and the process of dissemination continued. The CSO of First Army, Thursby-Pelham, made a complete tour of Eighth Army headquarters between 17 and 19 January 1943, and noted the extensive use of W/T. A Signals officer from Eighth Army went as a liaison officer to First Army on 20 February.[68] Montgomery held a 'study week' in Tripoli for generals and brigade commanders between 14 and 17 February 1943, which covered communications issues.[69] Although he wrote in his diary that all the invitees from Tunisia came, Montgomery told Brooke (by now the CIGS) that the party from Tunisia was very disappointing and that no generals or infantry brigade commanders attended.[70] This may have been because the dates coincided with a German offensive but, whatever the reason for their absence, it cannot have helped to achieve consistent practices between the two armies.

The most likely reason why First Army (presumably along with Home Forces, from which it had been drawn) had not absorbed some important lessons from Eighth Army is that some issues needed to be experienced first hand before they really were understood. As the war diary of 1 Division Signals put it, 'At the outset of a campaign, there is always a tendency to neglect the lessons of training at home [which] were founded on other people's battle experience'.[71] This understandable, if regrettable, tendency may have been exacerbated by a (possibly unconscious) reluctance by Anderson and other senior First Army officers to adopt Eighth Army's methods because of resentment of the superior attitude of Eighth Army personnel. Anderson wrote about the 'incessant accompaniment of belittlement, sneering, rumours and at times almost slander: all to the effect that 1 Army is no good and that had 8 Army had the job etc.'; he stressed the difference between the desert warfare of Eighth Army and the fighting in the Tunisian mountains.[72] Penney himself reported that Eighth Army did not 'admit the existence of anyone else' and could be 'perfectly bloody till you know them'. A hint that this may have been a contributing factor is given in Penney's diary early in February 1943 – 'Kenneth Anderson . . . difficult as ever and Thursby-Pelham has been through bad times'.[73] That many differences persisted up to the end of the campaign in spite of the fact that Penney (who was, after all, in overall charge of Signals) was aware of and dissatisfied with the disparities, suggests that some senior commanders in First Army were resistant to change.

In spite of the divergent methods of the two British armies, the collapsing supply lines of the Axis forces meant that they stood little chance after Mareth. The end came quicker than their commanders had expected and they surrendered on 13 May 1943.[74]

The Godwin-Austen Committee; designing a consistent army-wide communications system

As requested by Penney, a War Office committee under the chairmanship of Major General Godwin-Austen was given the task of resolving the material differences in methods of command, signals organization, equipment and technique that had emerged between First and Eighth armies. It was to define future policy and recommend necessary changes to manning levels. The committee had four members. Godwin-Austen himself had been GOC of XIII Corps in North Africa during 1941–1942 but, in one of the many changes of personnel in the Middle East, returned to England to become Commandant of the Staff College at Camberley. During 1942–1943, he was rehabilitated to become Director of Tactical Investigation at the War Office, and it was in this capacity that he chaired the committee looking into communications after the Tunisian campaign. The second committee member was a senior Royal Signals officer, Brigadier Nalder (the future historian of The Royal Signals, who had been OC 1 Division Signals at Dunkirk and who later succeeded Penney as CSO 15 Army Group in Italy); and there were two staff officers, Major Haslegrave and Major Lewis (secretary). The main evidence that they collected was given by Royal Signals officers – the SO in C Middle East; the CSO North Africa; the SO in C Home Forces; and the CSO 15 Army Group. They also interviewed several commanders and senior staff officers. The majority of the committee's recommendations were accepted and implemented by the War Office and the report was widely circulated in March 1944 for information but 'not . . . [to] form the basis for re-opening discussion on the topic' – there was to be no repetition of commanders creating their own personal communications systems.

The Committee found that the main reason for the disparity was 'the wide delegation of the War Office to Commanders in Chief of the Mediterranean theatre, of power to adapt their organisations and procedures within the resources at their disposal to meet in the most economical and efficient way the conditions peculiar to their own theatres'. The terms of reference of the Committee included the injunction that no gross increase in manpower could be accepted, but an overall increase was one of its main recommendations, along with a rebalancing of manpower resources and an increase in equipment. It argued that since several of the additions had already been made in the Middle East, the impact of the recommendations was less than it might have been.[75]

In reviewing the application of signals doctrine to operations in North Africa, the Godwin-Austen Committee found that the rapid pace of operations in North

Figure 6.4 Major General R. F. H. Nalder, Historian of the Royal Signals.

Born in 1895 and educated at Dulwich College. Served in France, Belgium and Italy during the First World War, becoming battalion signals officer in the East Surrey Regiment from 1916 to 1918. Seconded to the Royal Engineer Signal Service in 1918 and transferred to the Royal Signals in 1922. He served in France and Belgium as OC 1 Division Signals in 1939–1940 and was CSO IV Corps in 1940.

Between 1941 and 1943, he was at the War Office, acting as liaison officer with the Middle East and then serving on the Godwin-Austen Committee. He became CSO 15 Army Group in Italy between 1943 and 1945.

He retired in 1947 and became Colonel Commandant of the Royal Signals in 1955.

He wrote the two official histories of the Royal Signals – The History of British Army Signals in the Second World War. General Survey (London 1953) and The Royal Corps of Signals. A History of its Antecedents and Development (c1800–1955) (London 1958). He died in 1978.

Africa had made it impossible to provide adequate line communications quickly enough even at the Army level, so that it had been necessary to rely very largely on wireless. No major revisions of policy on when to use which means of communication were made, but the Committee recommended that a larger number of command vehicles should be provided at divisional and brigade headquarters and that extra wireless sets should be added to them. The Committee made a number of detailed adjustments to manpower and equipment to reconcile the differences between the First and Eighth Army establishments.

Another major area of investigation by Godwin-Austen was of the Phantom and 'J' services that had been developed independently to provide information to commanders controlling the battle. These systems were set up because it was found impossible to obtain sufficient and sufficiently rapid information from subordinate commanders through normal routes. Phantom, originating in the Hopkinson Mission in the BEF, provided information by means of officers making contact with forward formations and units, and reporting what they had heard and observed. 'J' originated in the Western Desert in 1941 and provided information by intercepting British wireless transmissions in the forward areas, which after a certain degree of filtering were reported straight to Army headquarters. The most important difference between the two services was that 'J' provided facts while Phantom largely gave opinions, often those of young and possibly inexperienced officers who were not always welcome visitors at busy headquarters.

There appeared to Godwin-Austen to be certain disadvantages in both systems. Phantom reported opinions, was expensive in personnel and tended to short-circuit intermediate commanders by connecting those in forward areas to the army commander. Since 'J' relied entirely on wireless interception, there were problems if reception conditions were poor or if wireless was not being used extensively. Because of this, Eighth Army (which had invented 'J') had augmented it with 'J' patrols (LOs who made personal contact with forward commanders). Provided they reported facts and not opinions, this solution appeared satisfactory to the Committee. It therefore recommended that there should be independent 'J' squadrons with each army, incorporating 'J' patrols. At the same time, it recommended that a separate Phantom Squadron should exist to work with Allies other than the Americans, presumably because language difficulties would be encountered if 'J' were used.

The resources provided for the replenishment of signal stores in the field were found early in the war to be inadequate. Resulting from operational experience, Middle Eastern forces had devised a system for meeting their operational needs that transferred to Signals a considerable part of the responsibility that had previously been vested in Ordnance. Godwin-Austen recommended the adoption of a comparable system.[76] The reserves of different types of equipment needed to be greater for more vulnerable or less reliable equipment – it varied from 2½ per cent of divisional holdings in the case of Fullerphones, up to 10 per cent in the case of No. 18 infantry sets, and 12 per cent for reception wireless sets. The following table shows the reserves that were held for divisions in corps ordnance field parks in May 1943.

These figures enable the scale of Signals operations to be calculated, as well as showing its constituent parts. For example, an armoured division contained no fewer than 580 No. 19 sets, 440 telephones and 80 Fullerphones at this time. An infantry division contained over 400 No. 18 or No. 38 infantry sets, 600 telephones and 120 Fullerphones.

Reserve Items.

Item	% of division-al holdings	Numbers of each type of equipment in each type of division		
		Armoured division	Mixed division	Infantry division
Wireless sets:				
No. 22	5	1	4	4
No. 19 in AFVs	2½	6	5	0
Other No. 19	5	17	5	0
No. 21	5	0	4	4
No. 18	10	2	11	14
No. 38	5½	5	19	15
No. 12	5	1	0	0
Reception sets R 107	12	4	1	1
Charging sets	6	9	9	8
Wavemeters	2½	0	1	1
Switchboards U C 10-line	2½	1	1	1
Telephones	2½	11	16	15
Fullerphones	2½	2	3	3
Cable D3}	Held by RAOC			
Cable D8}				

Figure 6.5 Reserves held in corps ordnance field parks.[77]

In the Western Desert, Eighth Army Signals had come to realize that the sudden imposition of wireless silence was itself a sign that some important activity was about to take place. The geographical sources of wireless traffic needed to be considered as well, since although DF might not be sufficiently precise to direct an artillery barrage, it could certainly give an approximate location. Thus, if a formation were to be moved prior to an attack, a dummy headquarters might be maintained in the original location and dummy wireless traffic sent from it in order to deceive the enemy, the real headquarters remaining silent. The Godwin-Austen Committee recommended that these more sophisticated systems of wireless security should be adopted. Such measures had, in fact, already been recommended in *MTP No. 41* of July 1943, showing that notice was being taken of the feedback from Africa before Godwin-Austen.[78]

Godwin-Austen found that in the Mediterranean theatre, Royal Signals had been given responsibility for several matters of signal security that had previously been handled by the General Staff. He recommended that the General Staff should be responsible for laying down security policy, while Signals should be responsible for advising the General Staff on policy, for issuing detailed instructions, maintaining a watch to see that instructions were carried out, taking corrective action in respect of breaches of security committed by Signals personnel and reporting to the General Staff breaches committed by others. The main burden of the transfer to Signals was the preparation, issue and distribution of code signs, map preferences, R/T and authentication codes. Godwin-Austen stated that signal deception would be useless unless it were related to all other means of deception in one comprehensive General Staff deception plan. Signals must therefore be associated with any such plan from its inception. These additional responsibilities were another reason why Signals establishments needed to be increased.[79]

The Godwin-Austen recommendations provided a framework for an effective communications system involving line, wireless and messengers, with duplication and redundancy, so that if one method failed, another could take over. Wireless now extended within infantry companies and artillery batteries, as well as down to individual tanks. Inter-arm communications had improved, though infantry–tank communications were still not satisfactory. The new system had been made possible by improvements in technology and increases in the amount of equipment, allied with an improved allocation of resources and revised methods of operating, and Godwin-Austen had ensured that policy was consistent between Home Forces and the Mediterranean. Though shortages of manpower meant that some of the recommendations took a long time to implement, command and control OODA loops could now operate much more rapidly than before, in mobile warfare. As described in the next two chapters, the system did not operate perfectly in Italy and North-West Europe, but it was infinitely better than the primitive arrangements that had struggled to cope in France and Flanders in 1940.

In summary, several problems arose within First and Eighth Armies during Operation TORCH and the invasion of Tunisia, and even more occurred when the two armies linked up. It was clear that the British Army still had a lot to learn after Alamein. But to what extent were inadequacies in communications responsible for the length of time that the Allies took to expel the enemy from North Africa? Although communications were partly responsible for some problems, there were many more important reasons for the slow pace of events, particularly the terrain, the supply difficulties that both First and Eighth Armies faced and the strength of Axis resistance, along with the much written-about themes of the possible lack of drive of First Army and the perhaps over-cautious approach of the commander of Eighth Army. Poor communications were a relatively minor contributor.

7

Sicily and Italy, 1943–44

The Godwin-Austen committee did not visit 15 Army Group until 12 August, at the end of the Sicilian campaign, but the CSO in Tunisia, Major General Penney, remained in overall charge of Army Group Signals in Sicily. Penney was therefore in a position to influence the training of the formations that were to form the new Eighth Army, so that they all operated in a consistent fashion. To what extent did he achieve this in the two months following the capture of Tunis? Did the lessons that had been learnt in North Africa, both in combined and land operations, influence the way in which the new operation was conducted? What is the truth about the performance of Signals in Sicily – was it generally satisfactory, as some authors have maintained, or does the charge of serious inefficiency that others have made stand up to scrutiny?[1] Is there evidence that British Signals performed worse than those in the US and German Armies? Did faulty communications contribute to the length of time that it took to defeat the Axis in Sicily, and to the fact that the Axis forces largely escaped to fight again in Italy?

The invasion of Italy in September 1943 closely followed victory in Sicily, raising the question of whether there was time to incorporate the lessons from Sicily into its planning. It was clear from the start that the geography of southern Italy, with its chains of mountains and numerous fast-flowing rivers, would greatly favour the defence and would pose severe problems for an army attempting to force its way northwards. Moreover, the weather in the autumn and winter of 1943 was particularly severe, making both physical movement and communications difficult. The Germans had accepted that they would not be able to defend Sicily for long, but they were determined to fight for every mile of ground in Italy. The Allies, at the highest military level, regarded Italy as a means of keeping the Germans busy rather than going all out for a rapid victory, and consequently tended to be parsimonious with their allocation of resources.[2] How did Signals deal with these challenges and to what extent did communications affect the outcomes of the key battles at Salerno, Cassino and Anzio? It was during the Italian campaign that the Godwin-Austen recommendations began to be implemented; a further question area is over the extent to which these were successful.

In January 1943, the Allies decided to invade Sicily once the Axis forces in North Africa had been defeated. No definite plan was made to continue into mainland Italy at this stage, a decision that was not finally made until after the Sicilian campaign had begun in July 1943. The invasion of Sicily was carried out by 15 Army Group, commanded by Alexander and consisting of the US 7 Army under Patton and the British Eighth Army under Montgomery. Eighth Army was temporarily dispersed at the end of the Tunisian campaign, so it was no longer identifiable to the enemy as a single force, and the training of the British formations that were to be involved took place in Egypt, the UK and Tunisia. As a result of this and other deception operations that disguised where the Allies would strike next, German forces were widely spread across the Italian islands, Italy and Greece.

The invasion plan for Sicily was code-named Operation HUSKY. Unlike in TORCH, the British and Americans were completely separated below Army Group level; this avoided previous problems arising from the different methods, including in the area of communications, which were used by the two armies. The invasion took place on 10 July 1943, with the British landing in the south-east of the island and the Americans landing further west. It took some time for the Italian and German forces that were present in Sicily to respond, impeded in part by the disruption to line communications that had been caused by Allied paratroopers. The Italian forces in the invasion areas were weak and did not put up a vigorous opposition, so that the British and American seaborne armies found it fairly easy to establish satisfactory bridgeheads. British and American airborne forces, however, experienced serious operational problems. German forces then reinforced the Italians, and the opposition became much stiffer. Progress up the east coast of the island by the British XIII Corps was initially rapid, but it was completely halted at the Primosole Bridge. Montgomery controversially switched his effort towards the west of Mount Etna, using XXX Corps, while Patton advanced round the west of the island to Palermo, before progressing rapidly along the north coast to arrive at the ultimate destination, Messina, on 16 August 1943, just before the British. By the time the Allies got to Messina, virtually all the Axis forces had been evacuated to mainland Italy, making the victory feel somewhat unsatisfactory.

The Allies immediately began preparations for invading Italy and Eighth Army began crossing the straits of Messina in Operation BAYTOWN on 3 September 1943, initially finding little resistance. Six days later, the US 5 Army, commanded by General Clark and including British X Corps, landed some 200 miles further up the west coast at Salerno in Operation AVALANCHE, but here, they immediately met stiff opposition and only just avoided defeat. Eighth Army eventually joined up with the Americans on 16 September, and by 1 October, Fifth Army had taken Naples and Eighth Army had captured the important airfields at Foggia on the eastern side of Italy. The Germans had prepared a series of defensive positions to the north, each of which they held onto tenaciously before withdrawing rapidly to the next one northwards. It therefore took until the beginning of January 1944 for the Allies slowly to fight their way up to the most heavily fortified line (the Gustav Line), which ran eastwards through Cassino to the coast near Pescara. The Allied forces in Italy had become very large by the beginning of February 1944, comprising IX Corps altogether – three in Eighth Army, five in US 5 Army (including British X Corps and NZ division), and one in reserve.

In an attempt to outflank the Gustav line, US VI Corps, including British 1 Division commanded by the ex-CSO, Major General Penney, landed at Anzio in Operation SHINGLE on 22 January 1944. The landing itself achieved complete surprise and was virtually unopposed, but the force did not advance inland to occupy the hills that overlooked the bridgehead before a strong German force had surrounded them. Fifty miles to the south, the main Allied force was unable to break through Cassino and VI Corps was consequently trapped at Anzio. Both at Anzio and on the Gustav line, conditions were reminiscent of the static battles of the First World War, including the massive use of artillery and heavy casualties. Cassino was finally overwhelmed at the end of May; VI Corps broke out from the Anzio bridgehead and Rome was captured on 4 June 1944. The Germans, meanwhile, were moving to the next major defensive line northwards, the Gothic Line, repeating the previous cycle of events. Operations in Italy after this date are not covered because their characteristics remained largely the same as before and because the Allies were then primarily focused on France; the campaign in Italy became, to an even greater extent than before, a means of diverting German troops away from the main theatres of North-West and Eastern Europe.

Training between victory in Tunisia and the invasion of Sicily

The formations making up the reconstituted Eighth Army were built up and prepared in the UK (1 Canadian Division), Egypt (5, 50 and 51 Divisions, and 231 Infantry Brigade) and Tunisia (78 Division). With these different locations and the different prior experiences of the formations, there was a danger that the history of First and Eighth Armies in Tunisia would repeat itself, and that they would not fit together after arriving in Sicily. Considerable efforts were made to avoid this, but lack of time meant that they were only partially successful. The judgement of a report issued soon after the invasion of Sicily was that 'Changes in [communications] equipment, organisation and procedure were necessary in order to get some degree of homogeneity . . . throughout the Army Group . . . There can be no doubt that these late changes did, temporarily, very much impair the efficiency of units, even though . . . they have since proved justified. It is hoped that existing [remaining] differences will be eliminated [by] the committee under Major General Godwin-Austen'.[3]

New equipment was issued on a considerable scale. No. 22 and portable No. 46 wireless sets for assault landings were issued to 51 and 1 Canadian Divisions, along with new handcarts for carrying the heavy No. 22 sets, and new pattern waterproof bags for keeping the wireless sets dry during landing. The 5 and 50 Divisions, however, had No. 48 sets in place of No. 46, only a partial issue of No. 22 sets, and older types of handcart and waterproof bags. Receiving only sets were issued down to battalion commander level, so that units could be kept in touch with the overall course of events by an Army broadcast; this was to continue until corps tactical headquarters had landed.[4]

Figure 7.1 No. 46 set. Although bulky by modern standards, this set could easily be carried and operated by one man. Crystal control made it very suitable for amphibious landings.[5]

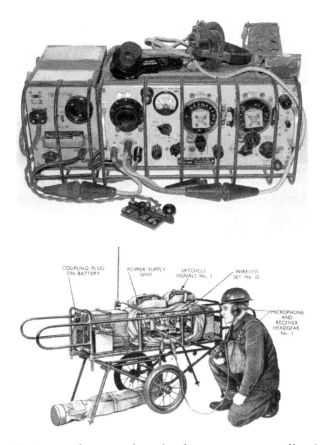

Figure 7.2 No. 22 set in close up and on a handcart in its waterproof bag.[6]

Troops needed time to become familiar with new equipment, which in some cases, arrived without essential instruction manuals, but it was not possible to give sufficient training in every case. A major issue in Tunisia had been the lack of signals security, and while many of the problems were caused simply by the careless use of R/T on the part of officers, others were the result of faulty and non-standard signalling procedures. The latter were addressed by issuing a new Link Call Sign procedure, and changes to codes and ciphers.[7] These were introduced in XXX Corps, 50 and 51 Divisions in June 1943, according to their war diaries, and it is assumed that they were implemented in all British formations. It may, however, be noted that no reference to them appeared in the Signals war diary of 78 Division, the ex-First Army formation that needed to pay particularly careful attention to security on the basis of its performance in Tunisia.[8] This absence does not necessarily mean that the new procedures were ignored, but it may be indicative at least of the attitude of mind of Signals in this division, either towards security or, bearing in mind the ill-feeling that had existed in some parts of First Army against Eighth Army, towards instructions from their new masters. Another development was the introduction of new combined R/T and W/T procedures for use when communicating with the forces of other nations and with other services.[9]

Each formation underwent individual training and took part in a series of combined operation training exercises. Afterwards, 15 Army Group felt that signals exercises during training were left too late, and there was insufficient time to correct the errors that emerged.[10] But taking 50 Division as an example, the problems in communications that were identified in an exercise on 12 June were rectified in an exercise a few days later.[11] The 51 Division was also fairly positive about their 'progressive' training exercises. First, a signals-cum-staff exercise was held at brigade level, in which all signal communication links were fully extended and all the landing craft that carried Royal Signals personnel were employed. This was followed by a series of brigade exercises involving troops and finally by a virtually full-scale divisional exercise. According to the report, these generated an 'extremely happy relationship between staff and signals', though it was felt that fewer exercises of longer duration might have been more useful.[12] Army communications worked well in all the 51 Division exercises, but naval wireless communications scarcely existed until the last exercise, and there were never any RAF communications at all.[13] This lack of involvement by the RAF in training and planning was noted at 15 Army Group – 'RAF signal planning was consistently late [and] caused anxiety and lack of confidence in army formations'.[14] The lack of co ordination of signals planning between the three services was blamed on the wide geographic separation of their planning headquarters, and the document summarizing the lessons from the preparations for HUSKY concluded that planning for all services should in future be concentrated in one place.[15] There was insufficient time to implement this recommendation before the invasion of mainland Italy, the planning of which was already underway by this time. Nevertheless, the issue of this document, and the many other summaries of lessons drawn from operations, demonstrates clearly that Eighth Army made great efforts to learn from its experiences. The Director of Military Training at the War Office reinforced these efforts and made frequent requests for 'hot news' on topics that would be of value in training in the UK and other theatres.[16]

The magnitude of the task of retraining the formations involved in HUSKY in the light of lessons learnt in Tunisia was too great to be accomplished in the short time available. Nevertheless, some progress was made and although preparations for HUSKY were imperfect, they were far better than they had been for TORCH.

The major amphibious landings and river crossings

The army laid more emphasis on learning from the experience of amphibious landings than it did from land operations. In part, this was because of the relative novelty of amphibious operations, but also because everyone was aware that the inevitable and highly dangerous invasion of North-West Europe (Operation OVERLORD) was not far ahead. An improvement in communications took place over time, and the lessons learnt were certainly of great assistance in the preparations for OVERLORD. Amphibious techniques were also adapted for major river crossings, the crossing of the River Garigliano in January 1944 providing a good example.

HUSKY (Sicily)

Operation HUSKY was a success. Communications problems occurred during the seaborne landings, but many of the recommendations made after TORCH had been implemented, and problems were fewer this time. Moreover, the lack of determined opposition from the Italians meant that the overall success of the invasion was not prejudiced. But the simultaneous operation by the British 1 Air-landing Brigade was chaotic, with its communications problems predominantly the result of all the wireless sets of the few effective troops being lost or damaged during landing.[17]

Communications during the seaborne landings were primarily by wireless (some flares were used in addition), and a very large number of frequencies was needed. The system of frequency allocation adopted was the same as that used in Tunisia when First and Eighth Armies met – overlapping frequencies were allowed on low power nets that were geographically separated, but more powerful transmitters had their own unique frequencies. This system had just been used in the preceding Operation CORKSCREW, the invasion of Pantellaria, but it worked better in HUSKY and there were very few cases of interference.[18] Formations observed wireless silence as they embarked from their training grounds while dummy wireless traffic was maintained in their original locations to disguise what was happening. Wireless sets were netted immediately beforehand and frequencies were calibrated using standard wave meters. The tuning dials of non-crystal sets were then locked and left untouched until immediately before the assault (this was not, of course, necessary with crystal sets, which were by definition, tuned to their pre-determined frequencies). The ships within each convoy communicated using V/T during the voyage. When wireless silence was broken, there was generally little difficulty in establishing contact in each net, proving that the overall system had worked well.[19]

The centres of communications during the landings were the HQ ships, the most important ones being HMS *Bulolo* (HQ XIII Corps) and HMS *Largs* (HQ XXX Corps). They communicated with the landing craft as they approached the beaches, and then with the troops on the beaches. Communications from the HQ ships were generally good in spite of the fact that, in many cases, arrangements only came together at the last minute and no time for testing was available. It was later concluded that more time should have been allowed to test communications thoroughly and to correct any errors that were found.[20] The personal interest that commanders had in signalling issues influenced later success. An after-action report stated, 'Communications on HQ ships would be more satisfactory if commanders displayed an earlier interest. [Commander] 1 Canadian Division did not visit his ship before [HUSKY] and was entirely dissatisfied with arrangements, whereas [Commander] XXX Corps paid a visit to *Largs* at Suez some weeks before the operation'.[21]

Failures of communication occurred in some larger landing ships due to a combination of unsatisfactory equipment and insufficient training among the naval rating operators; it was felt that, in future, the crystal-controlled No. 46 set was the only wireless simple enough for these operators to handle properly in their existing state of training. In some cases, the problems caused confusion about the progress of the landings until troops were established on the beach and could set up their own sets. Had there been heavier opposition, this might well have affected the course of the battle.[22] The seas during the landings were very rough, causing many sets to be thrown about and damaged by water as well as incapacity among the men through sea-sickness. The diary of one Royal Signals officer, Captain Mayhew, illustrates some of the problems.

During the invasion of Sicily, Captain Mayhew was in command of a Phantom patrol whose job was to monitor the forward wireless communications of British units and formations and then to pass interesting information straight back to higher commanders. Nearly all wireless messages were (or should have been) encoded or enciphered and Phantom operators therefore had to have knowledge of each unit's and formation's call sign and coding information. On 6 July 1943, Mayhew embarked on a landing ship tank (LST), bound for Sicily. 'My little patrol is complete and on good form. I clutch my precious map case inside which is a précis of the entire Corps plan with all the innumerable codes. There is a map reference code, a code for W/T frequencies, a time code, lists of code signs of formations, list of code words for objectives, and of code words for common words of operational significance. Also a personnel code and a Codex machine. All of these we must use and understand. Decoding is going to be a headache'. His patrol transferred to a smaller boat, a landing craft assault (LCA) capable of sailing right up to the beach for the final assault. It was, he wrote, 'Blowing a gale and extremely rough. Much distressed over prospects of operations. How can an LCA possibly be launched let alone land in a sea like this. Find my three operators absolutely prostrate with sickness. Wireless aerial not put up so get Miller on set and climb about the wet boat deck trying to fix aerial. Eventually fix aerial through wind funnel by jamming knife through gauze cover'. But they landed successfully and did not find that the Italians put up much opposition, 'It has been a very dull battle – thanks to the enemy'.[23]

The success with which sets were waterproofed depended on whether the new pattern of waterproofing bag was used; some sets in older types of bag and those that had been used before were 'drowned', while new bags were so effective

Figure 7.3 Landing Craft Assault.[24]

that sets could be floated ashore in them. To avoid the sets 'sweating' in the bags, it was desirable to fit them as late as possible.[25]

The planning of HUSKY was a complicated logistical operation and some errors were made. There were several instances when signals personnel were loaded in one ship and their transport and equipment in another; this was obviously disastrous if the two ships did not set out simultaneously or became separated in the rough seas – personnel and equipment were sometimes separated for long periods after arrival (in one instance, for 14 days). These problems were caused by the reorganization and re-equipping of formations that were taking place at the same time as the operation was being planned. After landing, beach signals units were set up in accordance with combined operations doctrine to act as temporary signals offices for each assaulting formation in turn, pending the arrival of their own signals units. But the greater number of landing craft available meant that it was often possible to implement the recommendation made after TORCH, and to land assaulting formations complete with their own signals, rendering this function of the Beach Signals Unit unnecessary. Some flexibility was therefore needed in the way in which these units operated; for example, they were used on occasion by both XIII Corps and 5 Division for their original function, but they also did other valuable work in providing tactical wireless networks onshore. The system of broadcasting news of how the assault was going, to keep troops in touch with overall progress and to maintain their morale, was a technical success but, according to one report, 'owing to a failure . . . to give any news whatever, [it was] not much use'. It required more thought.[26] As a result, during AVALANCHE and subsequently, force-wide news broadcasts included air raid warnings, situation reports and other information in their content.[27]

Inevitably, there were successes and failures in communications on the beaches. The overall verdict was that communications within beach groups were satisfactory, but communication between beaches was poor because of intervening mountains, and this made co ordination of attacks inland extremely difficult.[28] Even within beaches, some problems occurred. In 50 Division, for example, the HQ ship was out of position and beyond the range of the wireless sets of the assault battalions when they started transmitting. Wireless links to brigades failed during the first night because some batteries had not been kept charged during the voyage and some No. 22 sets proved unreliable as operators lacked experience with this new type of set. Wireless improved after the first night. Bad communications from its leading brigade meant that 5 Division was unclear on how its assault was proceeding. Light cable on the beaches was constantly being broken by tracked vehicles and shrapnel, and opinions about its value were mixed.[29] Visual signalling using Verey lights to indicate success was too easily confused with enemy signals and it was difficult to tell from the sea from which beach they came. In general, however, the new wireless equipment was felt to have acquitted itself well. The No. 46 set was easy to use and uniformly successful, given a sufficient supply of crystals; the larger, longer-range No. 22 set required more expert usage, but was also highly successful in the right hands; the No. 48 set, issued to 50 Division in lieu of No. 46s, had a better range than a No. 18, gave a reasonable performance, but was not crystal controlled and its tuning dials were difficult to use in the dark.[30]

HUSKY took place eight months after TORCH, so there should have been plenty of time to incorporate the lessons from TORCH in the planning. To some extent, this did take place and HUSKY was more successful. However, the planning of HUSKY was overshadowed by the struggle to achieve victory in Tunisia and the discussions on exactly how the invasion of Sicily should take place. In the end, planning and training had to take place quickly and this accounted for some of the remaining problems. Others were due to adverse weather and geographic conditions, the inadequacy and difficulty of use of some equipment, and human error.

AVALANCHE (Salerno)

The degree to which Signals were successful in the strongly opposed landing at Salerno was the subject of heated discussion immediately afterwards. A highly critical report was written by Major Thompson, a Royal Signals officer in 46 Division, and issued over the signature of the commander of the Divisional Signals.[31] This enraged the CSO of X Corps, who described the report as written by a 'young and apparently irresponsible officer', 'grossly impertinent' and 'containing a multitude of misleading and unfounded allegations'. He went on to say that it had been established beyond doubt that AVALANCHE was a success from a Signals point of view, and that it could never have succeeded if there had been any truth in the accusations levelled by Thompson at the planners of the operation.[32] Further up the chain of command, the CSO of Allied Force headquarters described Thompson as having 'power without responsibility' and said that he had taken insufficient account of the operational difficulties facing senior commanders.[33] Nevertheless, many of Thompson's criticisms were confirmed by other reports and he was quoted by Nalder (by then, the CSO of 15 Army Group) in a private letter to Major General Phillips, Director of Signals at the War Office, some months later, showing that he had credibility.[34] The final report on Signals in AVALANCHE pointed to several shortcomings.

British X Corps comprised 46 and 56 Divisions, neither of which had fought in Sicily, and the planning for AVALANCHE took place before a full analysis had been made of how communications had performed in HUSKY. So, it is not surprising that some of the lessons learnt in HUSKY were not implemented in AVALANCHE and some of the same mistakes were made. The 46 Division Signals report stated that no close support aircraft were seen during the landings and this may have been caused by the RAF being late in putting forward its frequency requirements. Another problem common to both HUSKY and AVALANCHE was that formations had insufficient time to train on the unfamiliar equipment issued just before the landings and much of that supplied from the Middle East was found to be faulty or inadequate and in need of replacement by UK-sourced equipment. Once again, there was insufficient time to test communications on the HQ ships and this proved to be a serious problem for 46 Division on USS *Biscayne* (a small converted aircraft tender), where mutual interference between sets and static from the ship's equipment was described as 'chronic'. As a result, communications were established to the brigades under command, but 46 Division could not hear corps headquarters because of interference. Insufficient time was again left for testing when *Biscayne* was used at Anzio four months later and exactly the same problems occurred. The headquarters of brigades were carried on LCIs (infantry landing craft), from which communications were broadly satisfactory, though generally established very late because of enemy action.[35]

Most brigades were self-sufficient in their communications as soon as they landed at Salerno, but 169 Brigade of 56 Division used the central Main Beach Signals Office because its own signals had been sunk by enemy action. No. 22 sets were landed to provide longer-range communications, but there were insufficient personnel to move them on their poorly designed handcarts and many sets were shoddily constructed, developing faults due to dry soldered joints. As a result, they were initially left at the beach signal offices while units moved inland, carrying No. 46 and No. 18 sets. Since the pace of advance was slow in the face of strong opposition, the latter afforded sufficient range, but their dry-cell battle batteries gave much trouble, just as they had done in Tunisia. Thompson said that 80 per cent of the batteries were useless, while the rest only lasted half an hour, and replacement batches had to be rushed from the UK by air. The consequent demand for telephones on the beach was difficult to meet because of a lack of personnel and the continuous damage to lines caused by vehicles; it was concluded that an extra line-laying detachment was needed by corps Signals, and that lines should be suspended on poles.[36]

Turning to security issues, Ultra decrypts in the middle of August revealed that the Germans knew that Salerno was likely to be used as a landing place, but this did not cause the Allies to change their plans.[37] The source of the Germans' information is uncertain, but seems most likely to have been due to agents' reports stemming from a general lack of security during the preparations rather than from the interception of signals before embarking – a junior Signals officer wrote of his pre operation briefing that 'The Brigade commander gave us all the interesting facts of the operation including formations and destination . . . For subalterns to know the destination of an operation of this magnitude is shocking. If we have a warm welcome I shall not be surprised'.[38] How right he was. The first convoys were discovered by enemy reconnaissance aircraft as they approached Salerno and when it was realized that surprise had been lost, wireless silence was broken in advance of H hour. Once again, the standard of R/T security during the landings themselves was poor, particularly among officers of 201 Guards Brigade, whom Thompson accused of 'hogging the airwaves with largely senseless conversation' (an example of the tactless style of his many criticisms). Many codes had to be withdrawn because they had been compromised or captured in the close fighting, showing that plenty of alternative codes needed to be provided in future to avoid R/T deteriorating into clear or 'veiled' speech.[39]

Communications in AVALANCHE were sufficiently successful for the landings to establish themselves on the beachhead, but they could have been much better if sufficient time had been available for planning, training and testing equipment. In addition, far too little attention was given to disguising the intended landing point.

SHINGLE (Anzio)

SHINGLE started on 22 January 1944 and, this time, the Germans were taken by surprise. Nalder (then CSO) wrote that he had gone to considerable pains to make a wireless cover plan for the landings at Anzio, foreshadowing the preparations for OVERLORD.[40] Indeed, as decrypts showed, the strict wireless silence observed by the Allies was the principal reason given by the German regional commander for failing to foresee the landings, coupled with an absence of agents' reports, an inability to mount air and sea reconnaissance and radar failure.[41] The Anzio landings were not strongly opposed as a result of the tight security, and were successful. British communications generally worked well.

The 1 Division was the only British formation involved in the landings. It was fortunate to have *Bulolo* as its HQ ship, communications from which were good. US VI Corps was given *Biscayne*, which had proved subject to heavy interference at Salerno. It was now a general recommendation by the CSO of 15 Army Group that a thorough rehearsal should take place before embarkation, but *Biscayne* had arrived too late for this to happen and, as a result, communications back to US 5 Army were very poor until after VI Corps headquarters had landed. It was resolved after SHINGLE that *Biscayne* should not be used again until the problems were solved.[42]

The 1 Division Signals diary reported no amphibious training in December 1943, but there was one thorough rehearsal, Exercise OBOE, just three days before SHINGLE. During the actual landings, wireless conditions were good, and the No. 46 sets were particularly praised. Communications worked well in the relative tranquillity that reigned in the beachhead in the first week after landing, which gave time for supply and other systems to be well established. It is clear that communications problems were not responsible for the much-criticized failure of VI Corps to push inland.[43]

The crossing of the River Garigliano

Some of the principles of amphibious landings were adopted in major river crossings. As an example, Operation PANTHER was mounted on 17 January 1944 to cross the River Garigliano, a formidable obstacle that formed the south-western end of the Gustav Line, to the south of Cassino and 60 miles from Anzio.

The 5 Division assaulted the river at its seaward end, with 13 Brigade on the right and 17 Brigade on the left, at the mouth of the river. Once a bridgehead had been established on the other side, the intention was to build bridges over the river. Plans for the initial stages of the assault were reminiscent of the crossing of the minefields at the start of the battle of Alamein, as far as communications were concerned – prior to the assault, lines would be laid at night up to terminals close to the river, the crossing by boat and the initial landing would be controlled by wireless, and light lines would then be drawn across the river to be replaced later by heavy multi-channel cables, which would be weighted down so that they lay on the bottom of the river. Rafts would be used by 13 Brigade to cross where the river was narrower, and its assault here turned out to be completely successful. But 17 Brigade would use sea-faring landing craft to go round the mouth of the river with the intention of establishing a beach maintenance area on the north side. The beach commander was provided with a No. 22 set, duplicated by a second No. 22 set, and shorter-range No. 46 sets were provided as well. The problems encountered by 17 Brigade provide an instructive illustration of how well-laid plans could go wrong and how communications could fail.[44]

Owing to faulty navigation in bad weather, many of 17 Brigade's landing craft failed to reach the north side of the river, but mistakenly landed on the same side that they had set off from. Thinking they were on the north side, they unloaded tanks that then drove at right angles inland, cutting through the cables that had been pre-laid between main and tactical brigade headquarters beside the river. In the meantime, the beach commander's DUKW (amphibious vehicle) was grounded on a sandbank, but he maintained communications through his No. 22 set until his vessel was rammed and partly submerged by another landing craft, drowning his wireless. At this point, he released two pigeons, the method of last resort, to inform division headquarters of what had happened. In addition, it was found that wireless reception was unusually bad near the mouth of the river, causing breakdowns in several wireless nets, which could not be overcome even with the use of intermediate 'step-up' sets. Because of all the problems in the south-west, the divisional commander switched the main axis of the assault to the right hand, 13 Brigade, sector and a second main cable was laid across the river there. These cables were subjected to continuous shellfire from German artillery on the surrounding hills, so the main axis was later switched back to the left hand sector, which by that time had sorted itself out, and the division eventually crossed the river.

The whole episode can either be viewed as an illustration of the fragility of communications, or alternatively as a vivid justification of the benefit of multiple backup systems; it is not surprising that different writers have been able to view similar incidents in entirely contradictory lights, depending on the points that they have wished to make. In the author's view, the overall communication *system* at the River Garigliano did not fail – it was sufficiently resilient to overcome a large number of unexpected set-backs, most of which were caused by factors beyond the signallers' control.

To summarize, communications during HUSKY and AVALANCHE were imperfect, but did not lead to a major disaster, while British communications in SHINGLE were good. The techniques learnt in the landings assisted in the many river crossings that were required during the land operations in Italy, and were invaluable in the planning for OVERLORD. The latter additionally benefitted from a much lengthier and more orderly planning process, putting right one of the key remaining faults identified in Italy - the lack of time allowed for planning and training because of late decisions and changes of plan in the highest political and Army levels. The question arises of how much account senior commanders took of the length of time needed to complete the complicated logistical plans for large operations and the extent to which rushing them might prejudice their chances. It is well known that Montgomery had to resist ferocious pressure from Winston Churchill to launch the attack at Second Alamein before he was ready and the timing of the amphibious landings was equally contentious. There was great urgency to press on and senior commanders may simply have judged that the systems would be able to cope; inasmuch as the operations were broadly successful, they were correct. An example of Brooke's attitude in such matters is shown by his reported introduction to Lieutenant General F. E. Morgan of his job of planning the invasion of North-West Europe – 'Well, there it is. It won't work, but you must bloody well make it'.[45]

Airborne operations

Airborne operations were used by both the British and the Americans during the Sicily campaign, but were found to be fraught with difficulties. One of these operations, the attempt to capture the Primosole Bridge near Catania, had an extremely negative effect on the campaign, and is therefore examined here in detail. Primosole Bridge blocked XIII Corps' advance up the east coast, and in order to secure it before the Germans could blow it up, the British planned that 1 Airborne Division should land by parachute and glider. The Division should capture the bridge and then defend it for 24 hours against the expected armoured counter-attack until 50 Division advanced from the south to join up. The action commenced on 13 July 1943. Several problems occurred with the landings, so that fewer than 300 out of the intended 1,850 airborne troops were available for the battle. They then had serious problems in communicating with the ground forces and, because of the resulting confusion, the Germans were able to consolidate their hold on the area.

A major reason for the failure was that a large proportion of the main means of communication, the No. 22 wireless set, was dropped by parachute in the wrong place. Although it was afterwards concluded that, in future, wireless equipment should as far as possible be dropped 'on the man' – portable sets attached to the operator – this would not have been appropriate at Primosole Bridge since portable sets would not have had the range to communicate back to the leading elements of XIII Corps. More powerful No. 22 sets were essential for this task, but they were heavy and required at least three men to carry them. The difficulty of manhandling No. 22 sets meant that future airborne operations included sets mounted in jeeps and flown in by glider.[46]

Of the sets that were retrieved after landing, some had been damaged in the drop and others were 'drowned' when fording the river. There were also more easily avoided mistakes – a No. 22 set was in working order, but 1 Airborne Division was still unable to make contact with the relieving ground troops because the latter were not monitoring wireless communications within the airborne forces and because the No. 22 set's operator did not know the frequencies and call signs of the ground formations. Furthermore, after accidental wireless contact had been made with another formation, 4 Armoured Brigade, the two sides could not understand each other's map reference codes. The CSO of 15 Army Group recommended that in future airborne operations, all forces must know each other's frequencies and call signs, that regular watches should be kept on the airborne forces' lateral frequency, and that lateral ciphers should be simplified. More generally, it was felt that much more training was needed before further operations could be attempted.[47]

Referring to this action, the American historian Carlo D'Este blamed the problems of communications on the 'notoriously inefficient British wireless sets.'[48] But he was wrong to express it in this way because it was the absence of undamaged sets and the way the communication system was set up and operated that was to blame, not the wireless sets themselves. D'Este's insinuation that British wireless in Sicily was worse than the American equivalent also appears dubious – a report on communications in 1 US Infantry Division identified many problems and a military observer of the American landings at Licata wrote that 'a layman was left with the impression that wireless was a totally unreliable means of communication, [although it] improved as the campaign went on . . .'[49] Axis forces also suffered from poor communications in Sicily.[50] All sides had communication problems and a judgement on whether one side was better overall than another is extremely difficult, if not impossible, to make and is beyond the scope of this book.

Nevertheless, in making his comments about British wireless, D'Este was undoubtedly expressing the view held at the time by many junior British officers. Therefore, an important question is why senior officers generally appeared satisfied with wireless communications when they were questioned by Royal Signals whereas junior infantry officers frequently complained.[51] One reason is that wireless communications for senior officers were simply better, because more attention was given to them, because their sets were usually handled by Royal Signals rather than less expert regimental signallers and because, being motorized, they could use heavier and more powerful sets.[52] By contrast, junior infantry officers tended to use portable Nos. 18 and 38 sets, which were light enough to manhandle over rough terrain, but were not very powerful and often had battery problems. It is also possible that senior officers were more aware than their subordinates of the realities of the power-to-weight relationship in wireless sets, explained below, and that when they said communications were satisfactory, they meant that they were as satisfactory as could be expected within the bounds of existing technology. The expectations of the users were also important; Royal Signals operators could often fight through fading and interference to communicate, but if officers expected the reception to be like a telephone, they would be disappointed and might simply give up.

The failure to achieve a breakthrough at the Primosole Bridge had serious consequences, for the British did not finally move northwards from the Catania area until 5 August, and were then only able to do so because the Germans withdrew as a result of being outflanked by operations further west. Failure to make a rapid breakthrough at Primosole was an important factor in the length of time taken to finish the Sicilian campaign and communications problems contributed to the failure.

Land operations

Communications in land operations in Sicily and Italy exhibited a number of themes that developed in parallel with the main battles. The mountainous terrain in Sicily and Italy caused land operations to be akin to those in Tunisia and to have a completely different character from the campaign in the Western

Desert. Truly mobile operations were usually impossible, so armoured divisions played a minor role and tanks were primarily used to interact with infantry. Thus tank–infantry communications were particularly important. The inability to achieve mobility meant that many of the key actions in Italy became battles of attrition involving massive artillery barrages, causing high casualty rates and consequent shortages of trained signallers, and making it difficult to implement the increased manpower scales that had been recommended by Godwin-Austen. The mountains themselves interfered with wireless communications and made it difficult to lay lines. They also caused problems with the transportation of heavy wireless and other signalling equipment, particularly in the extremely wet weather that occurred in winter. Tanks, guns and trucks could not travel cross-country and were restricted to the few narrow roads, which were easily blocked and defended. By contrast with the wide open spaces of the desert, formations were crammed together, causing congestion on the ground and making the operation of a large number of wireless links without mutual interference difficult. Moreover, traffic control – avoiding blockages and making sure men and equipment passed along the roads in the right order – became an extremely important issue so that elaborate communications systems were needed between the traffic control points.[53] First Army had faced many of these difficulties in Tunisia, but the senior commanders of Eighth Army were relatively inexperienced in mountain warfare, and had to adapt quickly.

A major problem with forward infantry communications was the short range of portable wireless sets and the weight of longer-range sets – the power-to-weight relationship. The No. 19 set (primarily designed for use in tanks) had an R/T range of 10 miles with an eight-foot rod aerial, but it was cumbersome, weighed at least 65 lbs and was usually carried in a vehicle. The No. 22 set had a similar range and was only slightly less heavy; a handcart was sometimes supplied to enable it to be manhandled, but this was unsatisfactory on very rough ground encountered in the mountains and the sets were sometimes left behind to be brought forward later.[54] The No.18 set was much smaller and weighed 32 lbs, so it could be carried and operated by two men (or one man when fitted with a low capacity battle battery); but it only had a range of 1–3 miles with a ground aerial or 2–5 miles with a six-foot rod. The single-man No. 38 set weighed only 22 lbs and had a range of 0.5 miles with a four-foot rod or 2 miles with a 12-foot rod.[55] This power-to-weight relationship posed a dilemma for the infantry, illustrated by the experience of the Hastings and Prince Edward Regiment of 1 Canadian Division at Assoro in Sicily on 21 July 1943.

The hinge of the Germans' defensive position in central Sicily was the mountain that rose 1,000 feet above the plain, at the top of which was the village of Assoro. On the highest point, above the village, was its ruined twelfth-century castle, which had never previously been successfully stormed. The battalion commander, Colonel Lord Tweedsmuir, planned to take the village by making a flanking march by night to the foot of the steepest cliff below the castle, scaling it and making a surprise attack at dawn. The regiment had earlier found their back pack radios 'useless' (by which, they probably meant insufficiently powerful), so that when they commenced the attack on 21 July, Tweedsmuir insisted that his signallers brought along a heavy No. 19 set, which was normally used in tanks. They managed to get the set to the foot of the cliff on a mule, but this then collapsed and died of exhaustion. Somehow, the set was hauled manually up the precipice, along with Bren guns and two-inch mortars.

When they reached the top by the castle, the Canadians found it manned only by an artillery observation post because the Germans had thought the cliff impossible to climb. The observation team was quickly overwhelmed. From the vantage point of the castle, the Canadians were then able to attack the main German force on the plateau just below the village. Ferocious German counter-attacks were mounted throughout the day, but the No. 19 set enabled the Canadians repeatedly to call up artillery barrages from their batteries on the plain below and were thus able to stave off them off. This would have been beyond the range of a more easily portable set. A battalion of Panzer Grenadiers mounted a final series of attacks an hour after sunset, but these too were beaten off with the aid of the Canadian artillery, and the Germans gave up Assoro the following morning. Tweedsmuir attributed the success of the operation both to the wireless set and to the deceased mule, which had almost certainly saved the lives of 500 men.[56]

In addition to problems caused by the mountainous terrain, wireless was often affected by other factors – for example, the magnetic, dusty soil around Mount Etna had an adverse effect on the communications of 78 Division, which could only slightly be ameliorated through experimentation with different kinds of aerial and earth.[57] Heavy winter rain in Italy meant that sets had to be waterproofed in the same way as in amphibious landings (and in the jungles of Burma). There were many instances of the same failures with the dry, un-rechargeable battle batteries for Nos. 18 and 38 sets that occurred at Salerno, though their reliability had improved by February 1944.[58] Poor wireless communications were also often attributable to inexperienced operators. As a result, training was given in the selection of suitable sites and aerials; the courses given by 1 Canadian Division, for example, contributed materially to the excellent communications that were maintained during the assault on the Hitler Line at the end of May 1944.[59] Compared with previous communications, there was a greatly increased scale of wireless infantry communications down to company level, though they remained inadequate below that. Wireless was now the primary means for forward communications, but cable was also laid when there was time; in this respect, infantry signals had finally broken free from the Jackson doctrine of the mid-1930s. This meant a large increase in the number of wireless sets, but there was no proportionate increase in Royal Signals personnel, so that operators needed to be found from within units, reducing the number of 'bayonet carriers'.[60]

There was also an increased demand for line further back, for example to link up additional tactical headquarters at brigade level. This made the increased number of cable laying detachments, already agreed as a result of the Tunisian campaign, doubly necessary. If mules were not available, laying forward line communications in the mountains sometimes necessitated the secondment of drivers to act as porters for the equipment. Use was made of single-stranded light assault cable, which employed a less secure earth return rather than another wire in order to save cable, but because this was not robust, it needed to be upgraded to stronger paired field cables as soon as positions stabilized, buried to provide protection from shellfire and vehicles.[61] Visual signalling using lamp was frequently used when W/T was unreliable and line could not be laid, but these methods were slow and extravagant in personnel since they required two men per V/T terminal, one to operate the lamp and one to read out or write down messages. V/T operators also needed to be careful to avoid betraying their location, particularly when misty weather at night diffused the light from their signalling lamps.

There was a stark contrast between the slow pace of advances in Italy and the rapid movement that had taken place in the Western Desert. There were a number of reasons for the slow pace, including the problems of movement in the mountains and commanders' judgement that the risk was too great of forward formations being cut off from their supply lines if they advanced too rapidly, as well as the strength of resistance of the enemy. Another reason was that wireless had insufficient capacity to meet the demands of divisional headquarters in Italy – elaborate line systems therefore had to be laid, which could only be done at a rate of approximately five miles a day. Brigades could move faster than this, but they had to wait for higher formations to catch up. All this combined to mean that on the rare occasions when movement of the large armies in the Italian campaign was achieved, it was slow and deliberate.[62]

Infantry, armour and artillery all needed effective communications between each other as well as within themselves. Systems were improved during the Sicilian and Italian campaigns, but communications between tanks and infantry in particular were unsatisfactory and remained so in North-West Europe, as discussed in detail in the next chapter. Artillery communications in early 1944 '[stood] out a mile by itself' according to Penney in contrast to those within the infantry, which were 'very backward and [did not] receive nearly enough attention'.[63] By contrast with the situation between the infantry and armour, communications between the infantry and artillery was nearly always excellent in Italy, a performance attributable not only to the fact that it was within the technical capabilities of the existing equipment, but also because infantry and artillery units had normally trained and lived together for long periods.[64]

As forces were massed to try to break through the Gustav Line in January 1944, it was agreed that V Corps Royal Artillery should have separate line and wireless networks so that the commander-in-chief of the Royal Artillery (CCRA) could control the entire corps artillery.[65] This also occurred during the final, decisive battle for Cassino in May when the CCRA of XIII Corps had his own separate headquarters five miles in front of the corps commander, together with an elaborate laddered line system connecting all the RA regiments and a wireless network, including a continuous broadcast of artillery reconnaissance reports. It was the largest build-up of artillery communications since Alamein. The system imposed a much more complicated system of command, requiring a greatly increased number of communication networks. It worked well within the artillery, but the decision to locate the CCRA in his own headquarters impaired communications between him and the corps commander, and it was decided that, in future, the CCRA should always remain at main corps headquarters.[66] The use of very large amounts of artillery meant that forward formations had to remain within reach of the ordnance depots, which also took over the supply of some signalling equipment (for example, the disposable battle batteries for portable sets) from Signal Parks in early 1944.[67]

During static periods, for example, on the Gustav line in the first months of 1944 and in the Anzio beachhead, line communications predominated. At Anzio, all outposts and gun positions were connected by line, placing an increased demand for telephones and small switchboards. Since the entire beachhead was in reach of enemy artillery, lines were laid in the extensive system of drainage tunnels or were buried using field ploughs. They were laid in a laddered system so that if one section was cut, a communication route could still be found, and lines were duplicated, triplicated and sometimes even quadruplicated to provide backup. This naturally placed a heavy demand for line maintenance crews. Communications back to Army headquarters further down the coast was of necessity by wireless; it was possible to use high speed VHF sets connected to automatic teleprinters because a direct line-of-sight existed from a headland near Army headquarters to Anzio.[68]

During pursuits, it became possible even for Corps headquarters to operate entirely by wireless, though they had to borrow extra equipment from Signal Parks to do so. Generally, however, the rule was for wireless to be supplemented by the maximum line that could be provided, because of the latter's greater traffic carrying capacity, security and 'intimacy'.[69] After the breakthrough at Cassino, 1 Canadian Division advanced at a rate of five miles a day, laying line as it went along the axis of the advance, with laterals being laid to the brigades on either side, while good wireless links were maintained to the brigades and to reconnaissance as well. As they prepared to attack the next German defensive position, the Hitler Line, cables became more difficult to maintain because of enemy fire and damage by their own tracked vehicles, but during the attack on 20 May 1944, no line was out of action for more than 30 minutes, with connections available to all formations at all times. Wireless also worked well during the attack, assisted by the short intensive training course that had been held just beforehand.[70]

The campaigns in Sicily and Italy were costly both in terms of casualties among signallers and loss of signalling equipment. Malaria disabled more men in Sicily than battle casualties, and became a threat again at Anzio the following spring, while battle casualties were very high during the battles at Anzio and Cassino. Overall, monthly 'wastage' rates from battle casualties and sickness were considerably lower in Royal Signals than in the infantry and the Royal Armoured Corps. In July 1943, for example, 4 per cent of Royal Signals officers were out of action, compared with 20 per cent of infantry officers, 11 per cent of Royal Armoured Corps officers and 9 per cent for the overall Army. Wastage rates for other ranks were about two-thirds of the rate for officers in all cases.[71] Casualties in Royal Signals varied by trade with occupations such as despatch riding and line maintenance being much more at risk than wireless operating at divisional headquarters, for example. There was also pressure on manpower from the conflicting requirements of the forthcoming operations OVERLORD and ANVIL (southern France). An example of the scale of the loss of equipment was the destruction of over 200 wireless sets in 1 Division in its first month at Anzio. By early 1944, it had become easier to replace equipment than to recruit and train new signallers, and lack of experienced operators certainly led to some communications failures. As examples, 1 Canadian Divisional Signals was 70 men (about 10 per cent) below strength in October 1943, particular shortages being in wireless and line operators and driver mechanics, and 56 Division had a deficiency of over 40 wireless and line operators at that time.[72] Regimental signallers were particularly targeted by the enemy when they were carrying portable wireless sets and suffered high casualties; to make them less conspicuous, the normal rod aerial was sometimes replaced by a trailing wire.[73] In December 1943, Nalder reported that 15 Army Group was 15 whole Signals sections short of the new Godwin-Austen manpower scales, in addition to shortages within existing sections. By February 1944, he had made a start, 'in a small way', on the Godwin-Austen reorganization, but it was not possible to do much in the absence of manpower and with continuous active operations.[74]

Turning to signals security, considering the many problems in Tunisia and the changes that had been instigated by the CSO in the two months before the invasion, it might be expected that a noticeable improvement would have occurred in Sicily. However, CSO XXX Corps described the standard of security in July 1943 as exceedingly poor, and a review by Eighth Army at the beginning of September 1943 also concluded that security in Sicily had been of a low standard, and that serious security breaches had occurred. It said that the main problem was now regimental R/T rather than the areas controlled by Royal Signals directly – as a result of the excitement of battle combined with lack of practice, R/T messages often gave away important information; there was misunderstanding or ignorance of the rules of signals security; and there was downright stupidity and carelessness. A German prisoner of war reported an example in which the exact location of British tanks was given away, prompting an immediate attack by enemy tanks. The efficiency of enemy interception was illustrated when troops at Salerno reported in clear that enemy mortars were landing to the left of their position and immediately found the mortars shifted over towards them.[75] Idiosyncratic private codes were used by 50 Division, 51 Division and various units, which had a low security value. These problems continued in spite of the emphasis given to security in wireless instruction courses. General Alexander issued a letter to the whole Army group in October 1943, describing signals security as being of a very low standard, and identifying the principal offenders as 'commanders and other officers and other ranks who use R/T'. It seems clear that it was the officers who were mainly to blame and that operators' chat was not very common.[76] By December 1943, the CSO reported that security monitoring had revealed a considerable reduction in the number of violations, but problems continued after this date. For example, 1 Division reported frequent breaches of security at Anzio and a report of 1945 described the 'apparent impossibility of maintaining, in battle, any degree of wireless security in veteran units of a British Army'.[77] This was not a peculiarly British problem – German security was also faulty and British intelligence gained valuable information from intercepts.[78] Eighth Army was also alive to the insecurity of line communications – telephone was always regarded as insecure, but the Fullerphone was considered secure enough for all traffic, apart from messages classified as 'most secret', to be sent in clear. All 'most secret' messages had to be enciphered whichever way they were sent.[79]

Wireless deception, which utilized wireless insecurity to gain an advantage, was extensively used to disguise the movement of formations. For example, during Operation DIADEM when formations on the east coast of Italy were moved to the Cassino area, they observed wireless silence while dummy signals continued to be transmitted in their previous location to give the impression that nothing had changed. A pattern of silent, neutral and active periods of transmissions was also regularly carried out to change the norm rather than act as an indicator of impending action.[80]

By the time that Rome was captured, the Army had much greater experience of the problems of communicating in the mountainous conditions prevailing in Italy, and had made many improvements to its techniques. It would, however, be over-optimistic to say that all problems had been solved and indeed, with the equipment that then existed, it was impossible for communications to be perfect. The effect that these limitations had on the overall progress of the campaign is considered below.

The effect of communications on the outcome of the campaign

As has been described, a careful analysis was made of communications in the main amphibious landings immediately after the events, but this was not done to any great extent for the ongoing land operations. There remained the normal tendency in contemporary reports to focus on the difficulties that occurred rather than to mention periods when everything worked smoothly. This tendency was partly in order to alert others to problems and to find solutions, and partly because a lack of difficulty was not newsworthy. It is noticeable that the impression given by the records of individual formations becomes more positive as they gained experience in the local conditions – as time went on, formation Signals became increasingly confident. This may mean that, to an extent, the overall performance of their communications improved over time, as they found ways round the difficulties. But it may also be that they grew to accept the impossibility of achieving good communications under certain adverse conditions and gave up reporting the fact.

Steady improvement did not take place in the overall performance of communications because the problems encountered varied from location to location and because different formations were involved. Eighth Army experienced numerous problems with both wireless and line communications in Sicily. These were particularly severe during the first night after landing due to inexperienced wireless operators and faulty wireless batteries, and also due to lines constantly being cut by tracked vehicles and shrapnel. However, a summary by 50 Division Signals stated that, on the whole, both wireless and line were satisfactory after this. 'Satisfactory' did not mean trouble-free, since the same war diary mentioned several difficulties on an almost daily basis, leading to the impression that the overall summary was rather over-optimistic.[81] Similar difficulties were mentioned by 5 Division and 231 Infantry Brigade.[82] Major General Simonds, GOC of 1 Canadian Division, stated that infantry wireless behind brigade headquarters was excellent, but that forward communications had fallen behind requirements because the No. 18 set had insufficient range. Many commanders suffered from the lack of longer-range sets.[83] These views reflected a pattern of failed forward communications and the general impression is one of intermittent problems with both wireless and line. But with the important exception of the action at Primosole Bridge described earlier, no specific major negative consequence of these failures in Sicily has been found. Rather than being caused by poor communications, the slow pace of the Allied advance in Sicily was primarily caused by the difficulty of overcoming determined enemy resistance in well-prepared defensive positions in the mountainous terrain.

Communications also appear to have been unreliable to start with, in Italy. The 15 Infantry Brigade, for example, found W/T communications 'completely useless' on 4 and 5 September 1943, and issued an instruction to lay lines right up to forward elements.[84] For the first two days after landing by sea at Taranto in September 1943, 4 Parachute Brigade's wireless worked well, but then, their batteries ran out and were impossible to replace. This caused wireless to break down completely, leading them to depend on runners for communication; but the operation was nevertheless successful.[85] After 7 Armoured Division had landed at Salerno and advanced to Pompeii at the end of September 1943, it found wireless conditions 'appalling' because of the proximity of Mount Vesuvius and because of trees and buildings. 7AD had not been in Sicily and needed time to adapt to the conditions, which were very different from the desert. In fact, Italian conditions, in general, were not conducive to the use of armoured divisions – one reason why 7AD was withdrawn to the UK in November.[86]

As experience was gained during the remainder of 1943, communications improved to some extent. By contrast with the numerous problems that he had reported after landing at Salerno, the CSO of X Corps said that communications during the attack across the River Volturno in October were satisfactory and reported no further major problem during the rest of 1943.[87] This assessment is confirmed by a more general review of the action at the Volturno, which makes no mention of communications – it is assumed that silence means an absence of problems.[88] Similarly, 6 New Zealand Brigade reported their communications to have been 'excellent throughout' between the crossing of the River Sangro on 28 November 1943 and their arrival at Fontegrande on 24 December. This made a 'pleasant contrast to many experiences in Africa' and was attributed to the establishment of a brigade forward signal centre close to assaulting units, from which short lines could run to units and where a 'J' system to intercept forward wireless traffic was established.[89] In December 1943, 46 Division found that their lines were often damaged by enemy shellfire, but they always had alternative circuits laid, and could maintain communications.[90]

In early 1944, however, problems re-emerged. The communications in the Anzio beachhead relied principally upon the multiplication of lines, buried in tunnels or trenches. There was a constant need to repair the lines and the casualties that linemen suffered caused great difficulty in doing this in a timely fashion. The area was very confined and crowded, causing frequent wireless problems with mutual interference, and it was difficult to maintain a supply of fresh battle batteries for the portable sets used by company headquarters while the area was covered by enemy artillery fire. Infantry communications below company headquarters relied on runners, just as they had done in the First World War. Though they were satisfactory immediately after the landings at Anzio, it then became as much of a struggle to maintain communications as the soldiers found it to survive at all.[91]

Further south, in front of the Gustav Line, conditions were also difficult at this time though, because it was not quite such a confined area, it was possible to escape from enemy shellfire. In the assaults, however, infantry communications were similarly erratic; telephone lines were continually cut by fire, and wireless sets were not improved by rough handling and wet conditions. The combined effect of these factors, sets slipping off frequency, reception being screened by obstacles and batteries failing, made it difficult to maintain wireless.[92] The GOC of V Corps believed that battalion headquarters were sometimes so far forward that their COs could find themselves stuck in a hole on a forward facing slope, with poor communications, and consequently unable to grasp the battle.[93] Perhaps it was because the communications problems were familiar that, in a report on the Cassino operations in March 1944, the somewhat complacent statement was made that 'no new [communications] lessons have been learnt from the air and ground action at Cassino. Established principles were confirmed'.[94] As stated earlier, familiarity with seemingly insuperable problems led to a reduction in their emphasis.

In summary, there were some periods during which communications were relatively trouble-free, but for much of the time, considerable problems were experienced. Since the Allies did not suffer a major defeat in Sicily and Italy, such failures in communications as occurred were clearly not catastrophic, but did they contribute to the length of time that it took to complete the conquest of Sicily and to advance northwards in Italy? The reporting of problems should not obscure the positive contribution that Signals made to the defeats eventually suffered by the Germans, even though this is particularly difficult to measure. It is obvious that without an overall level of effective communications, the Army could not have operated and, therefore, Signals must be credited with their contribution to the victory.

The failure to make a decisive breakthrough at the Primosole Bridge has already been described and it has been concluded that this was, in part, attributable to poor communications. Had Eighth Army been able to pass over the bridge and move on across the Plain of Catania, it is likely that the Germans would have had to accelerate their evacuation of Sicily, and they might not have been able to get so many of their forces out. Poor signalling did contribute to the delay in achieving victory in Sicily. Whether a more rapid victory in Sicily would have speeded up the advance into Italy is debatable since it was, in any case, a logistical struggle to organize the BAYTOWN and AVALANCHE landings in the time available. But the capture of a large number of German troops in Sicily would have been very beneficial to the initial Italian campaign.

Communications during the landings at Salerno were imperfect, but they did not prevent the overall success of the operation, and the delay before Eighth Army came within reach of the Salerno beachhead, precipitating the withdrawal of the German forces surrounding X Corps and Fifth (US) Army, was not due to communication problems per se. Rather, it was due to the length of time that it took to establish satisfactory supply lines and to overcome the many road blocks and blown bridges that the Germans had thrown in Eighth Army's way. It was, in any case, a matter of a few days, even if it must have felt much longer to those at Salerno. Similarly, the failure to break out from the Anzio beachhead was nothing to do with communications, but was due to poor generalship early on. To what extent did poor communications delay the main Allied forces in their efforts to take the Gustav Line? There is no evidence that communications were responsible, but rather that the problems of communications were caused by the Allies' inability to break out of a static position covered by German artillery fire. In summary, the conquest of Sicily was delayed by communications problems at the Primosole Bridge, but the slow pace of the advance northwards through Italy was not attributable to poor communications.

8

North-West Europe, 1944–45

OVERLORD commenced on 6 June 1944. The British 21 Army Group landed at three beaches in the Bayeux – Caen area, with US forces landing further west. Once the beachheads were secured, a three-week military build-up took place before operations to break out began. These battles continued for two months, with the British fighting at Caen being particularly ferocious and of an attritional nature. Eventually, the Allies succeeded in breaking through and began a rapid advance across northern France, liberating Paris on 25 August and forcing the Germans to retreat across the River Seine by 30 August.

In order to make use of the momentum gained, Montgomery launched Operation MARKET GARDEN on 17 September, a single thrust north over the branches of the Lower Rhine to bypass the German Siegfried Line and attack the Ruhr. Paratroopers were dropped to secure key bridges and towns, the furthest north being the drop by 1 Airborne Division at Arnhem, but it had to retreat before it could be relieved by the main force. The attempt to cross the Rhine therefore failed and it was not until the port of Antwerp and its approaches had been captured and brought back into operation in late November that the supply situation improved sufficiently for another attempt to be made. A further delay was imposed by the German counter-attack through the Ardennes, principally along the US-held sector of the front. The subsequent battle was fiercely fought, lasting from mid-December through to the end of January 1945, but after they had been forced to retreat, the Germans were fatally weakened. Operation PLUNDER at the end of March 1945 was the final, successful, attempt by the Allies to cross the Rhine, after which they advanced rapidly into Germany until the war in Europe finally ended on 8 May 1945.

The British D-Day landings went very well and it is relevant to ask whether communications matched this overall success. But the advance inland from the bridgehead was slow. In the face of stiff opposition, close tank–infantry cooperation was needed to move through the 'bocage' country of Normandy, made up of farmland criss-crossed by hedgerows and trees. A major question is whether difficulties with front line infantry communications and tank–infantry communications, in particular, contributed to the failure to make faster progress. After the Allies eventually broke out of the coastal area, the L of C struggled to deal with the large distances between the rapidly advancing front line and the supply bases in Normandy, prompting questions about the efficiency of L of C communications. The failure of the airborne operation at Arnhem needs to be put in the context of the two other major British airborne operations, on D-Day and during the crossing of the Rhine, both of which were generally successful. Was it due to differences in the performance of communications that the disparity in the overall operations occurred? Finally, Signals security was another area that remained inadequate during the campaign in North-West Europe. Why was this, given all the experience of previous campaigns?

There were three important factors governing the performance of signalling in North-West Europe. First, the topography of the area was relatively flat compared with the mountainous terrain that had made life so difficult for signallers in Tunisia, Sicily and Italy. Secondly, while resources were always rationed in the Mediterranean because they either did not exist or were being held back for use in France, supplies were much more plentiful in this campaign. Thirdly, the campaign benefitted from nearly five years' experience of armed combat and, not surprisingly, communications had improved as a result. As always, discussion of communications issues in contemporary documents reflected the areas where there were problems; the fact that relatively little was written about artillery and armoured communications indicates that they worked satisfactorily on the whole. It was in the infantry and the airborne divisions that the primary problems lay. The contents of this chapter reflect this.

Operation OVERLORD

The principal reasons for the success of communications during OVERLORD were the experience gained and lessons learnt from previous amphibious operations, careful planning before D-Day, the large number of training exercises and the abundance and improved quality of equipment. Planning started in April 1943 while the Tunisian campaign was still underway, but the invasion was finally launched after the three major amphibious operations in

Sicily and Italy had taken place. The planning process was highly complex, but at the end was judged to have proceeded smoothly overall. It was easier in some respects than previous amphibious operations because the build-up of forces was at home and subsequent supply of equipment also emanated from the UK. This eliminated some of the earlier difficulties in planning when formation headquarters had been widely separated – in some cases, in different countries. Experience of earlier landings had also resulted in a revised War Office pamphlet on communications in combined operations, which governed the overall strategy for communications during OVERLORD.[1] The doctrine followed the same general principles as earlier versions, but the vastly greater quantity and the improved quality of transport and equipment meant that fewer compromises on preferred practice had to be made than in previous landings. A particularly important suggestion in the pamphlet was the warning against laying lines too hastily after landing, something we shall come back to later.

In addition to planning, the period between autumn 1943 and June 1944 saw numerous signal training exercises, though their thoroughness was contested. According to Lieutenant Colonel Cole, the acting CSO of I Corps, training benefitted from being unhampered by the usual disadvantages of shortage of time and lack of special equipment.[2] By contrast, a report by Brigadier Childs, his predecessor at I Corps who had been temporarily sick, stated that training had been greatly hampered by the diverse geographical location of units and restrictions on wireless working so that no full signals exercise was possible during the six months prior to the assault.[3] As always, the way in which the same events were reported thus depended on the attitude of mind of the individual reporting. XXX Corps did not have a complete corps signal exercise because of the late arrival of equipment and the corps staff having other priorities. Nevertheless, the training in assault roles at divisional level and below was considered by the CSO to have been fairly thorough. This positive view of training is also confirmed by the war diaries of 3 Canadian Division Artillery and 27 Armoured Brigade.[4] The topics that were covered in the training exercises appear, naturally enough, to have focused particularly on the assault itself and some felt in hindsight that the action to be taken *after* landing had not received enough attention.[5] There was, however, a conference on tank–infantry communications in March 1944, attended by all brigade commanders and Signals officers and all regimental and battalion commanders, so it cannot be said that no attention was devoted to the subject that appears to have been particularly problematic during the Normandy campaign.[6]

Both security and deception played a vital part in OVERLORD. Operation FORTITUDE was the name given to one of the deception plans, to which Signals contributed in important ways. In addition to the combined headquarters at Plymouth and Portsmouth that were primarily involved in the actual landings, a headquarters and Signals centre was established at Dover. The wireless traffic from this centre was designed to give the impression that an assault on the Pas de Calais was likely to occur, causing the Germans to spread their forces across northern France. Fifteenth German Army remained in the Pas de Calais even after the Normandy landings had taken place, though there may have been other reasons beside FORTITUDE for this.[7] Wireless traffic also simulated two fictitious corps in Scotland designed to indicate an invasion of Norway.[8] The security of genuine wireless traffic received much attention and periods of wireless silence in the UK were imposed at the end of 1943. During the planning period, most communications in the UK were by telephone, but wireless was also employed.[9] The combination of security and deception was very effective – the Germans knew an invasion was coming, but they did not know when or where.[10] During the build-up of forces after the initial landings, some wireless security problems arose, however – various codes needed replacement because they were compromised and delays occurred in ciphering as a result of lack of practice. Although no major security threat resulted from these, according to a report by a Signals security officer on the staff of the SO in C, they did partially justify the preference of some commanders for line communications when practicable.[11]

Wireless equipment had improved over the previous year, with the crystal-controlled No. 46 replacing the No. 18 as a short-range set, and the No. 22 being used for medium-range use. At the discretion of the Signals officer of each formation, additional equipment for use in the landings could be requested, beyond normal establishment levels. Although some equipment (crystals for the No. 46 sets and waterproofing kits, for example) was late to arrive, the CSO of XXX Corps conceded that 'in the end we were equipped magnificently'. As ever, it was still possible to put a negative gloss on this abundance – the CSO of a Canadian division wrote that 'the sets required came in great heaps and the [Quartermaster] was swamped'.[12] The increase in supplies was such that the CSO of I Corps described one formation, 27 Armoured Brigade, as 'extremely well equipped . . . in fact I think it was probably over-equipped' in terms of the quantity and types of wireless.[13] The latter seems a surprising statement even in the context of OVERLORD, but in earlier operations, it would have been unthinkable. Since OVERLORD was on such a large scale, wireless frequencies could only be separated by four Kilocycles instead of the previous minimum of five Kilocycles. The consequent need for very accurate tuning meant that crystal control was essential on links further up the chain of command, which would previously have used adjustable frequencies.[14]

After the event, many senior Signals officers wrote reviews of the performance of the equipment during OVERLORD, and in most cases gave positive opinions. The CSO of Second Army wrote that communications worked well between command headquarters in England and the HQ ships in the invasion force; because of crystal control, they were established within 35 minutes of wireless silence being broken. He felt that mutual interference in the HQ ships was negligible. The lack of complaints from most officers suggests that this was generally true, but it was not the experience on HMS *Largs*, the HQ ship of 'Force S', on which too many high-powered sets were fitted according to the CSO of 3 Division. Static from the HQ ship of 69 Brigade also prevented communications.[15] Once the sets had been landed, the general experience was that mutual interference was slight, and although instances did occur, they were usually speedily eliminated by checking frequencies with a wave meter.[16]

In considering the relative absence of mutual interference, it is important to note that the majority of British sets used Morse as well as R/T and operated on short wave, not VHF. Comparing his own set with an American VHF set that only used R/T, a British signaller noted that he could vary the pitch of his Morse signal – if interference had a low pitch, he could move up the scale to make his signal audible against its background. He wrote that 'in the incredibly heavy radio traffic of D-Day . . . the Americans found that their FM signals broke up and speech was impossible. Morse code was the only sure way of getting through'.[17]

A particular reason for British success was the duplication that plentiful equipment allowed, as explained in a letter to the War Office from Lance-Corporal Underwood, Royal Signals, who was the NCO in charge of a brigade rear link wireless detachment. This letter is one of a series of replies from other ranks to a request in early 1945 for first-hand accounts of D-Day experiences, another example of the desire of the British Army to learn for the future. This detachment was equipped with a No. 22 set mounted on a handcart in one of the first landing crafts, with a later craft carrying an M14 half-track vehicle that contained the detachment's main No. 19 set and a reserve No. 46 set. Underwood tested his No. 22 set as his landing craft was on the way to shore and found it immediately worked perfectly in spite of having been tuned in, sealed and waterproofed 10 days earlier. He and the No. 22 set landed and set up communications, awaiting the arrival of the main set. The craft carrying the M14, however, was sunk close to the shore. The M14 itself was eventually towed ashore by a bulldozer and it was found that the waterproofing of both the vehicle and the sets had been effective. The No. 22 set was loaded onto the M14 with the other sets for carriage inland.[18]

In the light of previous experience, much attention had been given to waterproofing sets and vehicles, with new types of waterproof bags being introduced a short time before the assault. As a training film demonstrated, these bags had to be used carefully, and the CSO of I Corps believed that no unit that carried out the procedure properly had their equipment drowned. Some signallers found their sets perfectly dry after a rough landing, but for whatever reason, some other sets were damaged by water. The duplication of sets meant that there was normally an alternative means of communicating in the latter case.[19] Duplication also kept communications going when casualties occurred on landing, though because of the surprise achieved, casualties were lighter than had been feared in the British sectors.

Immediately after landing, there was a heavy demand for telephones. This was not because wireless failed to work well – all reports stated that wireless communications remained excellent during the build-up of forces – but because commanders found the telephone a much easier and quicker way of communicating in a secure way, free of the fear that codes might have become compromised and free of the delays of enciphered W/T. The net result was that the bridgehead rapidly became strewn with cable. Consequently, lines suffered continual breaks from vehicles and from telegraph poles collapsing from the weight of cables added to them – damage from enemy action was very slight by comparison. The extent to which lines and line damage became a theme of the establishment of the lodgement area is demonstrated by the cover to the report on OVERLORD by the CSO of Second Army (see below).[20] As a consequence, the biggest problem facing Signals in the bridgehead was line maintenance, to which may be added strain on both cable supply and line personnel.[21]

It is interesting to speculate on whether this cover design was intended to be ironic or merely humorous. There certainly is an irony in the fact that after all the attention devoted to providing wireless for commanders, they immediately reverted to telephone as soon as they could. The extensive use of line was not a direct cause of what has been described as unduly slow progress on the part of the Allied forces after OVERLORD, for wireless facilities were extensive and

Figure 8.1 Cover to report on OVERLORD.[22]

usually worked well when the need arose. But the large line system was clearly a symptom of the British Army's desire to construct a firm base for operations from which advances inland could take place.

The headquarters of some formations, including Army and Army group headquarters, remained in the UK until after the assault had begun, so that cross-channel communications were important from the start. These were achieved by a variety of means – both short-wave and VHF wireless were used for urgent messages, the latter being by line-of-sight between high points in France and England. Two days after D-Day, the laying of submarine telephone cables began in order to provide secure telephone links, with the first coming into service a week later on 15 June. Less urgent documents were sent by air and naval despatch services and a considerable flock of Army and RAF pigeons were provided as a reserve, if all else failed in the first days of the campaign. Some 80 pigeons were allocated to the Press Corps, which had increased greatly in size since the beginning of the war so that the public in the UK and the United States could be kept informed and supportive. Press communications placed a considerable burden on Army Signals, which had to provide wireless and line links for them.

An idea of what it was like to be involved in front line signals during OVERLORD is given by the letters of Lieutenant H. T. Bone, 2 Battalion, the East Yorkshire Regiment. Bone was the signal officer of the battalion when it landed on D-Day.

> Then the actual loading into craft – the swinging on davits – the boat lowering and finally "Away Boats". It was some distance to the beaches and it was a wet trip. Promptly at H Hour I began listening on my wireless sets for the first news and very soon crystal clear over my sets came messages from the assaulting companies: "Heavy opposition, pushing on" and "Heavy casualties, pushing on". Now was the moment – we clutched weapons and wireless sets, all carefully waterproofed. The doors opened as we grounded and the Colonel was out. The sea was choppy and the boat swung a good bit as one by one we followed him. Several fell in and got soaked through. I was lucky. I stopped to help my men with their heavy wireless sets and to ensure they kept them dry. As we staggered ashore we dispersed and lay down above the water's edge.
>
> I saw one of my signal corporals with a wound in his leg and I took his codes with me promising to send a man back for his set before he was evacuated. The other boat party was mostly missing, also three quarters of my sets. The Colonel was getting a grip on the battle and I was sent back on the beach to collect the rest of us. Under the side of a tank that had been hit I saw a bunch of my people and I bawled at them to get up and get moving. I felt a little callous when I found that nearly all of them had been hit and some were dead. But sorting them out I made up half a wireless team and then went in search of some more.
>
> The night of D-Day was spent back from the actual front in a cornfield. I spent the night in a signals vehicle half dozing as Ronnie and Chris shared spells of duty with me. Next day leaving our line laid we moved forward onto a ridge. My people had laid lines again. Now they had to dig in 400 yards away, move the exchange and relay the lines. Tanks and tracked vehicles all round used to move forward of us each dawn and return to laager in our rear at nightfall. Thus twice a day my lines were broken and my tired men had to turn out and repair them. We were short of men by now and we had to man wireless sets as well as lay and maintain lines and operate the exchange.
>
> The CO wanted lines laid. There was only one man and myself to lay them and we had to borrow a reel from the gunners nearby. The party of four under a corporal who had been laying line from the start line forward were no longer there, only one of them. The corporal had behaved magnificently, rejoining breaks, helping communication through to brigade, never taking cover and always calm and patient. When hit through his helmet, he bound the wound up

himself and carried on. Only when ordered back by the CO had he gone back to the RAP to be evacuated as a casualty. He deserves a gong. Another of these four was wandering around the back areas shell-shocked. The other two were still repairing the line. They came up later to report that it was through again.[23]

Overall, the performance of the British communications system during and immediately after the landings was very good. Some difficulties were inevitably encountered, but the luxurious level of equipment and the relatively light opposition as a result of the successful security and deception operation meant that these problems could be overcome without too much difficulty. The British Army and its communication system were then poised for the next stage of the campaign.

Infantry, Armoured and Artillery communications in North-West Europe

A key issue in the Normandy bocage was deciding the order in which infantry and tanks should advance (Figure 8.2); the presence of anti-tank guns, wire and

Figure 8.2 The Bocage country in Normandy, in which both tanks and infantry were highly vulnerable without close support from each other, but communications between the two arms was problematic.[26]

machine guns meant that sending in tanks before the infantry or vice versa, both had serious disadvantages. It was realized that they should advance together so that the infantry could be the eyes and ears of the tanks and could deal with the anti-tank guns, while the tanks were able to deal with the wire and machine guns to which infantry was vulnerable.[24] But good cooperation was difficult or impossible without good communications between the two arms and indeed some contemporary sources wrote that poor communications were the major reason for the lack of cooperation that frequently occurred.[25] The reason why communications within the infantry and between infantry and tanks were found to be so problematic was primarily technical but, overlaid upon the inadequacy of wireless equipment as well as being partly caused by it, was the negative attitude of many in the infantry towards wireless.

The increasing importance of infantry communications to the Army along with a recognition of their inadequacy led to considerable growth in the manpower of Divisional Signals regiments over time, as the table below shows.

Table 8.1 Number of signallers in an infantry Signals regiment[27]

Year	Number of signallers
1938	491
1941	516
1943	710
1945	743
1946	892

Accompanying the increase in the Signals regiment, the number of wireless sets in a division increased tenfold between 1940 and 1944, most of these sets being operated by regimental signallers rather than Royal Signals.[28] The large increase in the establishment in 1946, which did not result from a reorganization of responsibilities, appears to confirm that performance during operations in North-West Europe was regarded as substandard. This was nothing new. Forward communications in the infantry had caused many problems during the campaign in Italy, while those of the artillery were generally felt to be excellent and those between tanks were satisfactory. The situation was no different in Normandy. Infantry communications rearward of battalion headquarters were generally able to make extensive use of line, backed up by relatively powerful vehicle-mounted wireless but, since light weight assault cable was not found to be an adequate substitute, company communications in mobile situations were largely dependent on portable sets. It was these that caused extensive problems in the bocage country, particularly when they were used in combined operations with tanks.

Infantry communications in August 1944 were described by an armoured unit thus – 'Bad infantry communications. These are almost without exception deplorable. There is a general defeatist attitude among the infantry that their communications are bound to fail once the battle starts. The attitude is justified as they always do. The result is that the plan has to be too rigid and once troops are committed it is impossible for them to adjust themselves to the enemy's reactions'.[29] This view of the infantry was even included in an Armoured Corps training manual of 1945 – '. . . good communications between infantry and tanks is essential, although the value of this is still not apparent to most infantry units. The primary need is . . . to make [infantry units] understand the need for and value of good wireless communications'.[30] Thus, the pre-war conservative culture of the infantry regarding communications, which was previously effectively imposed by a lack of equipment, appears to have survived into a period when more modern equipment had become available. Other reasons for a less than perfect performance by infantry communications were insufficient sets and suboptimal equipment. A post-war review suggested that no fewer than 78 sets were needed in a battalion compared with the then current allotment of 41, with a particularly large increase needed in the allocation to rifle companies. It said that the company sets needed to be lighter (no more than 10 lbs compared with 22 lbs for the No. 38 set) and to use VHF rather than short-wave to eliminate interference and fading at night.[31]

The diary of the commander of the signals platoon of the 4 Battalion, the Dorsetshire Regiment, perfectly encapsulates the bias towards line in the infantry, showing that he at least was most certainly not 'wireless minded'. On 23 November 1944, he wrote, 'Lines had been very badly cut up and . . . this caused speech to be very poor . . . It would have been better perhaps to use the wireless network, but I was always a believer in telephone communications, even if the line was only through for a matter of 30 minutes a day, as this would give the commander personal contact and orders could be far more easily explained on the phone than over the air, because conversations on the air had to be limited for security reasons'.[32] It has to be recognized that there were good reasons for the preference of forward infantry towards line – their wireless sets were tricky to use and lacking in range; an R/T conversation was much less immediate than the telephone; and wireless was innately insecure, necessitating the use of codes, still further creating a barrier to understanding. Nevertheless, it does seem likely that habitual avoidance of wireless led to lack of practice and lower efficiency when there was no alternative.

The portable wireless sets available to forward infantry in the North-West European land campaign were primarily the Nos. 18 and 38 sets. In his paper on communications within the infantry battalion of December 1944, Lieutenant Colonel Honeybourne described the defects of these sets which were 'only too well known'. His biggest criticism was that they required expert handling, a particularly serious disadvantage when inexperienced operators had to be brought in because of high infantry casualties. The Chief of Staff of 21 Army Group had called for additional training to address this same problem early in September, but it had evidently been impossible to provide.[33] The sets were also insufficiently waterproof and robust; the No. 18 set was too heavy; their frequency band (high up the short wave band) made them very susceptible to interference, particularly at night; and it was too obvious that the signaller was carrying a set, rendering them prime targets for snipers.[34] Honeybourne might have added that the range of the No. 38 set was too short, which was one of the primary problems in tank–infantry communications.

There was very little overlap in the frequency range of the No. 38 set with that of the No.19 sets used in tanks, making it impossible for the infantry to communicate directly with tanks on the tank net.[35] This was in spite of the normal policy of ensuring an overlap in frequency bands between sets of different types to allow them to work to each other if required. Why was this frequency range chosen? It could have been because there was more effective radiation from a whip aerial at higher frequencies and that there were more available channels at higher frequencies. The latter was certainly the case, given the crowded lower frequency ranges utilized by more powerful sets. But perhaps the main reason was that if the low powered No. 38 set had utilized frequencies near those of the more powerful No. 19 sets, they would have been swamped, as had been found with the No. 18 set.[36] Thus front line infantry, being late on the wireless scene (a hangover from the 1930s), were pushed into an unsuitable band because there was no room elsewhere.

The conclusion of Honeybourne's report was that front line infantry needed a completely different wireless set and he put forward a specification that was similar to that of the American SCR 300, a crystal controlled VHF set. But the end of the war came before such potential developments could come to fruition. It is somewhat ironic that a VHF set for the infantry should have been advocated in 1944 when the development of such a set, the No. 13, had been abandoned in 1937.[37]

Given the poor performance of forward infantry wireless within purely infantry formations, it is scarcely surprising that tank–infantry wireless communications were problematic. Their importance was recognized and each of a series of War Office documents on tank–infantry cooperation contained a greater or lesser mention of communications. A training document (*ATI No. 2*) of 1941 recognized that tank units had good wireless communications, but infantry units were lacking in this respect; it therefore recommended that the infantry brigadier should place himself well forward and that the commander of his tank battalion should accompany him, communications thus being by personal meeting. Personal meetings were also advocated between tank and infantry battalion commanders and rendezvous points were to be selected in advance for this purpose. Beyond this, details were vague – flag signals were to be used between individual tanks and infantry while tank wireless could be used by the infantry for passing back important messages. Two years later, the May 1943 edition of the document was completely rewritten, but contained even less on communications than before. Tank commanders would 'initially at any rate have their heads out of the turret both in order that they may see better and in order that the infantry can communicate with them by word of mouth'. The limited view of the tank commander when closed down into the tank along with his inability to hear what was going on above the roar of the engine were key problems both for tank operations and intercommunication with infantry. The 1943 edition strongly advocated that tank and infantry needed the fullest knowledge of the methods of their partner in arms and that this should be achieved by training together; what this meant was that communications would be less important if the two arms instinctively knew each other's needs and methods – in other words, that intuition could make up for a failure of technology.[38]

The emphasis on training together was repeated in an Eighth Army document of November 1943, but for the first time, this also stated that a certain percentage of tanks were equipped with No. 38 sets operating on the infantry net while others carried external telephones that could be used by infantry commanders. However, 'it must be remembered by the infantry commander that it is difficult for a tank officer to find a company HQ in battle [which is often in a slit trench] and if he requires the assistance of tanks and cannot communicate by R/T he must make an effort to attract the tank commander's attention'.[39] This document also showed Montgomery's influence on doctrine, based on his own experience, with its emphasis on *all* tank units being expected to give close support to infantry, including Sherman as well as Churchill infantry tank units. The same doctrine on tank–infantry communications was given in the equivalent 21 Army Group document of February 1944.[40]

Meanwhile, battle conditions in Italy demonstrated that intuition was not enough and that a common doctrine of tank–infantry cooperation was essential; because a brigade of tanks might have to work with one of several divisions, it could not be assumed that the two formations would have trained together. A conference was held in XIII Corps in April 1944 to establish the doctrine and, as part of this, more detailed guidance on solving 'the problem of communications' was given. It said that wireless was unquestionably the only truly satisfactory method – its reliability could be improved by ensuring batteries were fully charged, connections were clean and wires were not loose; all company and platoon nets should utilize the same frequency so that any platoon could, in theory, communicate with any tank. But external telephones on tanks, LOs and visual signals should also be available for use since the survival of an infantry No. 38 set in battle was uncertain. Even if a good wireless connection were established between infantry and tank, it was often difficult for the tank commander to understand the location of a target described verbally by an infantryman; it could also be indicated by smoke, flares, tracer or even by laying a rifle on the ground pointing in the right direction.[41] The British Army was not alone in having these difficulties – in the absence of effective wireless communications, similar primitive methods were used by US armour and infantry in Normandy, sometimes involving the waving of a handkerchief as a signal.[42]

Although the lessons from Italy on low level tank–infantry communications seem to have been recognized by 21 Army Group, they do not appear to have been put into practice extensively before D-Day, perhaps because they had been learnt after Montgomery had left Italy. Training prior to OVERLORD did involve inter-arm cooperation; for example, Exercise LEAPYEAR of March 1944 included 3 Infantry Division, 27 Armoured Brigade and artillery. But the frequencies used by these formations indicate that low-level wireless communications between the infantry and armour were not included.[43] And it was only decided in late July 1944, some seven weeks after D-Day, that operations by 11 Armoured Division, reputedly one of the best trained armoured formations, should involve

the support of infantry; the fitting of No. 38 sets and external telephones to its
tanks was accordingly hastened.[44] Even when infantry sets had been fitted to
tanks, they were often unsuccessful. During an attack involving the division in
September 1944, for example, tank–infantry communications failed because of
lack of No. 38 set training among infantry reinforcements, drafted in to replace
heavy casualties. As a result, direct contact had to be established between tank
and infantry commanders on foot – a highly hazardous process in battle.[45] Failure
was not all the fault of the infantry, however – tank commanders did not always
make proper use of their No. 38 set communications because they had enough
to do in fighting the battle and managing their own No. 19 sets; also, wireless
discipline in tanks was sometimes bad with far too much chat swamping nearby
infantry No. 18 set communications.[46] An example of the many penalties paid
for the lack of efficient infantry – tank communications was that of 3 (Tank)
Battalion, The Scots Guards, on 2 November 1944 – their supporting infantry
mistook smoke laid to cover their work of extrication for the pre-arranged signal
to withdraw. The tanks, thereby left unsupported, were attacked by the enemy
infantry.[47]

Infantry needed to keep pace with tanks, but in the early stages of the North-
West Europe campaign, they either walked (which was too slow) or rode in
unarmoured lorries (which lacked any protection). On some occasions, they
rode on the outside of the tanks and while this made communications by word
of mouth easy, it led to heavy casualties. In order to overcome the problem,
improvized bullet-proof vehicles for carrying the infantry into battle were
initially created by converting US Priest self-propelled guns, and were used for
the first time by II Canadian Corps at the beginning of August 1944 in their
advance from Caen to Falaise. This development was regarded as a revolution
in the conduct of armoured warfare and improved versions of these armoured
personnel carriers, known as 'Kangaroos', were built shortly afterwards.[48]

Another advantage of carrying infantry in armoured vehicles was the
opportunity to provide them with more powerful, heavier, wireless sets, which
could communicate directly on the tank nets. The photograph below of one of
these 'defrocked Priest' vehicles shows a wireless aerial and the later Kangaroo
armoured personnel carrier also sometimes carried a wireless.[49] But, for whatever
reason, it does not seem that the Kangaroos of 7 Canadian Infantry Brigade had
effective wireless communications with their supporting tanks during Operation
VERITABLE of February 1945, since it was reported that Captain Burnett of the
Scots Guards 'set a magnificent example of bravery. During the heaviest shelling

5. A "defrocked Priest", used as an Armoured Personnel Carrier (7 August 1944)

6. Another view of the "Priest"

Figure 8.3 'Defrocked Priest' Armoured personnel carrier.[50]

he got out of his tank and went on foot from Kangaroo to Kangaroo getting the infantry out and guiding them to the objective. Unfortunately he was killed by a shell just after this'.[51]

When they were properly equipped, however, infantry were able to operate directly on the tank net, alleviating the communications problem, and this was successfully done during operations against the River Maas in April 1945. The attack was a combined operation involving tanks, artillery and infantry carried in Kangaroo armoured personnel carriers. It demonstrated the ample time allowed to practise for the operation and the really close liaison between arms that resulted, as well as the extreme care taken to ensure reliable communications between all arms – wireless links were triplicated through tank, infantry and artillery sets, while the Kangaroo net duplicated the tank squadron and infantry company links. Thus, the infantry, while they were in the Kangaroos, were able to communicate directly with the tanks. It also illustrated the use of counter-battery and counter-mortar organizations. In brief, the objective was to destroy an enemy bridgehead situated in a wood on the left hand side of the river. This was protected by heavy machine guns and rocket launchers in the wood itself, and by anti-tank guns based on the right hand side of the river, which were controlled by an observation post in the wood. Two previous attempts at night by infantry to clear the wood had failed. The attack on 8 January commenced with an approach at first light by the squadron of tanks. Once they had reached the edge of the wood, they called forward the infantry, who advanced in the Kangaroos, covering approximately one mile in only four minutes and suffering no casualties from enemy gunfire because of the rapidity of their advance and the protection offered by their vehicles. The infantry dismounted and then advanced alongside the tanks into the wood, taking prisoners as they went. There was no serious opposition at this stage, the bulk of the garrison having withdrawn in the face of the British force. The main British casualties were suffered when some of the Kangaroos struck mines after sections of the infantry had dismounted. A lesson from this was that there should be no movement of the Kangaroos while exposed infantry was close by.[52]

But in spite of these efforts, the overall standard of front line tank–infantry communications was unsatisfactory. Montgomery wrote in November 1944 that they presented 'considerable difficulties' in North-West Europe.[53] A review dated December 1944 stated that infantry battalion commanders had normally achieved satisfactory communications with commanders of accompanying tanks by being in the same location or by using a LO equipped with a No. 19 set. At the infantry company–tank squadron level, various wireless solutions had been tried with mixed success, but failure was normal at the infantry platoon–tank troop level because of the inadequacy, difficulty of use or cumbersome nature of the No. 38 set. It was considered that these problems could not be remedied until a set was provided for the infantry that could communicate on the tank command net.[54] Much the same conclusion was reached in Italy.[55]

Artillery communications, however, were highly successful and the liaison between infantry and artillery and between tanks and artillery was good.[56] Royal Artillery had its own centralized control organization utilizing both wireless and line communications. The fundamental reasons for the success of artillery wireless communications compared with the often poor performance of those in the infantry were, first, that observation officers and artillery batteries were removed from the very front line and were consequently under slightly less pressure, and secondly, that they were often provided with more powerful vehicle-mounted sets than infantry in the same position. For example, in Operation PLUNDER, the artillery forward observation officers accompanying the assault companies had No. 22 sets while the companies themselves only had Nos.18 and 46 sets.[57] In many cases, infantry commanders were accompanied by an artillery observer so that they could simply request support by word of mouth and this could be passed on over the artillery net. Alternatively, so long as front line infantry could communicate back to their battalion headquarters, artillery support could be requested from the RA representative, who was often the commander of the battery that was operating in support of that battalion. The contrast with infantry–tank communications in Normandy was stark – while infantry had difficulty communicating with a tank a few yards away, artillery support was often provided from a distance of several miles.

The problem of communication between front line tanks and infantry fundamentally remained unsolved at the end of the war. It was an important reason why the Germans were able to mount such an effective defence in the bocage despite their lack of resources and air inferiority, and hence why the pace of the Allied advance in Normandy was so slow.

Communications during the pursuit across France, the crossing of the Rhine and the pursuit into Germany

After the Allies eventually broke through the German defences in Normandy and overcame the German counter-attack, the fighting troops advanced rapidly across northern France, covering 250 miles in six days. The move created considerable difficulties for all the auxiliary services, including the supply chain. While the Army was in static conditions in the bridgehead after the OVERLORD landings, communications with its supply bases had mainly used line rather than wireless. As soon as the breakout occurred, verbal links between the advancing army and the supply bases in Normandy were disrupted since the civil telephone lines were all down; it was impossible to lay field cable over such distances quickly enough and the range was too great for normal wireless. Despatch riders were therefore extensively used, covering long distances and frequently suffering casualties in road accidents; DRs in the Second Army's rear areas were reportedly worked to the point of exhaustion. A system of road haulage headquarters was set up connected by No. 12HP wireless sets and intermediate relay stations. These sets worked day and night without respite, often under conditions of heavy interference, and suffered from generator trouble because of the heavy workload. The railway system was soon repaired and was used extensively for transportation of supplies.[58] A telephone system connecting all the railway stations was completed in only five days, eventually comprising more than 350 miles of line.

A report of 27 September 1944 stated that lack of communications greatly affected the flexibility of supplies, with the turn round between Brussels and bases at Bayeux taking seven days.[59] This version of events was disputed by the CSO of 21 Army Group in a memo issued in January 1945. He said that in the light of further information then available, it appeared that the earlier report was based on an isolated case and in fact 'communications provided for operations and administration stood the unusual strain imposed upon them by the rapid advance most successfully'.[60] Consequently, in a later report issued by Signals, it was stated that 'no really major breakdown in communications occurred' in the rear areas during this period.[61] It is clear that short-term difficulties with supply communications did occur, but the evidence suggests that these were fairly quickly overcome; if a telephone system could be laid in five days, it seems unlikely that communications problems were responsible for more than a minor portion of the overall delay in obtaining sufficient supplies to mount the invasion of Germany. Rather, it appears that the lack of adequate port facilities prior to the opening of Antwerp to Allied shipping at the end of November was the single biggest factor responsible for the supply problems.

Turning to command communications during the advance, those at high level (down to corps, and in some cases, divisional headquarters) used a system of long-range VHF No. 10 sets, with intermediate step-up stations between Normandy and the front line. These sets had insufficient capacity for anything other than urgent operational messages, and so routine messages had to be carried by DRs and air messengers.[62] Formations were widely dispersed, creating serious challenges for the Liaison Officer system that Montgomery used to keep in touch with his army group. This system required LOs to travel daily to formation headquarters, not only to find out what was going on, but to report on the state of mind of the commanders. They reported back to Montgomery every evening at what was described by Brooke as a 'séance' and an impressive sight. It was a unique information system that went beyond normal communications.

Many of the LOs were young and fairly junior officers and some commanders objected that the system short-circuited them, but Montgomery overruled their objections.[63] During the rapid advance, the LOs travelled by light aircraft each day to a point close to their destinations, following which there was 'a frantic chase in the jeep to reach the forward command posts and back again to the waiting aircraft'.[64]

Some lower level headquarters faced more mundane difficulties, as the following examples show. On 20 September, wireless communication on 4 Armoured Brigade's 'Q' link was almost impossible over a distance of 40 miles. Difficulties with the brigade's links also occurred during large-scale moves close to the German border in October, when its headquarters had to remain on line communication with XII Corps while the rest of the brigade moved. There were then problems with line communications to corps over a distance of 80 miles after brigade headquarters followed the rest of the formation.[65] The report by 7 Canadian Recce Regiment, however, stated that wireless communication with its divisional headquarters was excellent despite the great distances between them. This was achieved by placing relay stations as they travelled along.[66] Communications during 43 Division's assault crossing of the Seine were adequate even on the approach march by dint of the provision of two additional high-powered sets. A particular challenge in this case was extending lines over the damaged road bridge across the Seine and subsequently controlling the traffic across the bridge constructed by the Royal Engineers; the system for the latter worked extremely well.[67] These examples illustrate the variety of challenges facing Signals at this time, which were overcome to a greater or lesser extent.

The crossing of the Rhine may be seen as the point at which virtually everything had come together to ensure successful communications – there was enough equipment of all kinds to ensure redundancy in the systems, detailed planning took place and sufficient time was allowed for training. There was indeed a huge contrast between this and the operations of the British army of 1940. Shortage of manpower was the major problem – 21 Army Group Signals reported in March 1945 that they were in urgent need of an additional 2,000 men, with a further 2,500 needed in the near future. The War Office promised to provide some 800 men and 400 ATS immediately.[68] Large forces were assembled between the rivers Maas and Rhine prior to the Rhine crossing. The crossing was treated as an assault landing on an open beach and was achieved by a ferry operation requiring a considerable river bank control system. Prior to the operation, an extensive buried line network (205 miles in XII Corps alone) was laid from headquarters to the western bank of the river, requiring their location to be decided two weeks in advance. Once the initial assault had been completed, the lines were carried across the river by DUKWs to connect the eastern bank with the previously created west bank system. The line system was duplicated by a wireless network in which infantry assault forces were equipped with crystal controlled No. 46 wireless sets (10 per battalion) in a similar way to an amphibious landing from the sea. Artillery FOOs were originally intended to have No. 68R sets on a scale of six per division, but it was decided that these might have insufficient range; they were replaced by No. 22 sets carried either by handcart or broken down into man packs, both methods being successful. While the preparations were in train, a total of four signals exercises were carried out and this highly organized approach, coupled with the increasing weakness of the opposition, paid dividends.[69] Communications in the operation were successful.

Another rapid advance took place after the breakout from the Rhine bridgehead, when the 250 miles to the Elbe were covered by VIII Corps in three weeks. The speed of the advance again meant that normal line communications were impossible even at corps level, so each afternoon, the main corps headquarters moved close to its leading division in order to shorten the range of wireless. Some distance needed to be maintained, however, to avoid mutual interference between wireless sets – for example, the high powered sets of main and rear VIII Corps headquarters were kept at least three miles apart. During this time, the wireless resources prescribed by the war establishment scales allowed adequate, if austere, corps communications. For the first time in land operations, the main sets were controlled by crystal and this proved to work well, with the four principal nets remaining in touch with all outstations during the entire period. The reliance on wireless meant that cipher offices were very congested, and operational messages took priority over administration. The latter generally had to employ messengers for their communications.[70]

To summarize, communications during the rapid advances eastwards from Normandy and between the Rhine and the Elbe were challenging, but were generally adequate. Nor does it appear that problems with supply line communications across northern France were responsible for the delay in crossing the Rhine. By definition, these advances only took place when the Allied position was in the ascendant, so such problems as occurred were not disastrous; it was during smaller movements by the infantry and paratroops in the teeth of opposition that communications were found to be so difficult. Communications during the Rhine crossing matched the overall success of the operation.

Airborne landings on D-Day (June 1944), at Arnhem (September 1944) and during the crossing of the Rhine (March 1945)

The attraction of airborne landings was that they used the vertical dimension to get into the rear of the enemy, but their record in Tunisia and Sicily was not particularly convincing and British paratroops were not involved in a major airborne operation in Italy. One of the difficulties experienced in Sicily was that ground and airborne forces could not understand each other's map codes. It had therefore been decided that all formations likely to be in wireless touch with an airborne force should hold a copy of the airborne force's code keys, but there was too great a risk of compromise for the latter to hold anyone else's codes.[71] Another feature of the earlier operations was that the proportion of men and materiel arriving at the correct location was low. Efforts to increase the accuracy of the parachute drops and glider landings continued, but this was difficult to achieve; the main lesson was that something like double the required number of signallers and wireless sets needed to be sent to ensure that adequate numbers arrived where they were required. Finally, it had been decided that heavy wireless sets, such as the No. 22, should be mounted in jeeps and landed by glider rather than dropped in containers by parachute.[72] These lessons were implemented in the operations in North-West Europe, two out of three of which were successful. Unfortunately, in the operation at Arnhem, where the stakes were highest, the operation and its communications failed.

The 6 Airborne Division was the first British formation to land in France on D-Day, with the objective of securing the eastern flank of the British seaborne force. The landings took place at night. The parachute drops were inaccurate, so no more than 60 per cent of those landing were able to take part in the early operations. Despite this, all the primary tasks of the force had been achieved by daylight.[73] The performance of the communications system within the division on the first two days was quite variable, but wireless was summarized in the after action report as having been 'in general . . . most reliable'.[74] Some wireless was in touch for 90 per cent of the time from the start, while in other cases, confusion over call signs meant a nine-hour delay.[75] Signals losses during landing matched those of the overall force – in the case of the parachutists, about 60 per cent of signals personnel had arrived at their designated locations by H Hour, carrying considerably less than 50 per cent of the equipment. The losses of equipment were partly due to independently dropped containers going astray and partly because the lines attaching lighter loads to parachutists as they dropped had a tendency to break. A higher proportion of glider-borne personnel and equipment arrived correctly. In spite of these losses, divisional headquarters wireless communications with England were established within 15 minutes of landing and supplies to replace losses arrived successfully 12 hours later. It had been intended that line should be laid as soon as possible within the division, but heavy shellfire meant that it was not reliable enough until 14 days after D-Day, and in the meantime, wireless continued to be used. This was the first major British airborne operation that could be described as a success, partly attributable to the early support and relief given to the division. The impossibility of such early relief meant that the operation at Arnhem was much more risky.

The role of 1 Airborne Division in Operation MARKET GARDEN has been the subject of many books, articles, television programmes and films.[76] Problems existed both within the Division itself and between 1 Airborne Division and higher formations. The internal wireless communications of 1 Airborne Division at Arnhem were faulty, but the main reasons for this have been attributed to command and procedural errors and mishaps due to the effect of battle, rather than technical or operational problems.[77] The primary errors were – the decision to swap a less powerful No. 68P set for the No. 22 set on 1 Parachute Brigade's rear link to divisional headquarters; the decision of Major General Urquhart, the divisional commander, to leave his headquarters without proper communications, thereby isolating himself from his division; and the fact that the CO of the recce squadron attempted to meet Urquhart as the latter had ordered, leaving his squadron without direction. There were reasons for all of these decisions, but they made an already difficult decision worse. Urquhart's leaving of his headquarters was, to some extent, in line with Montgomery's instruction that the divisional commander must 'not wait for information that may never arrive; he must go forward and find out . . . for himself'.[78] But Urquhart was not 'accompanied by a good staff officer who is constantly on the air', as required by another of Montgomery's instructions.[79] Although line and DRs were alternative means of communicating at Arnhem, wireless had to be relied upon in practice. Line laying was attempted within the division, but field cable could not be maintained in the heavy fighting; the British were reluctant to make much use of the Dutch civilian telephone lines on security grounds; and it was impossible for DRs to get through. Pigeons, the method of last resort, could have been useful, but they proved to be of little value here.

Poor communications between 1 Airborne Division, 1 Air Landing Brigade and I Airborne Corps situated 12 miles away resulted in problems with re-supply and lack of air support. In addition, there was great difficulty in communicating with the relieving force, which was attempting to advance some 60 miles up the Eindhoven–Nijmegen–Arnhem corridor.[80] The inadequacy of I Airborne Corps communications was due to an insufficient number of wireless links and the fact that it had to be supplied with US sets, British high-powered sets being unavailable – this caused problems because there was no time for personnel to be trained on the US sets. The inability of 1 Airborne Division to communicate rearwards was because there were not enough of the high-powered sets that were needed to cover the distances – the No.19HP set was capable of the task, but only two were available and were in the hands of the artillery, and the No. 12 sets were not powerful enough.[81]

Divisional Signals officers warned commanders in advance of the appreciable risk of failure in wireless communications, given the range over which the sets would have to operate, and this risk was accepted along with the overall risk of failure of the very bold plan; the risks were high, but the potential rewards were great. Only two air support sets were supplied with crystals of the wrong frequency, not a wholesale misallocation, as implied in the film *A Bridge too Far*, and these sets were, in any case, destroyed before they could begin to operate. However, regardless of the reason for their failure, had the air support links been operational and more air support organized, matters might have turned out differently. Resupply by air had worked well for 6 Airborne Division during OVERLORD, but only 7 per cent of material dropped at Arnhem could be collected because the dropping zones had been captured by the enemy, and a message from the divisional rear wireless link to change the drop locations failed to get through. Therefore, as wireless equipment was destroyed later in the battle, replacements were not available and communications deteriorated.[82]

A vivid personal account of operations at Arnhem was given by Captain J. S. D. Hardy, the Signal officer of a battalion of the Border Regiment, who landed by glider. The battalion was given the task of covering the western side of a defence circle, which turned out to be in much more heavily wooded country than had been expected, as a result of which wireless communications were difficult. Headquarters found that it was in wireless contact with A, C and D Companies, but B Company was completely out of touch on the western edge of the perimeter. Since they were likely to be the first to be hit by the advancing enemy force, it was imperative that they were in touch with headquarters. Hardy decided to run a telephone wire out to them using a jeep, but there were no spare men to do this other than Hardy himself and his Signals sergeant. Even though it was undesirable for both of these men to be away from headquarters together, it was decided that they should go.

The line was laid successfully, but on their way back, the men ran into the Germans. They took two prisoners, but were unable to get back to headquarters and returned to B Company, which was then instructed via the newly installed telephone line to fight their way back. There was a fierce fight, but the company managed to evade capture and returned to headquarters safely. For their part in this action, Hardy was awarded the Military Cross, and his sergeant, the Military Medal.

Later in the battle of Arnhem, Hardy was forced to release the two homing pigeons that he had taken with him as an emergency communications method, because he had run out of food for them. There was no operational message for the second of these birds, but Hardy felt that the recipients would find it strange if a bird returned without a message. He himself therefore wrote a message that he later described as absolute nonsense, not really expecting it to get through. The bird did arrive, however, and his message was featured in the newspapers as an epic example of British 'sang froid'. It read:

1. Have to release birds owing to shortage of food and water.
2. About 8 tanks laying about in sub-unit areas, very untidy but not causing us any trouble.
3. Now using as many German weapons as we have British.
4. Dutch people grand but Dutch tobacco rather strong.
5. Great beard growing competition on in our unit but no time to check up on winner.

Hardy wrote, 'As each day came along we were all quite sure that this would be the day that the Second Army would reach us . . . finally the message came that we were to pull out'. He made it safely back.[83]

As far as the effect of poor communications on the total operation is concerned, one view is that it was doomed from the start because it was inherently too risky and would still have ended in defeat even if communications had been perfect. However, poor communications caused four battalions to be fed piecemeal and with little coordination into the battle to reinforce the bridge.[84] Had they reached the bridge and been resupplied with equipment, it might conceivably have been held until ground troops had relieved them. Overall, the combination of wireless problems, both within and outside 1 Airborne Division, makes it clear that poor communication was a major contributor to the failure of the operation, even though the issues were much more complex than many accounts have stated.

The Army quickly drew what lessons it could from the failure at Arnhem so that improvements could be made in time for the airborne operation across the Rhine, Operation VARSITY, the objective of which was to disrupt the enemy's artillery positions and rear defences. This plan did not run anything like the same level of risk as the landings at Arnhem and made due allowance for the vulnerability, amply demonstrated at Arnhem, of airborne forces if left on their own for too long. The 6 Airborne Division therefore did not land until a viable bridgehead across the Rhine had been formed. Moreover, the dropping zone was within easy wireless range of the ground forces.[85] In the light of problems experienced at Arnhem, a more complete list of call signs for other formations was carried, but was kept in special destructor boxes for added security, which could be ignited if they were in danger of capture. A new system of artillery support call signs was also introduced. These innovations were successful.[86] The operation achieved its objectives despite the airborne troops suffering severely while the troops who had crossed the river by ferry joined up with them within 24 hours.

The limited carrying capacity of the available aircraft meant that reserves of signals personnel and equipment were reduced below the desired 100 per cent coverage, and losses during the operation were as high as ever – for example, only 13 out of 29 sets of 5 Parachute Brigade Signals arrived safely at the rendezvous point because all the brigade headquarters gliders had gone astray. This meant that communications at 5 Brigade were more difficult than those of 3 and 6 Brigades, but fortunately some US walkie-talkie sets had been acquired by officers in 5 Brigade for their personal use. The available communications proved just adequate; essential wireless links were quickly established and generally worked well. Unlike at Arnhem, they only had to last a short time, and so, the destruction of sets during fighting was not too serious a problem. Possibly because of more favourable geographic conditions, it was found that ground wave wireless ranges were, in many cases, considerably better than at Arnhem, up to 10 miles in the case of the Nos. 62 to 19HP set link. Another factor responsible for the improved performance was the fact that 6 Airborne Division had recent experience of active service, by contrast with 1 Airborne Division, which had been waiting in England for months prior to Arnhem. In a clear reference to this, the OC Signals said that his men were 'in an excellent state of training with their ears really in. So often airborne signals had to be committed to an . . . operation after months of waiting at base and no amount of ordinary training is a real substitute for operations'.[87]

The use of US walkie-talkies in VARSITY is of interest since they were small enough for commanders themselves to carry during parachute drops. Although US forces had used them since 1942, they were of an advanced design and resembled early mobile phones. Operating on short wave between 3.5 and 6.0 Megahertz, they had a range of about one mile over land, similar to the British No. 38 set, but much more compact, as shown in the illustrations below.

Figure 8.4 US SCR-536 'walkie-talkie' set in use during an amphibious landing.[88]

Figure 8.5 British No. 38 set.[89]

The walkie-talkies 'proved absolutely invaluable for immediate communications on the dropping zone without having to wait for operators and sets to
rendezvous'.[90] Brigadier Poett, the OC of 5 Parachute Brigade, believed that
their use meant that communications with battalions were established 30
minutes earlier than would otherwise have been possible. Security procedures
were ignored – they 'dispensed with all the mumbo-jumbo of RT procedure.
There were no link signs . . . and no station acted as control, it was in fact a
signaller's horror but it worked and worked well'.[91] The US official history of
Signals indicated that 'everywhere they were used, [Walkie-Talkie] sets served
outstandingly', but the mortality of the sets in battle was extremely high,
keeping them 'on the critical list of signal items' during 1944.[92] Clearly, there
were insufficient supplies for them to have been extended to British forces
on a wide scale. Moreover, they were not universally praised by US troops
on the ground. During VARSITY, Joe Rheinberger of 194 US Glider Infantry
Regiment was on a mission to find his battalion headquarters 'because the
radios didn't work as per usual'.[93] It seems that, like British sets, US wireless
sets were sometimes fickle.

The record of British airborne operations during the war showed that they
could be successful so long as the objectives were sufficiently limited, but that
where airborne troops were put in a position of having to fend for themselves for
long periods without support, they were likely to be defeated. Communications
was one of the aspects that broke down under these circumstances; it was an
important contributory factor in the overall failure of the operation at Arnhem,
as it had been at Primosole Bridge in Sicily.

Signals security in North-West Europe

As noted by *Signals Training Pamphlet No. 9* of August 1944, there was an inherent
conflict between security and speed of communication. It stated, 'The higher
the degree of security imposed, the more complex and cumbersome becomes
the method of transmission, especially in the more forward areas. Hence the
balance . . . must be decided by those on the spot'.

The lax security of 5 Parachute Brigade in VARSITY, described above, was
not the first time they had been guilty of security breaches, since prisoners of
war had testified that the Germans obtained much information from 6 Airborne
Division's W/T traffic in July and August 1944. The reports of the British Special

Intelligence service made it clear that many Allied formations were insecure. The preparations for OVERLORD and the build-up after the landings had been well disguised, but German signal intelligence services were much more successful in tracking Allied movements after the end of July 1944. While this was particularly the case with US forces, the order of battle of 21 Army Group was also regularly revealed by a combination of captured documents, traffic analysis and other signal intelligence. The Germans made good use of this knowledge in planning their Ardennes offensive and it helped them in their vain attempts to halt the Allied offensives in 1945.[94] After this point, it appears that Allied signals security was deliberately partially sacrificed to speed up the advance; for example, the CSO Second Army agreed that no code signs or security would be used on a network of borrowed American sets during XII Corps' crossing of the Rhine 'other than those dictated by common sense'.[95] The threat posed by poor wireless security was well known to Allied front line forces, not only from the warnings delivered by British Special intelligence, but from the fact that 'every [captured] German signaller testified to the carelessness of Allied soldiers on the air, especially the Canadians and some American units whose easy chatter provided priceless intelligence'.[96]

Evidence that the R/T procedure of some Canadian formations had been particularly poor prior to OVERLORD was given in the report on Exercise LAST (April 1944), which stated that 2 Canadian Corps' W/T security had been very good, but that of its R/T had been much worse due to unguarded conversation. It did not seem to have improved afterwards, for the interrogation of a German wireless intercept operator in September 1944 revealed that Canadian nets were much more useful than British ones – though the reason given was that there were fewer frequency changes rather than chatter. Because of this criticism, the Canadians instituted a wireless monitoring service of their own nets to identify offending units and operators and they believed that this resulted in some improvement.[97] Careless talk was not limited to the Allies, however, as the US interception of a German patrol's transmissions testified.[98]

But, if they could be somewhat cavalier about signals security, Allied soldiers over-estimated the ability of German direction finding, to the extent that they avoided occupying positions near major Signals units for fear that German radio locators would discover their exact position and direct artillery fire against them. *Current Reports from Overseas, Nos. 60 and 66* from October and December 1944 attempted to put soldiers' minds at rest concerning DF by pointing out that a captured German document had similarly aimed to calm overly-anxious

German soldiers about the power of Allied DF, clearly indicating that their own systems were capable of giving the general direction of a wireless transmission, but were insufficient for aiming an artillery barrage with any accuracy.[99]

The tendency to overestimate the capability of German DF, but to underestimate the potential damage of careless talk and other signals security lapses was a recurrent theme throughout the war. Security consciousness varied between units and individuals and, as a result, it is difficult to say to what extent it improved overall. The signal training document was right to state that the degree of security imposed was a matter of judgement, but soldiers' judgement was sometimes incorrect. However, wireless deception measures reached new heights of sophistication with Operation FORTITUDE prior to and after D-Day, the benefit of which is hard to overestimate.

It is concluded that many aspects of communications in North-West Europe worked extremely well, benefitting from the experience gained in Tunisia, Sicily and Italy, the flat countryside and the Allied air superiority that helped to protect signal links. But the biggest single factor helping to ensure success was the abundance of materiel and the consequent redundancy that could be built into the system. Communications during the amphibious landings in OVERLORD, the crossing of the Rhine by land forces, the advances across northern France and into Germany, as well as artillery and armoured communications generally, all achieved a high standard. Naturally, there were problems, but they were largely caused by enemy action rather than being endemic.

Despite this, it is clear that some fundamental problems remained. In the campaign in North-West Europe, the most obvious communications difficulties were within the infantry and between infantry and tanks in the front line. This was detrimental to tank–infantry cooperation, which in turn delayed progress through the Normandy bocage. When the battle reached more open country, the issue became less important, but it was still a potential threat. The inherent lack of security of wireless was also a continuing difficulty – if it was overcome by the use of codes and ciphers, the passage of information was delayed, sometimes with serious consequences; if it was ignored in the interests of speed or because of over-confidence, enemy intelligence benefitted. There do not appear to have been any large-scale security breaches (like the betrayal of the Salerno landings in Italy, for example), but the cumulative effect of more minor indiscretions was serious enough.

It would be unfair to describe the events at Arnhem as displaying endemic signalling failure, even though it is true that poor communications were partly responsible for the defeat. Rather, it appears that insufficient notice was taken of the warnings of the likelihood of signals failures given before the operation. The operation itself was arguably over-ambitious and so were the expectations of communications. It was clear that airborne troops were highly vulnerable if left unsupported for any length of time and that a very large over-supply of signals personnel and equipment was needed to make up for likely losses during the landings. That said, it seems quite possible that the same operation would have been attempted again in similar circumstances even with the benefit of hindsight, because the potential rewards of success were so great and, despite the terrible experiences of 1 Airborne Division, the consequences of failure for the total Allied cause less than catastrophic.

9

Conclusions

Communications are a vital part of an army's command system; without efficient communications, an army will struggle to operate at all, let alone successfully. The main purpose of this book has been to examine the impact that forward British Army communications (those at corps level and below) had on the outcome of the campaigns in Europe and North Africa during the Second World War.

The methods of communications available to commanders were – radio (generally known at the time as wireless), which either transmitted Morse (W/T) or voice (R/T); line, which was used for Morse messages and telephone conversations; messengers and liaison officers; and the less frequent methods of visual signalling and pigeons. The choice between wireless and line communications was the subject of much debate between the two World Wars. Far from ignoring the lessons of the First World War, the General Staff was determined from 1920 onwards to avoid a repetition of the attritional battles of the Western Front, and to use wireless to direct a mobile battle. During the 1920s, Royal Signals advocated a dual approach, utilizing wireless in mobile situations and line when stationary, to make best use of the strengths of the two methods. However, this policy was not universally accepted in the Army and, moreover, lack of investment meant that progress with wireless technology, in particular, was slow. When the German threat in the mid-1930s forced discussion to stop so that re-equipping could begin, signalling resources and capabilities were insufficient. The Jackson Committee of 1936 therefore allocated extensive wireless and no line to armoured formations while the infantry was given line with very limited wireless backup, even though this was bound to cause problems when the infantry was on the move. The difficulties faced during the rapid retreat to Dunkirk in May 1940 were therefore inevitable.

The extent to which an army requires an elaborate communications system depends, to some extent, on its command philosophy. The more commanders seek to know about and control events in the front line, the greater are the demands placed on communications. Most British commanders in the Second World War sought to impose a restrictive command system as opposed to the mission command system operated by the German Army in the early years of the war, maximizing the need for good communications. The links between the four elements of the command OODA (Observe–Orientate–Decide–Act) loop were highly dependent on good communications, often over considerable distances.

Poor communications undoubtedly contributed to some of the more notable setbacks, but from mid-1942 onwards, by dint of providing a system with built-in redundancy and multiple means of communication, signallers normally succeeded in providing the links required by commanders. A summary of the progress made by infantry and armoured wireless communications between 1940 and 1945 shows that only recent technological developments have offered the ability to resolve the security issues and the problems that remained with infantry communications at the end of the war.

The communications system of the BEF in 1940 could not meet the demands of the retreat to Dunkirk because there was an insufficient number of wireless sets and insufficient cipher staff. Wireless operators had had less practice during the static, Phoney War, period than was desirable, and staff officers had an inadequate understanding of the limited message carrying capacity of wireless, compared with the line communications to which they were accustomed.

The reasons for this primarily lay in the doctrine for the Field Force that was established before the war. There were also supply problems with wireless, so even 1 Armoured Division, which was supposed to rely on wireless, lacked equipment in May 1940 and there were problems with the reliability and information-carrying capacity of sets. The Army was very concerned about the insecurity of wireless, leading to the wireless silence that, in line with its command doctrine, was prevalent during the static period and was largely responsible for the shortage of training in the use of the wireless systems that did exist. It was also the reason for the imposition of cipher on all occasions. Finally, despite the fact that many in the Army and press commentators such as Basil Liddell Hart had advocated mobile tactics, it was envisaged that the British Expeditionary Force's main role would be to support the much larger French Army in a static defensive battle, in which line communications would be both feasible and appropriate. Even when it was decided that the first action of the British and French armies should be a rapid advance into Belgium, a static defensive battle was still envisaged, but further forward.

In spite of these fundamental mistakes in planning and doctrine, the judgement by many authors of the performance of BEF communications appears unjustifiably harsh. Operators were not practically untrained in the use of wireless, but their training was not as thorough or as realistic as was desirable. During the campaign, communications did not generally collapse, and wireless was not useless, but lines were frequently cut by enemy action, wireless communications on the move were very difficult, and DRs were often prevented from reaching their destinations or got lost. Nevertheless, signallers frequently overcame these difficulties even if it took some time to do so. The main problem was precisely this – lack of speed – it often took too long for communications to complete the OODA loop, contributing to the slow tempo of the British response to the German Blitzkrieg.

There were several aspects to the problem. In the first place, the reconnaissance resources of divisions in the BEF were inadequate, causing the initial O → ODA stage to break down. Then, the concentration of command at GHQ placed a great onus on its communications and these did not perform well. Pressure of work had not allowed the movement of GHQ to be practised in the static period, and it had seemed unlikely anyway that it would need to move. It had been intended that the two main parts of GHQ should remain at their location near Arras, but they were forced to move by enemy action. Gort's decision to create a third, moving, command post also caused many difficulties with internal GHQ communications, which had consequences for the entire command and control system of the BEF. Overall, there were key organizational defects at GHQ, which meant that the BEF's OODA loops could not operate properly and at a sufficient tempo to counter the rapid German advance. Furthermore, staff officers' attitudes of expecting efficient communications as a matter of course tended to contribute to problems, for example, when they moved their headquarters without informing higher command and when they sent excessively long messages.

A substantial proportion of the formations below GHQ were territorial. Analysing the difference between regular and territorial formations in the efficiency of their communications is complicated by the paucity of original documentation, the fact that some regular formations had Territorial Signals regiments anyway, and because territorial formations generally had less training time in France. Of great importance was the level of equipment that formations possessed. Where regular formations were deficient in signalling equipment, they had communications problems. Where territorial formations were properly equipped, their communications were no worse than those of regular divisions.

To what extent was the inadequacy of communications responsible for the defeat of the BEF? In some later battles, signalling problems clearly contributed considerably to defeat, but this was not the case at Dunkirk. At each stage of the retreat, systems were generally working, albeit sub-optimally, when the decision to retreat further was taken. It was the withdrawal that caused the biggest problems with communications, and not the other way round. Inadequate communications, in the British Army at least, was not therefore a primary cause of the defeat, but they exacerbated the problems facing the BEF, and therefore contributed to the number of men killed, wounded and captured.

The Bartholomew Committee of 1940 was set up to investigate the failures of the BEF. It redirected British policy towards the mobile battle, and re-emphasized the need for extensive provision of wireless as well as line in all types of formation, so that a return could be made to the communications doctrine of the 1920s, which advocated the use of both, depending on the circumstances. It also confirmed the restrictive, top-down, style of command that differed fundamentally from German mission command doctrine. However, it was not until the autumn of 1942 that sufficient resources were available for that Eighth Army to fully implement Bartholomew's recommendations on communications. In the Home Forces, the remainder of the period between 1940 and 1943 was devoted to putting this basic policy into effect, to refining signals doctrine, to training personnel and to developing and producing appropriate equipment. Verifying this process in Home Forces was, however, a largely theoretical exercise and lacked the test of battle. Communications in Eighth Army developed along somewhat different lines, learning from the experience of the many battles in the Western Desert and adapting to its particular geographic conditions. When the First and Eighth Armies combined together in Tunisia at the beginning of 1943, the two systems were found to be incompatible and both had to be altered and coordinated to meet the challenge of fighting the Germans in new types of terrain.

The great distances involved in many operations in the Western Desert meant that reliance often had to be placed on wireless. Wireless communications during the first major battle (Operation COMPASS in December 1940) were sufficient to enable the British to defeat the large immobile Italian Army, helped by the compact size and relatively thorough training of the Western Desert Force (the forerunner of Eighth Army). However, several inadequacies in communications were exposed and these became manifest when 2 Armoured Division was routed and driven back by Rommel's forces in March 1941. Inadequate wireless communications were undoubtedly a major contributor to the failure of BATTLEAXE in June 1941. Some progress was made between then and CRUSADER in November 1941, where the British could claim a victory. But considering how the British outnumbered the Axis Army, CRUSADER was scarcely convincing, and inadequacies in wireless communications contributed to the disappointing overall result. Considerable improvements were then made so that the British defeat at Gazala in May 1942 cannot be attributed to Signals failures. Instead, defeat was due to a combination of the British forces being in an offensive rather than a defensive disposition at the start of the German attack, failure to interpret reconnaissance information correctly, failure to disseminate appropriate information across all the formations in Eighth Army and failure of higher command to react to events in an optimal way. The entire organization, including its communications system, was in disarray after Gazala, and the successful resistance of the attack at First Alamein in July 1942 was achieved in spite of communications problems, while Alam Halfa at the end of August 1942, was a static defensive position that presented much less of a challenge to communications. The success at Second Alamein in November 1942 was assisted by improvements in the communications system, particularly the laying of extensive line networks prior to the battle, so that reliance on wireless was reduced. However, wireless problems compounded other failures in command during the inconclusive subsequent pursuit of the Axis Army following its defeat. Between 1940 and 1942, many improvements were made in wireless communications, but the greatest lesson learnt in the desert was the need to avoid total reliance on wireless and to use line or other means whenever feasible. This was the converse of the lesson drawn from the BEF; both experiences showed that extensive line *and* wireless systems were needed in both infantry and armoured formations.

The improvements that occurred over the period were driven by a combination of enhanced systems, increased resources and technical developments. The duplication of systems – multiple line connections, wireless, LOs, DRs, runners and even pigeons – was a key factor in ensuring success, but it required large amounts of equipment. Of the many technological developments, the introduction of the No. 18 portable infantry set was arguably the most important; even though the set was imperfect, it extended wireless communications for the first time down to front line infantry. Equally, the status of infantry in desert warfare greatly increased over the period, as the limitations of purely armoured formations became apparent.

Communications were also an important driver of changes in the organizational structure of the artillery where, generally speaking, communications were relatively trouble free. If command was at a low level, it was difficult to concentrate firepower when required, but if command was at a high level, it was difficult for individual units to get help when they needed it. In both cases, this was due to imperfect communications as well as to the complexities of the command structure and sometimes to lack of cooperation between commanders. Artillery (and the Army generally) ended under highly centralized control, as evidenced by the massive barrages at Second Alamein. The idea of creating brigade groups involving infantry and armour as opposed to keeping them separate was driven by similar considerations.

The habit of creating tactical headquarters close to the action was another major change. It enabled commanders to communicate much more easily with reconnaissance units and to make use more easily of the other mechanisms for obtaining information from the front line, such as the 'J' wireless monitoring system. Closer involvement also meant that commanders could understand the battle more readily. Thus, it helped both the Observation and Orientation aspects of the OODA loop as well as shortening the OOD → A link. The creation of these tactical headquarters required extensive communications links back to main and on to RAF headquarters, but these became available in a way that had been completely impossible when Gort attempted to set up a similar organization in May 1940.

As the Eighth Army pursued the enemy into Libya, the British First Army and the Americans landed in North-West Africa. The two British armies later joined together as 18 Army Group, and a series of new communication challenges were encountered, not least because the signals doctrine that had been developed over the previous three years in Eighth Army had evolved differently from that of Home Forces in the UK. Because of this disparity, a major conclusion from Tunisia about communications was that the War Office needed to decide upon and impose a consistent signals doctrine on the whole British Army. This was the task given to the Godwin-Austen Committee during the second half of 1943, the report of which defined communications doctrine for the rest of the war.

Operation TORCH was the first major amphibious operation in the Second World War and although communications were better than had been the case during the Dieppe raid, they were unsatisfactory in many ways and it was fortunate that there was no serious opposition. This meant that TORCH was close to being a very large-scale training exercise, which gave clear indications on how methods should be improved and, in particular, pointed to the need for fixed frequency, crystal-controlled, as opposed to variable frequency wireless sets to pre-dominate. There was ample time before the invasion of Sicily for these lessons to be assimilated.

The overall performance of First Army signalling in the Tunisian land campaign was poor. There were four main causes of the problems – lack of training; adverse geographical conditions; inadequate line supplies and poor security. Communications training in Home Forces had been imperfect, so that the completely 'raw' First Army was bound to struggle when it first went into combat. The mountainous conditions in Tunisia made wireless difficult, and this should have been better foreseen. The inadequacy of line supplies and personnel should have been anticipated from the increases in cable sections that had taken effect in Eighth Army, and the failure to adhere to Eighth Army practice contributed to the lack of security. While Eighth Army security was better, it too was imperfect and was the main communications failure that occurred between Alamein and Tunis, the most serious consequence of which was to make the attack on the Mareth line in southern Tunisia more difficult than it need have been. As a result of these problems, the Godwin-Austen Committee paid particular attention to the security of communications.

The overall conclusion about communications in North Africa between November 1942 and May 1943 is that the British Army still had a lot to learn after Alamein – First Army (and Home Forces) had failed to assimilate the lessons from the Western Desert, but these were not necessarily applicable in other terrains anyway; furthermore, the techniques used in amphibious landing and parachute operations had not been sufficiently practised. Many inadequacies emerged in the Allies' communications systems. It was therefore fortunate that the Allies faced a fundamentally weak foe in Tunisia and that they were given another chance to improve their performance before they encountered the Axis at full strength.

TORCH and the Tunisian campaign were successful in driving the Axis forces out of Africa, but it had all taken much longer than had been hoped, thereby delaying the invasion of Italy and arguably prolonging the war. Inadequacies in communications played their part in the delays, but it is not felt that they were primarily to blame. In the first place, expectations of the speed with which victory could be achieved were probably too high, given the relative resources of the Allied and Axis forces, the distances involved in the pursuit by Eighth Army, and logistical problems. Secondly, there were many more important factors contributing to the disappointing pace of events, such as – the decision to concentrate the TORCH landings in Morocco and Algeria rather than to attempt to invade Tunisia directly; the weather during the Tunisian winter; a lack of drive and skill in Anderson's First Army and the US II Corps; and the cautious approach of Montgomery's Eighth Army.

The communications training that took place before the invasion of Sicily was only partly successful in putting right the problems that the Tunisian campaign had uncovered. A start was made on improving methods of operation and on providing new equipment, but there was insufficient time to complete the process and for units and formations to become familiar with different arrangements. The arrival of additional formations, of all sorts of nationality, meant that there was a continual struggle to achieve consistency in the 'British' Army. In fact, as a result of the conflicting priorities of Italy and the impending operations OVERLORD and ANVIL, many of main recommendations of the Godwin-Austen Committee, particularly those relating to increased manning levels, had scarcely begun to be implemented before the capture of Rome.

The three most important amphibious landings were HUSKY (Sicily), AVALANCHE (Salerno) and SHINGLE (Anzio). The lessons from TORCH were taken into account during HUSKY even though the time available for planning was short, and there were fewer problems than before. As with TORCH, opposition during HUSKY was light, so the consequences of communications failures were not too severe. AVALANCHE took place before further improvements in technique could be implemented and also revealed serious security breaches, mainly from sources other than communications. It ended successfully despite strong opposition. Tight security was ensured in SHINGLE and other lessons from HUSKY and AVALANCHE were also taken into account. The landing was very successful and it was only later that Anzio turned into a near catastrophe. The experience gained in the three amphibious operations together was highly instrumental in ensuring the later success of OVERLORD.

Different authors have given conflicting views on the performance of communications in the land campaigns in Sicily and Italy. The fact that the Allies suffered setbacks, but no actual defeat in Sicily and Italy, and in the end achieved victory, suggests that communications, albeit imperfect, were sufficiently successful. But where they undoubtedly failed was in airborne operations; the setback at Primosole Bridge, for which poor communications were partly responsible, was seriously damaging to the progress of the Sicilian campaign. It must be said in mitigation that it was not just communications, but the entirety of the airborne operations that was at fault, leading to their abandonment as a concept during the rest of the Italian campaign while methods were improved.

The positive overall judgement of the British communications system in Italy, airborne operations apart, does not absolve it from criticisms. R/T insecurity was a considerable problem; the portable wireless sets used by the infantry lacked sufficient range; the manufacturing quality of the wireless sets and batteries was often poor; and inadequately trained personnel struggled to operate the equipment. Although the supply of sets increased very considerably, there were still insufficient sets at the front line and, moreover, many infantrymen were not 'wireless-minded'; as a result, front line infantry communications remained primitive. But further back, at company level and above, infantry communications gradually improved along with those between infantry and artillery. Within the artillery, communications were generally excellent. Infantry–tank communications were difficult, however, and remained so in North-West Europe up to the end of the war.

As a result of previous experience and facilitated by the improving supply situation, great emphasis was placed on multiple backup systems, so that when one line failed, another was available; if all lines failed, wireless could take over; when wireless failed, visual signalling or a runner could be used, and in the last resort, pigeons still had a role. It would be wrong to criticize a communications system just because one method failed; some failures were inevitable in battle and the question is whether alternative means were available. The system failed in the case of Primosole Bridge, but in most cases, it worked and forward formations were able to communicate.

With the launch of Operation OVERLORD in June 1944, the main action in Europe switched from Italy to France. Many aspects of communications in North-West Europe worked extremely well, benefitting from the experience of the previous five years, the flat countryside and Allied air superiority. But the biggest single factor helping to ensure success was the abundance and higher quality of material, and the consequent redundancy that could be built into the system. Not everything was positive, however. Forward infantry communications generally and tank–infantry communications, in particular, remained problematic; there were still many breaches of security with R/T, from which the enemy derived appreciable benefit; and poor communications at Arnhem were partially responsible for the failure of Operation MARKET GARDEN.

The signals doctrine used in the invasion itself was the result of an evolutionary process based on past experience, but whereas the operations in Sicily and Italy had often been rushed and were subject to restrictions in material, OVERLORD was planned over a long period and all possible resources were put into it. The abundance and duplication of signalling equipment meant that few compromises had to be made on preferred doctrine. There was also great emphasis on training, though this was perhaps slightly too much concentrated on the landings themselves and too little on the subsequent advance inland. Security to cover the point and timing of the invasion was excellent, reinforced by an extensive deception plan that involved communications aspects. Generally speaking, British wireless communications during the invasion performed well, helped by the fact that the Germans were taken by surprise.

Communications in the lodgement area made very extensive use of line, some of which was laid earlier than was advised by Combined Operations doctrine. It might be imagined that the desire to establish a firm line network could have been a cause of delay in striking out inland, but this was not the case – advances were attempted without delay, but became bogged down in the Normandy bocage.

Poor tank–infantry cooperation has been put forward by others as an important reason for the lack of progress through the bocage and poor tank–infantry communications was a major contributor to this. In fact, forward infantry communications were generally unsatisfactory. This was partly because of inadequate technology – portable infantry sets did not perform well and, in any case, communicated on a different frequency range from tank sets. Moreover, many front line infantrymen seemed to be resistant to wireless in spite of all the efforts to counteract the inter-war culture of relying on runners. These two elements, poor technology and a negative attitude, were of course interlinked – front line infantrymen distrusted wireless because it often failed them. It was recognized that a new and more satisfactory infantry set was required, but this had not been produced by the end of the war. As in Italy, artillery communications both within artillery itself and between infantry and artillery were good, and communications within armoured units also remained satisfactory.

After the eventual breakout, the rapid advance across Northern France imposed considerable strain on both L of C and command communications. But it has been concluded that the problems posed were generally overcome without pre-judicing overall operations – the slow progress and inability of the L of C to supply the Army's needs for advancing into Germany at this time were not due to poor communications. The Rhine crossing itself was meticulously planned and was preceded by four signals exercises; it was planned as an amphibious landing on an open beach and the performance of communications matched the high standard of the total operation.

There were three major airborne operations, of which the two by 6 Airborne Division on D-Day and during the Rhine crossing went satisfactorily. They were characterized by high losses of wireless sets during the landings, but this was expected and resupply worked well. Moreover, the forces did not have to hold out for very long on their own. By contrast, the Arnhem landings by 1 Airborne Division were much more risky because the drop was far ahead of relieving forces. Signals warned in advance of the likely difficulties that they would face, but the decision was taken to go ahead anyway because of the potential rewards, had the operation been a success. There is no doubt that failed communications for a number of reasons contributed to the failure, but the faults were complex and in many cases difficult to avoid.

The final aspect of communications that remained unsatisfactory in North-West Europe at the end of the war was security. Despite all the warnings that careless use of wireless could give the enemy a considerable advantage, many officers failed to adhere to the rules, particularly when they were under pressure to act quickly. Thus, for example, the Germans were able to track 21 Army Group's order of battle with considerable success and this helped them to plan the Ardennes offensive.

'Voice Control': Developments in wireless between 1939 and 1945

One of the major developments in British Army communications during the Second World War was that wireless contact became possible much further down the command chain than had previously been possible. This did indeed help to restore a measure of voice control of front line troops, the aspect of command that was absent in the First World War. A key issue addressed by this book has been to assess the extent of that measure. From the beginning of the inter-war period to the end of the Second World War (and beyond), the biggest technical challenge facing British Army communications lay in the development of wireless sets that would meet their requirements. The sets themselves are shown for reference, with their basic statistics, in Appendix I, but the objective here is to analyse the end results of the developments over time, not in technical terms, but in terms of effective capability. While the existence of wireless links can be verified from countless diagrams of communications networks that appear in the war diaries, the judgement of reliability is necessarily subjective. The judgement contained here has been based on the impression gained from the war diaries and other War Office documents.

It should be noted that the concentration on wireless here does not imply that technical developments in line communications did not occur or that they were unimportant. It has been demonstrated that wireless did not render line communications redundant. On the contrary, by the middle of the Second World War, wireless still had multiple drawbacks and not all the problems associated with it had been overcome. Consequently, the Army still had a great need for line communications and the increasing ability to construct multiple telephone lines and to operate them over long distances was extremely important. By 1943–44, a sophisticated communications system had been developed that relied on *both* means. Line networks were especially important with artillery communications because the gun emplacements were less subject to sudden movement than were infantry and armoured units. For the latter, however, the laying of line could never take the place of wireless in mobile situations and it was communicating in these circumstances that presented the Army with its greatest challenge.

The judgement of infantry and armoured wireless is summarized in the tables below – a clear box means that wireless communication at the particular level was practically impossible at that time; light shading means that it was possible, but unreliable; and dark shading means that it was usually reliable. The overall judgement on communications at a given level (e.g. battalion) refers to communications to higher headquarters (e.g. brigade) and communications within the (battalion) headquarters itself, where applicable.

These tables demonstrate that the generally unsatisfactory state of wireless communications in 1940 carried on into 1941 and did not finally improve substantially until the latter part of 1942. Infantry wireless then found it difficult to cope in the mountainous terrain in Tunisia, Sicily and Italy. Communications within armoured divisions were generally satisfactory in North-West Europe, but the interaction with infantry remained problematic, while infantry communications were reasonably robust at battalion level, but unreliable nearer to the front line. This analysis has only been concerned with the possibility of communicating; the security of wireless communications remained an issue and

Table 9.1 Infantry wireless communications

Period / HQ comms.	May 1940 France/ Flanders	June 1941 Western Desert: BATTLE-AXE	October 1942 Western Desert: Alamein	September 1943 Italy	June 1944 Normandy bocage	March 1945 Rhine crossing
Corps	Reliable, but limited	WDF wireless unreliable due to range	Reliable	Reliable	Reliable	Reliable
Division	Reliable, but limited	Insufficient equipment and unreliable due to long range	Reliable	Unreliable due to the mountains	Reliable	Reliable
Brigade	Limited and unreliable	Unreliable	Reliable	Unreliable due to the mountains	Reliable	Reliable
Battalion	Very limited and unreliable	Unreliable	Generally reliable	Unreliable due to the mountains	Reliable	Reliable
Company	Non existent	Non existent	Available for the first time, but unreliable	Unreliable	Unreliable (No. 18/38 sets)	Fairly reliable (No. 46 sets)
Platoon	Non existent	Non existent	Non existent	Unreliable	Unreliable	Unreliable

Table 9.2 Armoured division wireless communications

Period HQ comns.	May 1940 France/ Flanders	June 1941 Western Desert: BATTLE-AXE	October 1942 Western Desert: Alamein	September 1943 Italy	June 1944 Normandy bocage	March 1945 Rhine crossing
Division	Equipment deficiencies in 1st Armoured Division	Reliable, though some equipment shortages	Reliable during attack, but not during pursuit	Armoured Divisions not much used in this campaign	Reliable	Reliable
Brigade	Exact extent of communications unclear,	Several problems with old sets, shortages and charging problems	Reliable during attack, but not during pursuit		Reliable	Reliable
Regiment	but appears to have been very limited	As above	Reliable		Reliable, but tank–infantry unsatisfactory	Reliable, but tank–infantry unsatisfactory
Squadron	Non Existent	As above	Reliable		Reliable, but tank–infantry unsatisfactory	Reliable, but tank–infantry unsatisfactory
Individual Tank	Non Existent	Not all tanks had sets	Reliable		Reliable, but tank–infantry unsatisfactory	Reliable, but tank–infantry unsatisfactory

was often far from perfect throughout the war, sometimes with serious negative consequences.

It is beyond the scope of this book to give a detailed account of the developments of British Army communications since the Second World War. But it is a measure of the difficulty of the technical issues facing the Army in 1945, that the two principal remaining problems, of security and front line infantry communications, were not adequately solved until the Bowman system was introduced in 2004. Perhaps it would be wiser to say 'solved in theory', since reality may not always have lived up to the technical promise.

Although not everything was satisfactory in 1945, the story of British Army communications during the course of the Second World War is overwhelmingly positive – learning from experience to devise a more effective signals doctrine; large increases in the quantity and quality of wireless sets and other equipment and improved performance. By the end of the war, most aspects of the signals system worked satisfactorily within the limits of available technology, and the system was designed with built-in redundancy so that it was resistant to the results of enemy action. The fog of battle had indeed been lifted to a considerable extent, but not entirely. The endemic problems that remained in front line infantry communications and with security were intractable and arguably impossible to solve with contemporary technology.

Appendix I: British Wireless Sets

Main army wireless sets in the 1920s

Type	Purpose	Mode	Range	Dates	Comments
'120 Watt'	Down to Infantry Div. HQ	W/T	60 miles		Origins in the First World War. Some fitted in motor or horse-drawn transport. There were also 250 and 500 Watt sets
'A'	Infantry Bde – Bat	W/T	4–6 miles	1923 →	Unreliable
'C'	Infantry Div – Bde	W/T	10–20 miles	1924 →	Quite good results. Also used in vehicles. Remote control added in 1925
'F'	Long range	W/T	400 miles+	1925 →	Aldershot-Cologne
Artillery	Link OP to battery	R/T	3 miles	1928 →	Far from satisfactory
'MA'	Armoured car Regt HQ	W/T & R/T	30–100 miles / 20–30 miles	1928 →	Lorry borne. Weighed nearly 2 tons. Not satisfactory
'MB'	In armoured cars and medium tanks	R/T mainly	5 miles	1928→	Satisfactory on move, but inter-set interference. Inadequate range.
'MC'	In light tanks	R/T mainly	2–3 miles	1928 →	Unreliable due to loose connections. MB more powerful version of MC. Sometimes called MB/MC

Army wireless sets specified in 1929[1]

Type (Number)	Main purpose	Mode	Range	Replaces	Transport/ comments
1	Inf Bde – Bat Within Inf Bat?	R/T, W/T, Dial W/T	5 miles on move	'A'	To be transportable by car, armoured car, or 2 men (too heavy, in fact)
2	Div – Bde Within Tank Bns	R/T, W/T, Dial W/T	20 miles on move, 100 miles W/T stationary	'C' and MB/MC	To be transportable in AFV or lorry. Did not fit into light tanks
3	GHQ – Corps Corps – Div	R/T,W/T, High speed W/T	20–25 miles R/T on move, 100 miles W/T stationary	120 Watt and 250 watt	To be transportable in two (later, one) lorries
3a	AFV HQ to next higher formation	R/T	R/T above 25 miles	MA and MA/MB	Necessity for this set not yet decided (and never made)
4	GHQ – Corps	W/T	250 miles	500 watt set	To be transportable in a lorry. Never introduced
5	Base – GHQ	W/T	1,000 miles	'F'	
6	Home to distant commands/ theatre of war	W/T	Worldwide	–	

Additional sets added in 1930s[2]

7	AFV	R/T, W/T	3–5 miles		Designed to fit light tanks
9	AFV and Divisional Signals	R/T, W/T	8–20 miles	Nos 2 and 7	
11 LP	Short-range infantry	R/T, W/T	5–10 miles		
11 HP	Mechanized cavalry, Tank Bns, Div Signals	R/T, W/T	10–30 miles	No 1	High power version of 11 LP

Main army wireless sets at corps level and below, introduced from 1940[3]

Number	Main purpose	Issued from	Mode	Range (miles)	Replaced	Transport/ comments
12	General purpose. Armd and Inf Div HQ, Corps HQ	1941	R/T	10–15	Nos 2, 3	15 cwt truck
			W/T	25–60		HP version also developed
14	AFV set for short-range communications between HQ tanks or ACVs	1940	R/T	1,000 yards		Could be used alongside the No. 9 set without mutual interference
18	Portable manpack	1940	R/T	2–5	No 8 and No 13 prototypes	Normally 2 men, one carrying and one operating. Weight 32 lbs
	Battalion – Company HQ		W/T	4–10		
19	AFV set, later developed as a general purpose set. 'A' set HQ – tank	1941	'A' R/T	10	No 9	Tanks, then later in other vehicles and ground stations. Also inter-tank crew communications. Also known as No 24/19 (the '24' being the B set)
			W/T	15		
	'B' set inter-tank using VHF		'B'R/T	1000 yards		
21	Infantry Brigade and RA regiment HQ's	1940	R/T and W/T	Up to 5 miles	No 11	Vehicle or ground station. Smaller lighter and cheaper to make than No 11
22	General purpose	1942	R/T	10	No 11 (HP)	Primarily vehicle, but also ground station and could be carried as a manpack
			W/T	20		
33	Corps and Army transportable set	1941	R/T W/T	Up to 200		Similar to No. 12, but with increased range

(Continued)

(Cont.)

Main army wireless sets at corps level and below, introduced from 1940[3]

Number	Main purpose	Issued from	Mode	Range (miles)	Replaced	Transport/comments
38	Infantry Company and platoon. Also used for infantry–tank communications	1941	R/T	Up to 2 miles		Lighter than No 18 and carried by one man. Weight 22lbs
46	Portable manpack set primarily designed for beach landing operations	1942	R/T W/T	8–10 miles		Completely waterproof. Option for 3 pre-set crystal controlled channels. Weight 24 lbs
48	As for No 18 set	1942	R/T	1–5		US version of No 18 set Weight 29 lbs
			W/T	2–10		
52	General purpose Brigade and division HQ	1943	R/T	40	Canadian No 9 set	Vehicle or Ground station. More powerful version of No 19 HP
			W/T	100		
53	General purpose set primarily used in ACVs and lorries Division HQ and army Phantom services	1944	R/T	100	No 12 HP	The long awaited '100 mile' R/T set
			W/T	500		
68	As for No 18 set. Primarily intended for airborne operations	1943	R/T	Over 5		Longer-range version of No 18 set, using lower frequencies. Weight 32 lbs
			W/T	Over 10		

Production rates for important army wireless sets[4]

Set	Deliveries started	Peak year	Monthly average in peak year	Total during war	Remarks
No. 9	Pre-war			4,000	Ceased 1942
No. 11	Pre-war			19,000	Ceased 1942
No. 19	1941	1943	3,500	115,000	
No. 22	1941			55,000	
No. 62	1944			7,350	
No. 33	1941	1943	25	540	
No. 12 HP	1943			675	
No. 53	1944			2,300	
No. 18	1940	1943	2,310	76,000	
No. 38	1942	1943	7,000	187,000	
No. 46	1942	1945	2,500	24,500	
No. 36	1941			1,600	
All types		**1943**	**16,000**	**552,500**	
Receivers		1945	2,800	87,500	
Secondary Batteries		1944	178,300		In 2-volt units

Notes

Chapter 1

1   G. Sheffield, *Forgotten Victory. The First World War. Myths and Realities* (London 2002), p. 120. See also, for example: John Terraine, *The Smoke and the Fire. Myths and Anti-Myths of War 1861–1945* (London 1980), p. 179; Michael Crawshaw, "The Impact of Technology on the BEF and its Commander" in B. Bond and N. Cave (eds), *Haig. A Reappraisal 70 Years on* (Barnsley 1999), pp. 167–8.

2   Major-General R. F. H. Nalder, *The Royal Corps of Signals. A History of its Antecedents and Development (c.1800–1955)* (London 1958); Major-General R. F. H. Nalder, *The History of British Army Signals in the Second World War. General Survey* (London 1953).

3   For example, authors such as Nicholas Harman, *Dunkirk. The Patriotic Myth* (New York 1980) and Brian Bond, *Britain, France and Belgium 1939–1940* (London 1990) had nothing positive to say about front line communications in the five weeks before Dunkirk, yet there were some successes, as described below. XII Lancers, for instance, were very successful in maintaining wireless communications.

4   See, for example, David S. Alberts and Richard E. Hayes, *Understanding Command and Control* (Washington 2006). 'Network Centric Warfare' describes a system in which all members of an army have access to information held on a central computerized network. 'Self-Synchronisation' describes a state in which all members of an army have access to the same information, share the same objectives and training, and therefore will act in the same way without the need to be ordered to do so. Restrictive and Mission command are explained below.

5   David S. Alberts and Richard E. Hayes, *Power to the Edge* (Washington 2003), p. 18.

6   Sandra Bell and Rebecca Cox, *Communications Inter-Operability in a Crisis* (RUSI, London 2006), p. 28.

7   Alberts and Hayes, *Power to the Edge*, pp. 20–6.

8   John Keegan, *The Mask of Command* (London 1987), pp. 149–54.

9 Jürgen Förster, "Evolution and Development of German Doctrine 1914–45" in John Gooch (ed.), *The Origin of Contemporary Doctrine* (Strategic and Combats Study Institute 1997), pp. 28–9.

10 French, *Churchill's Army*, pp. 48–9.

11 Jürgen Förster, "Evolution and Development of German Doctrine 1914–45" in John Gooch (ed.), *The Origin of Contemporary Doctrine* (Strategic and Combats Study Institute 1997), pp. 28–9.

12 David Potts (ed.), *The Big Issue: Command and Combat in the Information Age* (Strategic and Combat Studies Institute, Great Britain 2002), p. 77; Alberts and Hayes, *Power to the Edge*, pp. 201–10.

13 French, *Churchill's Army*, pp. 17–21.

14 WO 287/125, Truppenführung, 17 October 1933, Section 328.

15 *Army Doctrine Publication Volume 2, Command* (April 1995), paras 0210–0224.

16 A. Behagg, "Increasing Tempo on the Modern Battlefield" in Brian Holden Reid (ed.), *The Science of War: Back to First Principles* (London 1993), pp. 110–30.

17 Robert Coram, *Boyd. The Fighter Pilot Who Changed the Art of War* (Boston 2002), p. 344.

18 For example, the account of communications contained in Brian Bond and Michael D. Taylor, *The Battle for France and Flanders 1940. Sixty Years On* (Barnsley 2001) was extremely damning.

Chapter 2

1 I am indebted to Brian Hall for his advice on this brief summary of communications in World War I. A full account can be found in Brian N Hall, "The British Expeditionary Force and Communications on the Western Front, 1914–1918" (PhD, University of Salford, 2009).

2 WO 279/56, Report on the Staff Exercises, April 1923.

3 WO 106/1775, Bartholomew Report.

4 WO 187/1-15, Royal Engineers and Signals Board C Committee (non-secret proceedings) 1919/20–1927; WO 287/24, Summary of engineer and signal information, 1929–38.

5 Nalder, *Royal Corps*, p. 251; Nalder, *British Army Signals*, p. 9.

6 WO 287/24, Summary of engineer and signal information, 1929–38, 21 March 1933.

7 WO 187/1-15, Royal Engineers and Signals Board C Committee (non-secret proceedings) 1919/20–1927; WO 287/24, Summary of engineer and signal

information, 1929–38; TM 623.61 (41) Details of Wireless Sets MA, MB, MC; General Staff, *Army Training Memorandum*, 1930.

8   WO 279/55, Report on the Staff Exercise, April 1923, p. 18.

9   IWM Sound Archive, Seddon 887; TM RH5, 1st Bde RTC Report on Training, 30/9/1931.

10   WO 279/71, War Office Exercises, Nos 1, 2 and 4, Buxton and the War Office, 1930, p. 41.

11   WO 32/3057, Telegraphy General, 1929–36.

12   WO 287/24, Article 18, A review of the present position of existing apparatus, 27 March 1930.

13   WO 287/24, Wireless Sets, 1937.

14   IWM Documents, Colonel D. T. W. Gibson, p. 355.

15   General Staff, *Modern Formations*, 1931, p. 65; WO 32/3057, Discussion of the carriage of wireless sets in AFVs, 23 March 1932; General Staff, *Supplementary Memorandum on Army Training*, 1929.

16   WO 112/21-29, War Office Army Estimates, 1932–39.

17   Based on the Composite Price Index published by National Statistics. Note, however, that inflation of military hardware may have been different and probably higher than general inflation, making comparisons with today's military expenditure difficult.

18   Nalder, *Royal Corps*, p. 340.

19   WO 33/1318, Memorandum on the Wireless Telegraphy Board's rules for the allotment of wireless call signs in the Navy, Army, and Air Force 1933 (update of memo of 16 October 1928); WO 163/607, Report on the Interdepartmental Committee on Research and Investigatory Work on Wireless Telegraphy, July 1929.

20   Major-General D. A. L. Wade, "Those Early Years", *Journal of the Royal Signals Institution*, Vol. XV(1) (1981), pp. 47–8.

21   M. Postan, *British War Production* (London 1952), p. 358; Guy Hartcup, *The Challenge of War* (Newton Abbot 1970), p. 159.

22   TM 355.6, Report of Mechanisation Board, 1934.

23   TM 355.6, Report of Mechanisation Board, 1938.

24   WO 287/24, Summary of Engineer and Signal Information, 1929–38; Nalder, *Royal Signals*, p. 254.

25   Robert H. Larson, *The British Army and the Theory of Armoured Warfare, 1918–40* (Newark 1984), p. 176.

26   WO 287/24, Progress of Experimental Work and Design, 21 March 1933.

27   Courtesy Louis Meulstee.

28 This photograph shows the author's father and his signals platoon at a Territorial summer camp in 1936. Copyright: the author.

29 *The Times*, 17 February 1938 "Cable Laying at 30 mph".

30 WO 32/3345, Automatic Telegraphy in the Field, 1934; TM 355.6, Report of Mechanisation Board, 1936; Nalder, *Royal Corps*, p. 262.

31 Courtesy Louis Meulstee.

32 WO 33/1377, Second Interim Report of the Field Force Committee, June 1935.

33 Brian Bond, *British Military Policy between the Two World Wars* (London 1980), pp. 234–43, 257–8.

34 WO 197/102, Memo by SO in C dated 24 March 1940.

35 WO 33/1377, Second Interim Report of the Field Force Committee, June 1935, p. 24.

36 IWM, Fourth Army Records, Vol. 64 (XIII Corps narrative, October-November 1918), "Lessons Learnt During Recent Operations", 14 November 1918.

37 WO 33/1377, Second Interim Report of the Field Force Committee, June 1935, p. 24.

38 WO 237/26, Abstract of the Recommendations of the Principal Commissions, Committees and Conferences relating to Army Affairs, 1936.

39 Nalder, *Royal Corps*, pp. 255–7 (In an earlier book of 1953, Nalder expressed this slightly differently, 'Both line and wireless communications were required in forward and rear areas, the two being to a large extent complementary. This disposed of views in certain quarters that lines were no longer necessary in the more forward formations'. The two accounts agree on the key point that line was reintroduced in the forward areas).

40 Nalder, *Royal Corps,* pp. 243–64.

41 LHCMA, Hobart Papers 15/11/4, Memorandum on unpreparedness of RTC for War, 17 June 1936.

42 WO 167/17, War Diary GHQ SO in C, 30 November 1939, 13 December 1939.

43 General Staff, *Infantry Training* 1937, Sections 29–32, 44; General Staff, *Infantry Section Leading* 1938, Section 40.

44 CAB 35/34, Use of Wireless Telegraphy for War Office Secret Communications in time of War.

45 CAB 35/34, Memo from Colonel R. Chenevix Trench, 7 May 1936.

46 CAB 35/34, Memo from Colonel R. Chenevix-Trench, 25 June 1936.

47 WO 33/1073, Security Issues, 1925.

48 IWM Documents, Section L. H. Vollans 82/14/1.

49 General Staff, *Army Training Memorandum No 15,* 1935.

50 General Staff, *Army Training Memorandum No 22*, 1939.

51 General Staff, *Army Training Memorandum No 23*, 1939.

52 WO 33/1532, Royal Engineers and Signals Board C Committee, 27 May 1938; WO 197/103, Lessons on the intelligence security aspect of Signals (20 June 1940, Major-General R. Chenevix-Trench).

53 WO 33/1073, Secret Supplement to Signal Training, 1925; WO 33/1249, Memorandum on Security of Field Wireless in War, 11 May 1931; General Staff, *Field Service Pocket Book, Pamphlet No. 2*, 8 February 1939.

54 General Staff, *Field Service Pocket Book, Pamphlet No. 2*, 10 December 1941.

55 Captain P. F. Stewart, *The History of the XII Royal Lancers*, Vol. II (London 1950), p. 322.

56 General Staff, *Memoranda on Army Training*, 1926–39.

57 WO 277/25, Gravely, Signals Communications, pp. 307, 450.

58 General Staff, *Supplementary Memorandum on Army Training*, 1929.

59 Morgan, "Modern Communications", pp. 414–18.

60 General Staff, *Army Training Memorandum No 1*, 1930.

61 *The Times*, 9 July 1931 "Army Training Southern Command. A Signalling Scheme".

62 *The Times*, 30 June 1933 "Southern Command Signals".

63 *The Times*, 24 August 1933 "1st Division Exercise".

64 *The Times*, 18 September 1933 "The Army on the Plain".

65 WO 279/76, Report on Army Manoeuvres, 1935.

66 TM RH5, 1Bde Report on Training of 1st Brigade, Royal Tank Corps, 30 September 1931; Harris, *Men, Ideas and Tanks*, p. 225; Bond, *Military Policy*, p. 157.

67 *The Times*, 19 August 1931 "Army Training. Royal Tank Corps".

68 TM RAC 623.438 (41) Training and Tactical Handling of Tank Battalions, 31 March 1931.

69 Harris, *Men, Ideas and Tanks*, pp. 247–51; Harold R. Winton, "Tanks, Votes, and Budgets. The Politics of Mechanisation and Armoured Warfare in Britain, 1919–39", in Harold R Winton and David R Mets (eds), *The Challenge of Change. Military Institutions and New Realities, 1918–41* (Nebraska 2000), p. 93.

70 IWM Sound Archives, Seddon 887.

71 TM RH5 TB MH (41), The Tank Brigade Training Report, October 1934.

72 TM RH5 1TB, The Tank Brigade Training Report, October 1935.

73 LHCMA, Hobart Papers 15/11/4, Memorandum on the Unpreparedness of the RTC for War 17/6/1936.

74 TM RH5 1 TB, The Tank Brigade Training Report, October 1936.

75 Ibid.

76 IWM Sound Archives, Smijth-Windham 954.

77 LHCMA, Hobart 15/11/8. The Armoured Division Egypt. Training Report, 1939.

78 General Staff, *Army Training Memorandum No 29*, 1940.

79 General Staff, Memorandum on the Training of the Royal Artillery 1937, 26 January 1938.

80 *The Times*, 11 March 1930 "Decline in Army Recruiting". In the Tank Brigade, Signal officer turnover in 1936 was approximately 100 per cent per annum, and turnover of other ranks was nearly as bad. This may have been exacerbated by stress resulting from Hobart's demand for and expectation of perfect communications, and 'if he didn't get it there was trouble' (IWM Sound Archives, Seddon 887).

81 WO 112/25 and 112/26, War Office Army Estimates, 1936 and 1937.

82 General Staff, *Army Training Memorandum No 20*, 1938; General Staff, *Army Training Memorandum No 21*, 1938.

83 *The Times*, 14 August 1924 "Formation of a Supplementary Reserve".

84 *The Times*, 18 May 1931 "Army Training Southern Command".

85 *The Times*, 10 August 1934 "TA Training at Arundel".

86 Captain P. F. Stewart, *The History of the XII Royal Lancers* (London 1950), pp. 319–28; Brigadier Dudley Clarke, *The Eleventh at War (1934–1945)* (London 1952), pp. 17–60.

87 T. R. Moreman, *The Army in India and the Development of Frontier Warfare, 1849–1947* (Basingstoke 1998), p. 140; *Review of Important Military Events, 1931–39* (Army HQ, India) British Library L/MIL/7/12492; *Training Memorandums, 1929–1939* (Army HQ, India) British Library IOR/L/MIL/17/5/2199.

88 *Review of Important Military Events, 1931–1939* (Army HQ, India) British Library L/MIL/7/12492, 29 January 1937.

89 WO 279/796, Notes on Imperial Policing, 30 January 1934.

90 *Official History of Operations on the NW Frontier of India, 1936–1937*.

Chapter 3

1 For example, almost wholly negative accounts are given in: Brian Bond and Michael D. Taylor (eds), *The Battle for France and Flanders 1940. Sixty Years On* (Barnsley 2001), p. 9; Brian Bond, "The British Field Force in France and

Belgium 1939–1940" in P. Addison and A. Calder (eds), *Time to Kill: The Soldiers Experience in the West 1939–1945* (Pimlico 1997), p. 44; Harman, *Dunkirk,* p. 81.

2   WO 197/102, Memo by SO in C, 24 March 1940; RSM Anon, The Static Period [Uncatalogued].

3   WO 197/102, Memo by SO in C, 24 March 1940.

4   WO 277/31, Rearmament: provision of weapons and equipment Vol. 1.

5   Nalder, *British Army Signals*, pp. 30–3.

6   WO 197/102, Memo by SO in C, 24 March 1940.

7   WO 167/53, CSO II Corps War Diary.

8   WO 167/195, Signals 1st Division War Diary.

9   WO 167/17, War Diary GHQ SO in C, 19 October 1939.

10 WO 167/17, War Diary GHQ SO in C, 30 November 1939, 13 December 1939.

11 WO 197/102, Memo by SO in C, 24 March 1940.

12 WO 167/131, CSO I Corps War Diary, 20 January 1940; WO 167/153, CSO II Corps War Diary, 24 December 1939.

13 Blaxland, *Destination Dunkirk,* p. 113.

14 Ibid., p. 54.

15 Harman, *Dunkirk*, p. 81.

16 IWM Documents, Section 82/14/1, L. H. Vollans, Signals at a Brigade HQ.

17 WO 167/17, War Diary GHQ SO in C, 5 November 1939, 27 November 1939.

18 RSM Anon, The Static Period [Uncatalogued].

19 WO 167/154, II Corps Signals War Diary, 9 April 1940, 26 March 1940.

20 WO 167/178, War Diaries III Corps CSO, Instruction No. 11, 11 April 1940.

21 WO 167/154, Report by Major H. C. B. Rogers.

22 WO 167/195, 1st Division Signals, Instruction No. 29.

23 WO 167/153, CSO II Corps War Diary, 13 October 1939, 8 December 1939.

24 IWM Sound Archive, 6490 Brigadier Freeman (GSO3, II Corps in 1940).

25 Nigel Hamilton, *Monty: The Making of a General, 1887–1942* (New York 1981), pp. 350, 362.

26 WO 167/17, Memo regarding Signal Methods in the SAAR Operations.

27 WO 167/195, 1st Division Signals War Diary, 5 October 1939; WO 167/222, 3rd Division Signals War Diary, 1 November 1939.

28 Stewart, *Royal Lancers,* p. 350.

29 WO 167/195, 1st Division Signals War Diary, 31 March 1940; WO 167/222, 3rd Division Signals War Diary, 29 March 1940, 1–10 April 1940.

30 WO 167/17, War Diary GHQ SO in C, 30 November 1939.

31 Nalder, *Royal Signals*, p. 281.

32 IWM Documents, Section 83/48/1, W. C. Brodie.

33 LHCMA, Alanbrooke Diaries 5/1/2, 18 May 1940.

34 WO 167/289, War Diaries 48th Division GS; WO 167/293, War Diaries 48th Division Signals.

35 WO 167/131, War Diaries CSO I Corps; WO 167/124, War Diaries I Corps GS.

36 Richard Doherty, *Only the Enemy in Front (Every Other Beggar Behind . . .)* (London 1994), pp. 1–2; WO 232/1 The Infantry Divisional Reconnaissance Regiment, p. 1.

37 WO 167/452, 12th Lancers War Diary, 13 May 1940.

38 WO 167/452, 12th Lancers War Diary, 10 May 1940, 18 May 1940.

39 NAM 1989-09-68 Journal of Events written by Lt. Basil Hall, 12th Royal Lancers.

40 WO 167/417, No 1 Armoured Recce Brigade War Diary, 10 May 1940, 16 May 1940.

41 Ibid.

42 WO 215/2, Phantom in France. Reports on Phantom during October 1939–June 1940.

43 Ibid.

44 LHCMA, Alanbrooke 5/2/15, Notes on my Life, p. 171.

45 WO 106/1775, Written evidence from Major-General B. L. Montgomery; Final Bartholomew Report.

46 WO 197/76, GHQ Signal Instruction No. 60, 6 April 1940.

47 IWM Documents Section PP/MCR238. The Memoirs of Major-General A Wade.

48 Sir John R. Colville, *Man of Valour. The Life of Field Marshal The Viscount Gort* (London 1972), p. 190.

49 WO 106/1775, Bartholomew Report, evidence given on 12 June 1940.

50 WO 167/124, I Corps GS War Diary. Notes by BGS Brig W. C. Holden on events 10–17 May 1940.

51 WO 197/93, Summary of Signals Events at GHQ 10 May–1 June.

52 WO 197/103, Signal Lessons of the War in France and Flanders (report by Lieut Colonel D. A. L. Wade, 31 May 1940).

53 WO 106/1775, Bartholomew Report, evidence given on 12 June 1940.

54 WO 197/93, Summary of Signal events at GHQ 10 May – 1 June compiled by SO in C; WO 197/80, Letter from Wade to Chenevix-Trench, 17 May 1940.

55 The Royal Corps of Signals Association, *A Short History of Signals in the Army (Part 2). The British Expeditionary Force 1939–1940* (London c. 1948), p. 55.

56 WO 197/75, Operational Signal Instructions received by SO in C; WO 106/1775, Bartholomew Report, evidence given on 12 June 1940.

57 WO 167/124, War Diaries I Corps GS.

58 Ibid.

59 Glyn Prysor, "The 'Fifth Column' and the British Experience of Retreat, 1940", *War in History* 12(4) (2005), pp. 418–47.

60 WO 167/124, War Diaries I Corps GS.

61 RSM Report by 2nd Lieut. Geo. Wilson.

62 WO 197/77, Signal Circuits in France and Belgium; WO 197/78, Wireless Circuits in France and Belgium.

63 IWM Documents, Section 93/19/1, Nalder, War Diary 10 May – 2 June 1940; WO 167/195, 1st Division Signals War Diary.

64 WO 167/195, 1st Division Signals War Diary.

65 WO 167/208, 2nd Division Signals War Diary.

66 Captain Sir Basil Bartlett, *My First War. An Army Officer's Journal for May 1940* (London 1941), p. 61; Nicolson and Forbes, *Grenadier Guards,* p. 18.

67 WO 167/208, 2nd Division Signals War Diary.

68 WO 167/293, War Diaries 48th Divisional Signals.

69 WO 167/148, War Diaries II Corps GS, May 1940.

70 IWM Sound Archive, 6490 Brigadier Freeman (GSO3, II Corps in 1940).

71 LHCMA, Alanbrooke 5/2/15, Notes on my Life.

72 IWM Documents, Section 83/48/1, W. C. Brodie, Sergeant R. Signals, II Corps HQ, 19 May 1940.

73 WO 167/222, War Diaries 3rd Division Signals.

74 WO 167/222, War Diaries 3rd Division Signals. This is a different impression from that given in Piercy, "Manoeuvre", p. 62, where the movement was described as 'carefully controlled by wireless'.

75 IWM Documents, Section 82/14/1, L. H. Vollans, Signals at a Brigade HQ.

76 Meulstee, *Wireless for the Warrior*, Vol. I, WS3-1.

77 WO 167/154, II Corps Signals War Diary.

78 WO 277/5, The Development of Artillery Tactics and Equipment, p. 37.

79 WO 167/124, War Diaries I Corps GS.

80 Brigadier W. J. Jervois, *The History of the Northamptonshire Regiment 1934–1948* (London 1953), p. 74.

81 Lieutenant-Commander P. K. Kemp, *History of the Royal Norfolk Regiment 1919–1951, Volume III* (Norwich 1953), pp. 116–7.

82 Nicolson and Forbes, *Grenadier Guards,* p. 26.

83   Michael Howard and John Sparrow, *The Coldstream Guards 1920–1946* (London 1951), p. 46.

84   NAM 7709-18 Diary of 2nd Battalion Bedfordshire and Hertfordshire Regiment, 27 May.

85   Hugh Williamson, *The Fourth Division 1939–1945* (London 1951), p. 18.

86   WO 167/124, War Diaries I Corps GS.

87   LHCMA, Alanbrooke 5/2/15, pp. 150, 173.

Chapter 4

1   The information in this section is drawn from five sources: WO 106/1775, Bartholomew Report; WO 197/102, SO in C's Draft for C in C's Despatch for period 1 February 1940 – 1 June 1940; WO 197/103, Signals Communications during the Flanders Campaign: reports and recommendations; WO 208/2050A, Lessons in Organisations, Staff Duties, and Minor Tactics from BEF, July 1940; LHCMA, Bartholomew MSS, 3/1-3/11.

2   WO 106/1775, Bartholomew Report.

3   LHCMA, Wade MSS.

4   WO 166/13, SO in C's (Home Forces) Training Memorandum No. 1, 18 July 1940.

5   HMSO, *Statistical Digest of the War* (London 1951), p. 150.

6   Royal Artillery Historical Society, *Proceedings*, Vol. 11, No. 3, January 1969, p. 96.

7   WO 199/232, SPARTAN. Comments by C in C Home Forces, p. 21.

8   WO 166/13, CSO's Conference 1 – 2 December 1941.

9   WO 232/3, Expansion of Signals, Appendix B.

10   *ATIP No 1*, 1941.

11   WO 166/13, CSO's Conference, April 1941.

12   WO 166/13, CSO's Conference, December 1941.

13   WO 232/1, The Infantry Divisional Reconnaissance Regiment, pp. 10–13; WO 166/13, CSO's Training Memos No. 14, 14 May 1941 and No. 18, 25 August 1941; WO 260/47, Report of the Godwin-Austen Committee.

14   *ATM No 22*, April 1939.

15   WO 166/353, CSO XII Corps Conference 15 November 1940; WO 199/2019, Letter War Office to C in C Home Forces, 12 August 1940; *ATM No 47*, January 1944.

16 WO 232/2, The Influence on the Battle of Improved Signals, p. 14.

17 *ATM No 22,* April 1939.

18 *ATM No 29,* February 1940; TM 654.9 (41) Wireless Wing RAC School, Notes for Signal Officers and NCO's, May 1945.

19 *ATIP No 2*, March 1941; *ATIP No 2*, May 1943.

20 *MTP No 19,* April 1939.

21 *ATM No 39,* April 1941.

22 *ATM No 41,* October 1941.

23 WO 166/13, War Diaries SO in C July 1940 – December 1941, Training Memo No. 14, 14 May 1941; Training Memo No. 18, 25 August 1941.

24 *ATM No 46,* October 1943.

25 WO 232/2, The Influence on the Battle of Improved Signals, p. 13.

26 *MTP No 41,* July 1943.

27 WO 166/1146, HQ 34th Tank Brigade, 1 December 1941.

28 R. L. V. ffrench Blake, *The 17th/21st Lancers 1759–1993* (London 1993), p. 81.

29 *ATIP No 3,* 1941; Meulstee, *Wireless for the Warrior*, Vol. II, p. WS19-3.

30 *MTP No 41,* July 1940.

31 ffrench Blake, *17th/21st Lancers*, p. 86.

32 *MTP No 41*, Part II, June 1943; Courage, *15/19 Hussars*, p. 67.

33 Jeremy A. Crang, *The British Army and the People's War* (Manchester 2000), pp. 2,144,145; IWM Sound Archive, Foster 27194; Collins 18742.

34 WO 166/13, War Diaries SO in C, 1 – 2 December 1941.

35 Nalder, *Royal Corps*, p. 351; WO 166/10396, CSO II Corps, 11 June 1943.

36 WO 232/3, Expansion of Signals, pp. 6, Appendix A.

37 WO 365/133, Army Tradesmen, Situation at 31 October 1943.

38 WO 32/9813, Supply of Service Tradesmen: The Beveridge Committee Report, 1941.

39 Crang, *People's War,* pp. 13–14.

40 IWM Sound Archive, Philpott 19955.

41 WO 32/15656, History of 2nd Signal Training Centre and 2nd Holding Battalion Royal Signals.

42 IWM Documents, A. F. Metson 03/2/1; Newland 03/22/1; N. J. Smith 99/61/1.

43 Crang, *People's War,* pp. 21–39.

44 IWM Documents, Captain J. O. Wolstenholme.

45 WO 277/36, Lieutenant Colonel J. W. Gibb, Training in the Army, pp. 86–97; Nalder, *Royal Corps*, pp. 338, 351–2.

46 IWM Sound Archives, Brown 18343; Foster 27194; Weathers 22363.

47 IWM Sound Archives, Collins 18742.

48 IWM Sound Archive, Rosier 21651.

49 TM MH5 (41) Half Yearly Report No. 4, July–December 1941, Appendix F.

50 WO 166/353, CSO XII Corps Conference, 15 November 1940.

51 WO 166/6078, CSO II Corps, 1942.

52 WO 166/10312, Report by SO in C on Exercise SPARTAN, 19 April 1943.

53 WO 166/353, CSO's Inspection of Exercise MURPHY II, 5 April 1941.

54 WO 166/353, CSO XII Corps Conference, 15 November 1940.

55 WO 166/10312, Report by SO in C on Exercise SPARTAN, 19 April 1943.

Chapter 5

1 Liddell Hart, *Rommel Papers*, pp. 200, 523.

2 WO 167/107, 7th Armoured Division Signals, 1939/1940.

3 WO 169/31, GHQ CSO, 9 April 1940.

4 WO 167/107, 7AD Signals, 23 June 1940.

5 Major P. Richards, "Armoured Command Vehicle", *Journal of the Royal Signals Institution* Vol. XVI(4) (Spring 1984), pp. 177–83; LHCMA Creagh, Report on Operations since 9 December 1940 by Commander 7th Armoured Brigade.

6 WO 169/31, Memo SO in C to CSOs of regions, 11 September 1940.

7 WO 169/606, 4ID Signals, October 1939 – December 1940; WO 169/3293, 4ID Signals, June 1941.

8 WO 167/107, 7AD Signals, 8 August 1940.

9 WO 277/25, Gravely Signals, p. 382; WO 215/41, History of Phantom and of "J" Service.

10 LHCMA Creagh, Lessons from Operations, 18 January 1941.

11 WO 106/2133, Operations in Western Desert, December 1940 – February 1941.

12 LHCMA O'Connor 4/2/19, O'Connor to Beresford Peirce 14/12/40.

13 LHCMA Creagh, Operations during period 10 June 1940 and 8 February 1041; Playfair, Vol. 1, p. 358.

14 LHCMA Creagh, Report on Operations since 9 December 1940 by Commander 7th Armoured Brigade.

15 WO 167/107, 7AD Signals, December 1940; WO 169/606, 4ID Signals, December 1940; WO 169/59, CSO WDF, December 1940; WO 169/1107, XIII Corps GS, January 1941; WO169/1113, CSO XIII Corps, January 1941; Nalder, *Royal Corps*, pp. 295–6.

16 Vaux, Interview by Author.

17 WO 169/1179, 7AD Signals War Diary, May/June 1941.

18 WO 201/2482, Report on Operation BATTLEAXE by 4ID, pp. 9, 32.

19 WO 169/1179, 7AD Signals Diaries, July – October 1941; WO 201/559, Report on Operations of 4ID, November 1941–February 1942; WO 201/515, 1st South African Division. Report on Operations, November–December 1941.

20 Nalder, *Royal Corps*, pp. 317–18.

21 WO 169/4092, 7AD Signals Diaries, 26 May 1942.

22 RAC RH. 4 7AD MH. 5(6) Letter from Lord Carver to Ronald Lewin, 16 November 1978 and reply of 20 November 1978; WO 169/4092, 7AD Signals Diaries, 26 May–7 June 1942; Michael Carver, *Dilemmas of the Desert War. A New Look at the Libyan Campaign, 1940–42* (London: B. T. Batsford Ltd, 1986), p. 66; Vaux, Interview; R. M. A., "A Commander Royal Signals in Action", *Journal of the Royal Signals Institution*, Vol. VII(5) (Summer 1966), pp. 222–6; IWM 75/72/1 7 AD Signals. Technical report on operations 27 May to 31 July 1942, p. 2.

23 WO 169/4252, 22nd Armoured Brigade Signals Section, May 1942.

24 WO 169/4058, 1AD Signals, 6 April 1942; WO 169/4271, 69th Infantry Brigade HQ, 14 May 1942.

25 WO 169/7608, 3rd Indian Infantry Brigade Signals, June 1942.

26 LHCMA Creagh, Lessons from BATTLEAXE.

27 NAM Cunningham papers, 8303-104-19 Account of Crusader, November 1941; Daily record of Cunningham's movements.

28 NAM Cunningham papers, 8303-104-19 Godwin Austen to Cunningham, 24 November 1941.

29 Barnett, *Desert Generals*, p. 143.

30 Playfair, Vol. III, pp. 246–58; Carver, *Dilemmas,* pp. 108–9.

31 WO 201/555, HQ RA Eighth Army Report on El Alamein. Command and Control; WO 201/583, Lessons from Battle of Egypt, 22 February 1943; WO 169/3948, CSO Eighth Army, November 1942.

32 Playfair, Vol. III, pp. 213–17; P. G. Griffith, "British Armoured Warfare in the Western Desert, 1940–43" in J. P. Harris and F. H. Toase (eds), *Armoured Warfare* (London 1990), p. 80.

33 Barr, *Pendulum of War,* pp. 51–64, 87; Barnett, *Desert Generals,* pp. 131, 188.

34 Griffith, "British Armoured Warfare", pp. 82–3; French, *Churchill's Army*, p. 191.

35 R. J. T. Hills, *Phantom was There* (London 1951), p. 86.

36 WO 169/1179, Report on Operations, 18 November – 27 November 1941; WO 169/1016, Appendix 'B' to SO in C's Memo No. 5, January 42; WO 169/1016, Some Signal Lessons of the Libyan Campaign.

37 RSM 916.3, Evidence of Intercepts.

38 WO 201/357, Lessons from Operation BATTLEAXE.

39 LHCMA Creagh, Lessons from BATTLEAXE; WO 169/3289, 4ID GS, 17 June 1941; WO 169/3351, Lack of Security during BATTLEAXE, 21 June 1941.

40 Vaux, Interview by author; WO 169/1179, 7AD Signals War Diary, June 1941.

41 WO 169/1179, 7AD Signals, September – October 1941; WO 169/3293, 4ID Signals, 10 October 1941; for an explanation of the Single Call Sign system, see Chapter 4.

42 NAM Cunningham papers, 8303-104-19 Account of Crusader, November 1941, p. 1.

43 Liddell Hart, *Rommel Papers*, p. 156.

44 WO 169/1016, Notes on Inter-Communication. Libyan Campaign 1941/2, Section 7a.

45 WO 169/1179, Report on Operations, 18 November – 27 November 1941; WO 169/1016, Appendix 'B' to SO in C's Memo No. 5 January 42; WO 169/1016, Some Signal Lessons of the Lybian Campaign.

46 Ronald Lewin, *Ultra goes to War* (London 1978), pp. 167–8; John Ferris, "The Usual Source: Signals Intelligence and Planning for the ' Crusader' Offensive 1941", *Intelligence and National Security*, Vol. 14(1) (1999), p. 103; Playfair, *The Mediterranean and the Middle East*, Vol. III, p. 5; WO 201/369, Operation CRUSADER, Giarabub Oasis deception plan.

47 IWM 75/72/1, Brigadier H. N. Crawford, 7th Armoured Division Line communications diagrams, May/June 1942.

48 WO 169/4092, 7AD Diaries, 27–8 May 1942.

49 F. H. Hinsley et al., *British Intelligence,* p. 298; RSM 916.3 Evidence of intercepts, May 1942.

50 WO 169/4041, Report on Security, July 1942, Memo on Signal Security, 31 July 1942.

51 Barr, *Pendulum of War,* pp. 20–1.

52 WO 169/3948, CSO Eighth Army, 10 November 1942.

53 WO 169/3946, CSO Eighth Army, 23 July 1942.

54 WO 169/1150, 2AD Signals, 14–21 February 1941.

55 WO 32/9596, Narrative of Action of 2AD during withdrawal from Cyrenaica March-April 1941; Nalder, *Royal Corps*, p. 299.

56 WO 106/2161, War Office Report, 20 June 1941.

57 F. H. Hindley, Alan Stripp (eds) *Code Breakers* (Oxford 1993), p. 3; HW 5/19, Reports of German High Grade Decrypts, 12 June 1941–19 June 1941.

58 WO 169/1281, 4th Armoured Brigade HQ, 23–30 November 1941.

59 WO 169/3289, GS 4ID, November-December 1941; WO 169/3293, Signals 4ID, 23 November 1941.

60 John Connell, *Auchinleck* (London 1959), p. 341.

61 Nalder, *Royal Corps,* p. 316.

62 Ferris, "British Army, Signals and Security", p. 277.

63 IWM 75/72/1, Technical report, p. 1.

64 Carver, *Out of Step,* pp. 104–19.

65 Carver, *Out of Step,* p. 121; Barr, *Pendulum of War,* p. 29; WO 106/2234, Over-running of 3rd Indian Motor Brigade on 23/24 June 1942; WO 169/7617, 9th Indian Infantry Brigade, June 1942.

66 RSM 916.3 Lessons from Operations October and November 1942, p. 56.

67 WO244/111, Signal Instructions, Battle of El Alamein.

68 WO 169/3947, CSO Eighth Army, 5 September 1942.

69 C. A. Borman, *Divisional Signals* (Wellington NZ, 1954), pp. 315–19.

70 Howard Kippenberger, *Infantry Brigadier* (Oxford 1949), p. 165.

71 WO 169/3947, CSO Eight Army Training Memorandum, 29 September 1942.

72 WO 169/3947, CSO Eighth Army Training Memorandum, 29 September 1942; WO 169/7534, 4ID Signal Instruction No. 1 c., 20 October 1942.

73 WO 201/437, Lessons learned from operations 23 October – 5 November 1942; WO 169/4252, 22nd Armoured Brigade Signals, 20 October 1942.

74 Howard, *British Intelligence,* pp. 65–6; AIR 40/1817 Signals Appendix for Marshal of the Royal Air Force Lord Tedder's Despatch on Middle East Operations, May 1941 – January 1943; WO 169/1016, CSO 10th Corps Reflections on Operations May – December 1942; RSM 916.3, Lessons from Operations October and November 1942.

75 Gladman, "Air Power", p. 163; WO 169/3947, CSO Eighth Army Signal Instruction, 18 October 1942.

76 WO 215/23, Letters on "J", March and May 1943; Hills, *Phantom,* p. 87.

77 Littlewood, *Wireless Operator,* pp. 4–5.

78 WO 201/561, 4ID Operational Order No. 87, 9 October 1942.

79 WO 169/7612, 5th Indian Infantry Brigade Signals, October 1942.

80 WO 201/437, Lessons learned from operations, 23 October – 5 November 1942.

81 Cody, *21 Battalion,* pp. 196–207; Further examples are contained in C. A. Borman, *Divisional Signals* (Wellington 1954), pp. 319–20 (available on-line at www.nzetc.org).

82 WO 169/4092, 7AD Signals Diaries, 25 October – 2 November 1942.

83 WO 169/4092, 7AD Signals Diaries, 5, 7, 10 November 1942.

84 WO 169/3948, CSO Eighth Army, 19 – 21 November 1942; WO 210/653, 10th Armoured Division Account of Operations, 6 November 1942.

85 WO 201/606, 7th Armoured Division: Operations at El Alamein and Tunis, 11 November 1942.

86 RSM 916.3, Lessons from Operations, October and November 1942, p. 54.

87 WO 169/1016, CSO 10th Corps Reflections; RSM 916.3, Lessons from Operations, October and November 1942, pp. 54–8.

88 Playfair, *The Mediterranean and the Middle East,* Vol. IV, pp. 31–107; Winston S. Churchill, *The Second World War*, Vol. IV (London 1956), p. 484; Latimer, *Alamein,* p. 307; Bungay, *Alamein* (London 2002), p. 190.

89 Latimer, *Alamein*, p. 309.

90 Bungay, *Alamein*, p. 190.

Chapter 6

1 WO 287/162, Communications in Combined Operations, 1943.

2 HW 73/6 Letter dated 4 September 1942.

3 WO 204/1580, Reports on Exercises MOSSTROOPER and FLAXMAN, 18 – 20 October 1942.

4 *Combined Operations Pamphlet No. 1* (September 1942); *Combined Operations Pamphlet No. 6b* (February 1943).

5 WO 175/172, 78th Divisional Signals, October/November 1942.

6 *Combined Operations Pamphlet No. 6b*, p. 20.

7 WO 106/2753, Notes on Signals – Operation TORCH, 31 January 1943.

8 IWM Documents, Kinden MSS.

9 WO 175/196, 11th Infantry Brigade; WO 175/517, 5th Battalion Northamptonshire Regiment; WO 175/519, 1st Battalion East Surrey Regiment, November 1943.

10 Gelb, *Desperate Venture*, p. 209.

11 WO 218/37, No. 6 Commando, November 1942.

12 WO 106/2753, Notes on Signals – Operation TORCH, 31 January 1943.

13 WO 244/8, Appendix VI to Flag Officer Inshore Squadron's Report 71/084, 8 November 1942; WO 204/6940, Impressions gained from the Assault Phase of TORCH.

14 WO 106/2753, Notes on Signals – Operation TORCH, 31 January 1943.

15 WO 106/5234, Letter from BRA, First Army, 29 December 1942.

16 WO 106/2779, Extract from the War Diary of V Corps.

17 WO 201/789, Combined Operations Lessons Learned 1942 December – 1943 January; WO 244/8, Lessons from the Present Campaign – 78th Divisional Signals; Nalder, *Royal Corps*, pp. 362–3; IWM Documents, Neale MSS.

18 S. W. C. Pack, *Invasion North Africa* (London 1978), p. 102.

19 WO 175/172, 78th Division, November 1942; WO 244/120, Report by CSO First Army.

20 WO 244/120, Report by CSO First Army on North Africa.

21 Playfair, *The Mediterranean and the Middle East*, Vol. IV, pp. 165–91; WO 208/2821, Summary of Operations of First Army.

22 WO 175/68, CSO First Army, 15–18 November 1942; Playfair, *The Mediterranean and the Middle East* Vol. IV, p. 174.

23 WO 204/7416, Report by CSO, First Army, 15 April 1943.

24 WO 175/172, 78th Division Signals, November, December 1942.

25 WO 260/47, Godwin-Austen Report.

26 IWM Documents, Lieut-Colonel J. K. Windeatt 90/20/1.

27 WO 244/115, Training Directorate Questionnaire and responses.

28 WO 201/480, Lessons from North Africa, 2 May 1943; WO 244/118, 51st Divisional Signals, Notes on Campaigns August 1942 – September 1943.

29 WO 244/120, Report by CSO First Army on North Africa.

30 WO 244/115, 78 Division, Lessons from the Tunisian Campaign.

31 WO 106/2753, Notes on Signals – Operation TORCH, 31 January 1943.

32 WO 231/10, Royal Signals Lessons from the Tunisian Campaign.

33 WO 244/120, Report by CSO First Army on North Africa; WO 244/114, Report by CSO V Corps on Tunisian Campaign, 29 May 1943.

34 WO 244/115, Lessons from North African Campaign, June 1943; WO 232/14, Lessons from the Tunisian Campaign; WO 201/480, Report of a War Office Observer, May 1943; WO 204/8173, Lessons from Operations of 2nd NZ Division, 15 June 1943.

35 WO 244/119, Views of Lieutenant-Colonel Woodford.

36 WO 175/182, Report on Operation at Bone by 3rd Parachute Battalion.

37 WO 175/526, 2nd Battalion Parachute Regiment, November/December 1942.

38 WO 208/2821, Summary of Operations of First Army.

39 WO 175/89, CSO V Corps, 26 January 1943.

40 WO 175/23, Memo from tour of 18 – 22 February 1943; WO 166/6523, 11th Armoured Division, 14 July 1942; WO 175/151, 6AD Signals, 26 March 1943.

41 WO 106/2753, Notes on Signals – Operation TORCH, 31 January 1943.

42 WO 175/23, Cipher Security Memo No. 1, 5 March 1943; WO 175/129, 1st Infantry Divisional Signals, 24 March 1943; WO 175/151, 6th Armoured Divisional Signals, 26 March 1943.

43 WO 244/120, Report by CSO 1st Army.

44 WO 204/7516, Report by CSO First Army, 15 April 1943.

45 WO 175/129, 1st Infantry Divisional Signals, 18–29 April 1943; WO 175/140, 4th Divisional Signals, 14 April 1943.

46 WO 175/172, 78th Divisional Signals, April 1943.

47 WO 106/5234, Report by Captain Martin (1st Canadian Division Signals), 7 March 1943.

48 WO 169/8744, 7AD Signals, 12 February 1943; WO 169/8904, 22nd Armoured Brigade Signals, April 1943.

49 WO 244/118, 51st (H) Divisional Signals. Notes on Campaigns, August 1942 – September 1943.

50 Hinsley, *British Intelligence*, p. 600.

51 CAB 146/26, The Axis in Tunisia, p. 112.

52 CAB 146/25, Rommel's Appreciation of the Mareth Line, 9 February 1943.

53 HW 11/4, GC and CS Air and Military History, Vol. IV North Africa 1941–43, p. 304, 327.

54 Playfair, *The Mediterranean and the Middle East*, Vol. IV, p. 345.

55 WO 169/8530, CSO Eighth Army, March 1943.

56 WO 169/8530, CSO Eighth Army, 17 January 1943.

57 WO 169/8654, CSO XXX Corps, 9 January 1943.

58 HW 73/6, Report of 26 November 1943.

59 HW 73/6, Report of interrogation of Lt-Col Mario Revetria (Italian Y officer).

60 WO 231/10, Lessons from the Tunisian Campaign (18 Army Group).

61 HW 11/4, GC and CS Air and Military History Vol. IV, North Africa, 1941–43.

62 1 MHz ī 1000 Kcs.

63 WO 169/8654, CSO XXX Corps, March 1943.

64 WO 244/116. CSO IX Corps. Signal Report of the Tunisian Campaign.

65 WO 175/485, 3rd Battalion Grenadier Guards, 17 March 1943; WO 175/499, 2nd Battalion Hampshires, 30 December 1942, 2 January 1943.

66 WO 244/114, Report by CSO V Corps on Tunisian Campaign, 29 May 1943.

67 WO 244/115, Note by Penney to Deputy C in C, 14 June 1943.

68 WO 175/68, CSO First Army, 17 January 1943; WO 169/8530, CSO Eighth Army, 18 January, 20 February 1943.

69 WO 205/478, Notes on Middle East Conference for Higher Commanders, 15 March 1943.

70 IWM Documents, Montgomery BLM 31/1; Nigel Hamilton, *Monty Master of the Battlefield* (London 1985), p. 143.

71 WO 175/129, 1st Infantry Divisional Signals, 29 April 1943.

72 LHCMA Wynne: Anderson to Wynne, 18 May 1943; Report on visit to North Africa during period, 12 April – 23 May 1943.

73 LHCMA, Penney Diary, 8 February 1943, 9 April 1943.

74 HW 11/4, GC and CS Air and Military History, Vol. IV, North Africa, 1941–1943, p. 333.

75 WO 260/47, Report of the Godwin-Austen Committee on Signals Organisation; WO 193/211, Action from the Report of the Godwin-Austen Committee.

76 WO 260/47, Report of the Godwin-Austen Committee on Signals Organisation.

77 *MTP No 9*, May 1943.

78 WO 193/211, Report of Godwin-Austen Committee, p. 76.

79 WO 260/47, Report of the Godwin-Austen Committee on Signals Organisation.

Chapter 7

1 For example, Carlo D'Este was very critical in his book *Bitter Victory: the Battle for Sicily 1943* (New York 1988), pp. 368–71 but Nalder maintained that communications in Sicily were generally satisfactory in *Royal Corps*, pp. 374–9.

2 Alex Danchev and Daniel Todman (eds), *Viscount Alanbrooke, War Diaries 1939–1945* (London 2001), 11 December 1942, p. 348.

3 WO 204/7870, Notes on Signal Communications in Operation HUSKY, September 1943.

4 Ibid.

5 Courtesy Louis Meulstee.

6 Ibid.

7 WO 169/8798, 51st Division Signal Instruction No. 4, 5 June 1943; WO 169/8784, 50th Division Signal Instruction No. 1, June 1943; WO 201/657, XXX Corps Operational Order No. 5, 5 April 1943.

8 WO 169/8830, 78th Division Signals Diary, 1943.

9 WO 169/8469, Joint Signal Procedure in HUSKY, 6 April 1943.

10 WO 205/39, Lessons learned in North Africa during training for HUSKY, 30 July 1943.

11 WO 169/8784, 50th Divisional Signals, June 1943.

12 WO 244/136, Communication Report on Bark South Landing, Operation HUSKY.

13 WO 169/8798, 51st Divisional Signals, Report on Landing in Sicily, July 1943.

14 WO 204/7870, Notes of Signal Communications in Operation HUSKY; WO 205/478, Report of the Long Committee, 14 October 1943, p. 36.

15 WO 205/39, Lessons learned in North Africa during training for HUSKY, 30 July 1943.

16 WO 204/7559, Lessons from Operations in Italy, 17 November 1943.

17 Otway, *Airborne Forces*, p. 122; LHCMA, Penney 3/2 Diary, 10 July 1943.

18 WO 204/7870, Notes on Signal Communications in Operation HUSKY; WO 205/39, Report on Intercommunications in Operation HUSKY.

19 WO 106/3871, 1st Canadian Divisional Signal Instruction No. 1, 14 June 1943; WO 205/40, Digest of some notes and reports from HUSKY, October 1943.

20 WO 204/7870, Notes on Signal Communications in Operation HUSKY; WO 205/478, Report of the Long Committee, 14 October 1943, p. 37.

21 WO 204/7870, Notes on Signal Communications in Operation HUSKY.

22 WO 244/136, Communication Report on Bark South Landing; WO 205/40, Digest of some notes and reports from HUSKY, October 1943.

23 LHCMA, Mayhew 3/2.

24 http://en.wikipedia.org/wiki/Landing_Craft_Assault).

25 WO 107/135, HUSKY. Report on Beach Maintenance, August 1943.

26 WO 204/7870, Notes on Signal Communications in Operation HUSKY; WO 205/478, Report of the Long Committee, 14 October 1943, p. 38; WO 169/8784, 50th Division, Signal points from the Sicilian landings.

27 WO 169/8771, 46th Divisional Signals, 28 August 1943; IWM Film WOY661, Signals in Combined Operations, 1944.

28 WO 107/135, HUSKY. Report on Beach Maintenance, August 1943.

29 WO 169/8784, 50th Divisional Signals War Diary, 10 – 11 July 1943; WO 201/616, 5th Division Narrative, 10 July 1943.

30 WO 204/7870, Notes on Signal Communications in Operation HUSKY.

31 WO 244/7, Memo by CSO X Corps, 3 November 1943.

32 Ibid.

33 WO 244/7, Memo by CSO AFHQ, 23 October 1943.

34 WO 244/126, Nalder to Phillips, 12 February 1944.

35 WO 244/7, Signal Lessons from AVALANCHE, 27 January 1944.

36 Ibid.

37 HW 11/5, GC and CS Air and Military History, Vol. 5, p. 58.

38 IWM Documents, Rose 88/17/1, Diary 31 August, 6 September 1943.

39 WO 244/7, Lessons from AVALANCHE.

40 WO 244/126, Nalder to Phillips, 12 February 1944.

41 HW 11/5, GC and CS Air and Military History, Vol. 5, pp. 74–7.

42 WO 204/6593, Report on the use of USS *Biscayne*, 3 March 1944.

43 WO 170/388, 1st British Infantry Division Signals, January 1944.

44 WO 170/431, 5th Division Signals, January 1944.

45 Danchev and Todman (eds), *Alanbrooke Diaries*, p. 395 (authors' footnote).

46 Golden, *Echoes from Arnhem*, pp. 51–7.

47 WO 205/40, Report on 1st Airborne Division, 18 August 1943; Otway, *Airborne Forces,* pp. 126–9; WO 169/8469, CSO 15th Army Group Memorandum No. 18, 8 August 1943.

48 Carlo D'Este, *Bitter Victory: The Battle for Sicily 1943* (New York 1988), pp. 368–71.

49 WO 204/6591, Report by First Signal Company, 1st US Infantry Division, 29 August 1943; WO 205/40, Notes on the Planning and Assault Phases of the Sicilian Campaign, October 1943.

50 Molony, *The Mediterranean and the Middle East,* Vol. V, p. 83.

51 WO 169/8530, On 23 July 1943, CSO Eighth Army interviewed the commanders of XXX Corps, 1st Canadian Division, 51st Division and 231st Brigade. In all their opinions, Signal communications were very satisfactory.

52 See, for example, IWM Documents, PP/MCR/182, The Memoirs of Major-General Douglas Wimberley (GOC 51st Division in Sicily), p. 144.

53 WO 244/128, Lessons from Operations in the Italian Campaign, December 1944; WO 244/124, Historical notes regarding signal communications in the Italian campaign.

54 WO 204/6584, Communication Report on Operation AVALANCHE.

55 Meulstee, *Wireless for the Warrior.*

56 IWM Documents, 91/8/1 Colonel Lord Tweedsmuir.

57 WO 169/8830, 78th Division, Communications in the Etna region, August 1943.

58 WO 170/318, Signal Lessons of Recent Mountainous Operations, 15 February 1944.

59 WO 179/2738, 1st Canadian Division Signals, June 1944.

60 LHCMA, Penney 12, General Lessons by Commander 1st Division on the action at Campoleone Station, February 1944. Penney stated that intercommunications within the infantry battalion were still unsolved at Anzio.

61 WO 169/8771, 46th Division Signals, December 1943.

62 WO 170/361, CSO XIII Corps, Lessons of Operations, March – July 1944; WO 170/488, 56th Divisional Signals, 19 January 1944; WO 179/2738, 1st Canadian Division Signals, June 1944; WO 170/287, Notes on V Corps study day, 5 April 1944; LHCMA, Kirkman XIII Corps, Lessons from Cassino, 6 July 1944.

63 WO 204/7576, Penney to Kenchington, 23 February 1944.

64 WO 204/7559, Notes from V Corps, 9 October 1944.

65 WO 170/287, CSO V Corps, 6 January 1944.

66 WO 204/132, Signals in the Italian Campaign; WO 244/124, Historical Notes on Signals in the Italian Campaign.

67 WO 244/126, Nalder to Phillips, 12 February 1944.

68 WO 204/6593, Communications in the Anzio Beachhead, 20 March 1944; WO 244/128, Lessons from Operations in the Italian Campaign, December 1944; WO 170/488, 56th Division Signals, 24 February 1944.

69 WO 170/287, CSO V Corps, 7 April 1944.

70 WO 179/2738, 1st Canadian Division Signals, June 1944.

71 WO 162/291, Battle Casualties, Sicily; WO 162/279, Manpower and Wastage, Italy; WO 170/388, 1st Division Signals, 19 April 1944.

72 WO 179/1739, 1st Canadian Division Signals, 10 October 1944; 56th Division Signals, 3 October 1943.

73 WO 244/128, Lessons from the Italian Campaign, December 1944.

74 WO 244/126, Nalder to Phillips, 20 December 1943, 12 February 1944.

75 LHCMA, Burton, Diary, September 1943.

76 RSM 916.3 (3) Signals Security Issues – Sicilian Campaign, 2 September 1943; GOC 15th Army Group Letter on Signals Security, 17 October 1943.

77 WO 169/8469, Report on Security Monitoring, December 1943; 1st Division Signals, 4 February 1944; WO 244/131, Notes on Signals in the final campaign in Italy, 1945.

78 See for example LHCMA, Allfrey, Diary, 21 January 1944, 21 March 1944; Royal Artillery Historical Society, *Proceedings*, Vol. 11(3), p. 98.

79 WO 170/529, 2nd Infantry Brigade, 15 January 1944.

80 WO 170/215, CSO Eighth Army, 10 January 1944; WO 244/127, CSO XIII Corps, 22 March 1944.

81 WO 169/8784, 50th Division Signals, July 1943.

82 WO 201/616, 5th Division, Sicily; WO 169/8993, 231st Infantry Brigade Signals.

83 WO 204/7870, Notes on Signal Communications in Operation HUSKY, September 1943, Appendix F.

84 WO 169/8889, 15th Infantry Brigade HQ.

85 WO 204/7567, Lessons from Operations in Italy, 156th Parachute Regiment.

86 WO 169/8744, 7th Armoured Division Signals, September–November 1943.

87 WO 169/8600, CSO X Corps September–December 1943.

88 WO 201/1888, Lessons from Italy, 28 November 1943.

89 WO 204/7563, Lessons from Operations, 6th NZ Brigade, March 1944.

90 WO 169/8771, 46th Division Signals, 29 December 1943.

91 WO 170/388, 1st Infantry Division Signals, 27 February 1944; WO 204/7576, Operation SHINGLE, Lessons by DMT; LHCMA, Scott-Elliot Account of the Anzio Beachhead, February 1944.

92 WO 170/318, CSO X Corps, 15 February 1944; WO 170/469, 46th Division Signals, 1 March 1944.

93 LHCMA, Allfrey Diary, 18 January 1944.

94 WO 204/4354, AFHQ Training Memorandum No. 15, 4 June 1944.

Chapter 8

1 War Office, *Combined Operations Pamphlet No. 6a. Military Communications in Combined Operations* (February 1944).

2 WO 171/238, CSO I Corps, Signal Report on the Assault Phase of OVERLORD, 21 June 1944.

3 WO 171/238, CSO I Corps, Report on OVERLORD, 15 July 1944; Nalder, *Royal Corps*, p. 424.

4 WO 171/238, 3rd Canadian Division, Report on Artillery Communications in OVERLORD, 28 June 1944.

5 Ibid.

6 WO 171/238, Notes on Tank-Infantry Communications, 18 March 1944; Commander Signals, 27th Armoured Brigade, Report on OVERLORD, 21 June 1944.

7 Mary Kathryn Barbier, "Deception and the planning of D-Day" in John Buckley (ed.), *The Normandy Campaign 1944. Sixty Years On* (Abingdon 2006).

8 Nalder, *Royal Corps,* pp. 425–6; Ellis, *Victory in the West, Vol.* 1, pp. 103, 104, 127; Hastings, *Overlord*, p. 63.

9 WO 171/158, CSO 21st Army Group War Diary, January–June 1944; WO 171/238, CSO 2nd Army War Diary, January – June 1944; WO 205/906, Notes on and Lessons from OVERLORD Planning, November 1944.

10 HW 11/8 and 11/11, GC and CS Air and Military History, Vol. VIII, pp. 35, 63–4, Vol. XI, p. 229.

11 WO 171/158, Report of a visit on Security, 26–7 June 1944.

12 WO 171/238, CSO XXX Corps, Report on OVERLORD, 5 July 1944; Commander Signals 27th Armoured Brigade, Report on OVERLORD, 21 June 1944; 3rd Canadian Division, Report on Artillery Communications in OVERLORD, 28 June 1944; Remarks by CSO I Corps on the Report by 2nd Canadian Armoured Brigade Signals, 2 July 1944.

13 WO 171/238, Comments by CSO, I Corps on Report on OVERLORD by Cmd 27th Armoured Brigade Signals.

14 WO 171/158, CSO 21st Army Group War Diary, January–June 1944.

15 WO 171/238, CSO Second Army, Report on Communications in OVERLORD, 3 August 1944; OC 3rd Infantry Division Signals, Report on OVERLORD, 8 July 1944, WO 205/1227, Hope to Signals Co-ordination, War Office.

16 WO 171/238, 51st Division Signals, Report on OVERLORD (undated).

17 IWM Documents, 06/126/1, K. B Wakelam.

18 WO 205/1227, Underwood to Signals Co-ordination, War Office.

19 WO 171/238, CSO I Corps, Report on OVERLORD, 15 July 1944; WO 205/1227, Hetherington, Jones and Gordon to Signals Co-ordination, War Office; IWM Film WOY661.

20 WO 171/158, CSO 21st Army Group, June 1944; WO 171/238, CSO Second Army, Report on OVERLORD, 3 August 1944.

21 LHCMA, Pyman 5/24/1, An Account of the Operations of Second Army in Europe, 1944–1945, pp. 146–7.

22 WO 171/238, Operation OVERLORD. Report on Communications. CSO Second Army, 3 August 1944.

23 IWM Documents, H. T. Bone 87/31/1.

24 *Current Reports from Overseas No. 68*, 20 December 1944.

25 LHCMA, Allfrey 4/5, Summary of Corps Commander's Address to Senior Commanders of XIII Corps at Vanafro, 8 April 1944; WO 171/619, Report by Commander, 22nd Armoured Brigade, June 1944; WO 171/159, Lessons from the Battle issued by the Staffordshire Yeomanry, 16 August 1944.

26 Picture obtained from the Imperial War Museum.

27 WO 277/25, Gravely Signals, p. 310.

28 Ellis, *Victory in the West*, Vol. 1, p. 9, 134–5.

29 WO 171/159, Lessons from the Battle issued by the Staffordshire Yeomanry, 16 August 1944.

30 TM 654.9 (41) Wireless Wing RAC School, Notes for Signal Officers and NCOs, May 1945.

31 WO 232/2, Wireless Communications within the Infantry Battalion in the Infantry Division, pp. 1–3.

32 IWM Documents, Caines 90/20/1.

33 WO 171/159, Memo on Communications. Standard of Training within Infantry Battalions, 8 September 1944.

34 WO 232/77, Report by Lt-Col. Honeybourne, Royal Signals, 3 December 1944.

35 Frequency ranges were: No. 38 set, 7.3 – 9 MHz; No. 18 set, 6 – 9 MHz; No. 19 set, 2 – 8 MHz.

36 WO 171/159, Extract of Signal Interest, 4 September 1944.

37 WO 287/24, Wireless Sets 1937.

38 *ATI No. 2*, May 1943.

39 IWM Documents, Montgomery 52/17, Eighth Army. Notes on the Employment of Tanks in Support of Infantry in Battle, November 1943.

40 LHCMA, De Guingand 4/1/7, 21 Army Group. Notes on the employment of Tanks in Support of Infantry in Battle, February 1944.

41 LHCMA, Allfrey 4/5, Summary of Corps Commander's Address to Senior Commanders of XIII Corps at Vanafro, 8 April 1944.

42 De Lee, "American tactical innovation in Normandy 1944", p. 71.

43 WO 171/417, 3rd Infantry Division Signals, 23 March 1944.

44 WO 171/460, 11th Armoured Division Signals, 27–28 July 1944; D'Este, *Decision in Normandy*, p. 373.

45 WO 171/159, Extracts of Signal Interest from Battle Experiences, 17 September 1944.

46 WO 171/159, Notes from a Battalion Commanders Point of View, 4 September 1944.

47 IWM Documents, Llewellyn-Smith 79/38/1, History of 3rd Bn Scots Guards, p. 18.

48 Terry Copp, *Fields of Fire. The Canadians in Normandy* (Toronto 2003), p. 262.

49 WO 106/5844, BAOR Battlefield Tour; Operation TOTALIZE, September 1947; Ellis, *Victory in the West,* Vol. 1, p. 420; David Fletcher, email to the author, 4 December 2008. The Ram Kangaroo, of which an example exists in the Tank Museum, Bovington, has provision for a No. 19 set; WO 106/5846, BAOR Battlefield Tour, Operation VERITABLE, December 1947.

50 WO 106/5844, Report on Operation TOTALIZE.

51 IWM Documents, Llewellyn-Smith 79/38/1, 10 February 1945.

52 *Current Reports from Overseas no. 84.*

53 LHCMA, De Guingand 4/1/8, 21 Army Group. Some Notes on the Conduct of War and the Infantry Division in Battle, November 1944.

54 WO 232/77, Notes resulting from Visit by Maj. J. H. Arkell to units in the field, 19 November–2 December 1944; *Current Reports from Overseas No. 94*, 25 July 1945.

55 *Notes from Theatres of War No. 20* (May 1945).

56 WO 244/100, Report of a Visit to Signal Divisions, September/October 1944.

57 WO 171/4063, Operation PLUNDER Technique Instruction No. 4, 6 March 1945; LHCMA, Pyman 5/24/2, p. 405.

58 van Creveld, *Supplying War,* p. 215.

59 WO 171/159, Report No. 86, 27 September 1944.

60 WO 171/3898, CSO 21st Army Group, 25 January 1945.

61 WO 244/85, Report on Communications in the Second Army Rear Areas, June 1944 – May 1945.

62 WO 244/24, SHAEF Army Signals, 29 November 1944; Gravely, Signals, pp. 189–90.

63 Danchev and Todman, *Alanbrooke Diaries,* 2, 24, 25 March 1945; Ellis, *Victory in the West,* Vol. 2, p. 183.

64 Carol Mather, *When the Grass Stops Growing* (Barnsley 1997), p. 279.

65 WO 171/602, 4th Armoured Brigade Signals, October 1944.

66 WO 171/159, 7th Canadian Recce Regiment. Advance from Falaise to Calais, 22 August 1944 – 5 September 1944.

67 WO 223/50, Notes on 43rd Divisional Signals, Seine Crossing, 1947 Staff College Course.

68 WO 193/90, 21st Army Group Signals Requirements, 14 March 1945.

69 LHCMA, Pyman 5/24/2 The Signals Aspect in the R. Rhine Crossing; WO 244/39, The Signals Aspects of Operation PLUNDER.

70 WO 244/50, CSO VIII Corps, Notes on the Signal Aspects of the advance from the Rhine to the Elbe, 27 March – 21 April 1945.

71 WO 171/460, 11th Armoured Division Signals, May 1944.

72 Golden, *Echoes from Arnhem,* pp. 51–7.

73 Ellis, *Victory in the West,* pp. 155–6.

74 WO 171/429, Report on 6th Airborne Division Signals D-Day and D + 1.

75 WO 223/16, 6th Airborne Division Signals in OVERLORD.

76 For example: Buckingham, *Arnhem*; Golden, *Echoes from Arnhem*, Ryan,
    A Bridge Too Far on which the eponymous film was based; Urquhart,
    Arnhem; Deane-Drummond, *Return Ticket* (London 1953); Nalder,
    Royal Corps, pp. 433–5.

77 Greenacre, "Assessing the Reasons for Failure".

78 LHCMA, De Guingand 4/1/8, 21 Army Group. Some Notes on the Conduct of
    War and the Infantry Division in Battle, November 1944.

79 LHCMA, De Guingand 4/1/9, 21 Army Group. The Armoured Division in
    Battle, December 1944.

80 Nalder, *Royal Corps,* pp. 433–5.

81 WO 244/35, Operation MARKET GARDEN, Communication Report, October
    1944.

82 Otway, *Airborne Forces,* pp. 270–94.

83 IWM Documents, J. S. D. Hardy 93/1.

84 Greenacre, "Assessing the Reasons for Failure", p. 307.

85 Saunders, *Operation VARSITY,* p. 45.

86 LHCMA, Pyman 5/24/2, The Signals Aspect in the R. Rhine Crossing.

87 WO 106/5847, Personal account by Lieut-Col. P. E. M. Bradley, Commander of
    the Royal Signals Regiment of 6th Airborne Division.

88 Courtesy olive-drab.com.

89 Courtesy Louis Meulstee.

90 WO 244/46, The Crossing of the Rhine. Royal Signals, 6th Airborne Division
    Report on Communications.

91 Saunders, *Operation VARSITY,* pp. 121–2.

92 George Raynor Thompson and Dixie R Harris, *The Signal Corps – The Outcome*
    (Washington DC 1966), pp. 34, 144–5.

93 Stephen L. Wright, *The Last Drop. Operation VARSITY 24–25 March 1945*
    (Mechanicsburg 2008), p. 255.

94 HW 11/11, GC & CS Air and Military History, Vol. XI, pp. 229, 273–9.

95 WO 171/3977, CSO Second Army, 1 March 1945.

96 Hastings, *OVERLORD,* p. 200.

97 WO 179/2705, CSO 2nd Canadian Corps, April, September–December 1944.

98 WO 171/159, Battle Experiences No. 7, 7 December 1944.

99 A translation of this document is reproduced in WO 171/159 as an extract from
    Second Army Intelligence Summary No. 70, 31 August 1944.

Appendix

1 WO 32/3057, Telegraphy General, 1929–36.
2 WO 287/24, Summary of Signal Information, 1929–38.
3 For earlier sets, see Table 1.2. For a very full description of the sets see Meulstee, *Wireless for the Warrior*, Vols. 1 and 2. Additional information from WO169/8469, 11 June 1943 List of principal British wireless sets.
4 Nalder, *British Army Signals,* p. 364.

Bibliography

Unpublished primary sources

The National Archives, Kew

AIR 5
CAB 35, 106, 146
HO 341
HW 11, 73
T 160
WO 24, 32, 33, 106, 107, 112, 113, 162, 163, 166, 167, 169, 170, 171, 175, 179, 187, 191, 193, 197, 199, 201, 203, 204, 205, 208, 214, 215, 216, 218, 219, 220, 222, 223, 228, 231, 232, 237, 244, 252, 258, 259, 277, 279, 282, 285, 287, 291, 305, 365

Imperial War Museum, Department of Documents

Alexander MSS 13026 04/15/1
Baxendale MSS 12648 03/22/1
Beaumont MSS 4267 83/36/1
Bone MSS 1464 87/31/1
Bowley MSS 3533 85/9/1
Bradshaw MSS 10811 PP/MCR/203
Brandejs MSS 13239 05/46/1
Brodie MSS 4285 83/48/1
Brooks MSS 3892 84/13/1
Brown MSS 4163 83/16/1
Bryce MSS 3690 96/4/1
Burton MSS 2558 94/8/1
Caines MSS 306 90/20/1
Campbell MSS 9794 P182
Cowles MSS 2251 93/6/1
Cox MSS 5618 97/1/1
Crawford MSS 7485 75/72/1
Dawkins MSS 13363 05/74/1
Findlay MSS 636 91/13/1

Framp MSS 3579 85/18/1
Freer Roger MSS 10984 P382
Gore MSS 852 90/29/1
Hainsworth MSS 12578 03/2/1
Hardy MSS 2273 93/19/1
Harris MSS 5936 67/256/1
Hemsley MSS 3865 84/7/1
Hiley MSS 2092 93/2/2
Hutchinson MSS 95/12/1
Hyde MSS 14283 06/3/1
James MSS 7023 77/23/13 and 13A
Johnson MSS 5635 97/1/1
Kinden MSS 4051 84/50/1
King MSS 3508 85/6/1
King MSS 5543 96/29/1
Lane MSS 137 89/19/1
Leeper MSS 6632 79/30/1
Llewellyn-Smith MSS 6666 79/38/1
Lovett MSS 3060 95/12/1
Lymer MSS 12284 PP/MCR/131
Lyne MSS 13160 71/2/5
McClure MSS 2917 94/47/1
MacKellar MSS 11145 P382
Merrett MSS 3960 84/29/1
Metson MSS 11628 03/2/1
Misc 92 (1365)
Misc 154 (2393)
Misc 177 (2703)
Misc 3037 177 (2703)
Montgomery collection
Morrison MSS 7487 75/75/1
Nalder MSS 2393 93/19/1
Neale MSS 12896 06/41/1
Newland MSS 12197 03/22/1
Noble MSS 11223 PP/MCR/181
Osborne MSS 1322 87/15/1
Parker MSS 1591 87/44/1
Parry MSS 3432 86/82/1
Peakall MSS 13023 04/11/1
Priestly MSS 4214 83/24/1
Proctor MSS 5636 97/1/1
Reader pp/mcr/330

Roberts MSS 12437 Con Shelf
Rose MSS 487 88/17/1
Royle MSS 8533 99/72/1
Rhodda MSS 3704 85/34/1
Smith MSS 8132 99/61/1
Stannard MSS 2843 95/6/1
Stephens MSS 10206 06/39/1
Stiebel MSS 6980 98/3/1
Tateson MSS 1784 92/10/1
Taylor MSS 8510 99/46/1
Thompson MSS 261 89/1/1
Thraves MSS 7776 98/3/1
Thubron MSS 2662 94/8/1
Vollans MSS 4376 82/14/1
Wade PP/MCR 238
Wakelam MSS 15448 06/126/1
Walsh MSS 13101 73/7/1-2
Watson MSS 8610 01/32/1
Weatherall MSS 2088 76/143/1
Weightman MSS 7295 76/104/1
Westover MSS 8927 99/63/1
Windeatt MSS 305 90/20/1
Wolstenholme MSS 13555 05/44/1
Woodcock MSS 6043 67/266/1

Imperial War Museum, Films

WOY 110 Exercise Spartan (1943)
WOY 661 Signals in Combined operations (1944)
ADM 1163 Combined Operations: Beach Organisation (June 1943)

Imperial War Museum, Department of Sound Archives

Adams 14791
Allen 25061
Bell 16726
Bolton 23195
Brown 2705
Brown 11035
Brown 18343
Carver 13218

Clarkson 15748
Cocke 6378
Collins 6461
Collins 18642
Davey 11271
Deane-Drummond 20888
Dent 27393
Foster 27194
Freeman 6490
Gabbitas 2706
Grace 22344
Hackforth-Jones 13350
Hancock 6708
Harding 8736
Hay 23177
Henn-Collins 27395
Hill 11317
Holmes 6382
Lakeman 18335
Lane 13086
Langfield 21022
Leakey 14024
Mailey 13720
Mason 12037
McNish 12435
Norton 23442
Packer 23789
Philpott 19955
Pickering 12012
Procter 22499
Pullen 26979
Radmore 12609
Ray 27374
Rees 22677
Rosier 21651
Sealey 22360
Seddon 887
Smijth-Windham 954
Smith 22622
Sone 13593
Vaux 20950
Weathers 22363

Whiteley 6609
Wood 20936
Woodhouse 6184

John Rylands Library, Manchester University (JRL)

Auchinleck MSS
Dorman O'Gowan MSS

Liddell Hart Centre for Military Archives, King's College London (LHCMA)

Adam MSS
Alanbrooke MSS
Allfrey MSS
Bartholomew MSS
Bridgeman MSS
Brown MSS
Burton MSS
Cadogan MSS
Capper, J MSS
Capper, T MSS
Clarke, E H MSS
Creagh MSS
Cribb MSS
Davidson, F H N MSS
De Guingand MSS
Dempsey MSS
Divers, S MSS
Elliott MSS
Hackett MSS
Hamersley MSS
Hobart MSS
Ismay MSS
Kennedy, J N MSS
Kirke MSS
Laycock MSS
Lewis MSS
Liddell MSS
Lindsell MSS
McNeill MSS
Manley MSS

Maturin-Baird MSS
Metson MSS
Morgan, C MSS
O'Connor MSS
Penney MSS
Pyman MSS
Roberts, G P B MSS
Wade MSS
Warrack MSS
Wright, L W MSS
Wynne MSS

The Tank Museum Archive and Reference Library (TM)

623.61 (41), Details of Wireless Sets MA, MB, MC.
623.61 (41), W. T. Pamphlet No 77 Part 1. MB and MC Sets (1929).
654.9 (41), Signals.
355.6, Reports of the Mechanisation Board, 1934–1939.
RAC 623.438 (41), Training and Tactical Handling of Tank Battalions, 31 March 1931.
RH5, 1Bde Report on Training of 1st Brigade, Royal Tank Corps, 30 September 1931.
RH5 TB MH (41), The Tank Brigade Training Report, October 1934.
RH5 1TB, The Tank Brigade Training Report, October 1935.
RH5 1 TB, The Tank Brigade Training Report, October 1936.
RH5 1 TB, 1st Tank Brigade Training Directive No 2, 1938.
RH88 RAC Half Yearly Reports, 1939–1945.

The Royal Signals Museum Archive and Reference Library (RSM)

916.0 General Works 1939–1945.
916.1 UK Home Defence 1939–1945.
916.2 Anon. The British Expeditionary Force, September 1939 to June 1940.
916.3 – 6 Several Boxes containing documents on Western Desert and Tunisia 1941–43, Sicily and Italy 1943–5, and North West Europe 1944–45.
938.09 (6) Andrew Reid, *Royal Signals at War.*
938.09 (14) Letters from Major-General R. F. H. Nalder to Major-General L. G. Phillips concerning the Italian Campaign.
2nd Lieut G. Roberts, *Report of Events occurring between the Opening of the Command Post Signal Office "Robert" and our departure for the Beach prior to embarkation.*
Report of and on Tournai Table "A", 10 June 1940.
2nd Lieut H. H. R. Mole, *Report of my Actions from 17 May to 24 May 1940.*
2nd Lieut H. Dudley, *Operations – Lille Table A,* 13 June 1940.

The National Army Museum (NAM)

1989-09-68. Journal of Events in Belgium and France May to June 1940, written by Lt Basil Hall, 12th Royal Lancers.

1989-10-126. Short History of 3rd Divisional Signals, 1/9/1939 – 30/6/1940.

2001-03-52. Copies of Papers referring to 5th Battalion The Buffs in France May 1940.

2001-03-69. 5th Battalion, The Buffs War Diary France 1940.

2003-02-277. Transcript Diary of Capt H. C. W. Wilson, 2nd Bn. Gloucestershire Regt, France Flanders 14 May 1940-26 June 1940.

2004-02-118. Manuscript memoir by Cpl Charles Crisp, RE, associated with 44th Div.

2004-09-6. Transcript Diary of Lt Iain Murray's Service in France and Belgium as personal assistant to Lt-Gen W.G. Lindsell, QMG to BEF.

2004-10-180. Papers relating to service of Driver Cyril Marsh 505 Field Company Royal Engineers.

2005-05-11. Historical Account of the work of 1st Battalion Welsh Guards Carrier Platoon during defence of Arras May 1940.

7510-11. History of 9th Battalion. The Border Regiment.

7709-18. Diary of 2nd Battalion the Bedfordshire and Hertfordshire Regiment covering a period from May to the early part of June 1940.

8208-198. Oxfordshire and Buckinghamshire, Light Infantry.

9002-24-4. Interview with L/Cpl L. S. Palmer, Royal Signals.

Published primary sources

Official Publications

Amphibious Warfare Headquarters, *History of the Combined Operations Organisation 1940–45* (London 1956).

Anon., *Standing Orders of the King's Royal Rifle Corps 1930* (Aldershot 1930).

Central Statistical Office, *Statistical Digest of the War* (London 1951).

General Staff Publications:

Army Training Instruction Pamphlet Series

Army Training Memorandum Series

Combined Operations Pamphlet Series

Comrades in Arms. Three Talks to Junior Officers or Officer Cadets to Assist them in Handling their Men (London 1942)

Current Reports from Overseas Series

Field Service Pocket Book 1914 (London 1914).

Field Service Pocket Book (1939). Pamphlets 1-11 (London 1939).

Field Service Regulations, Part 1. Operations (1909) (London 1909).

Bibliography

Field Service Regulations, ii. Operations (1920) (London 1920).
Field Service Regulations, ii. Operations (1924) (London 1924).
Field Service Regulations, ii. Operations (1929) (London 1929).
Field Service Regulations, i. Organisation and Administration (1930).
Reprinted with Amendments (Numbers 1-11) 1939 (London 1939).
Field Service Regulations, ii. Operations General (London 1935).
Infantry Section Leading (London 1938).
Infantry Training, i. Training (London 1932).
Infantry Training, ii. War (1921) Provisional (London 1921).
Infantry Training, ii. War (1926) (London 1926).
Infantry Training, (Training and War) (1937) (London 1937).
Infantry Training, vi. The Anti-tank Platoon (1943) (London 1943).
Memorandum On Army Training Collective Training Period 1926 (London 1926).
Supplementary Memorandum On Army Training Collective Training Period 1926
    (London 1927).
Memorandum On Army Training Collective Training Period 1928 (London 1928).
Memorandum On Army Training Collective Training Period 1929 (London 1929).
Supplementary Memorandum On Army Training Collective Training Period 1929
    (London 1930).
Military Training Pamphlet Series (London 1938–45).
Modern Formations (London 1931).
Notes from Theatres of War Series
Signal Training (All Arms) (London 1936).
Signal Training Vol. I (London 1936).
Signal Training Vol. II (London 1936).
Signal Training Vol. III (London 1936).
Signal Training Vol. IV (London 1936).
Signal Training Vol. V (London 1936)

Chief of the General Staff publications:
    Army Doctrine Publication (Volume 2 COMMAND), April 1995 (*www.army.mod.uk/*
        doctrine/resources/publications).
HMSO, *Invasion Europe* (London 1994).
HMSO, *Statistics Relating to the War Effort of the United Kingdom* (London 1944).
HMSO, *Statistical Digest of the War* (London 1951).
Joint Warfare Publications, *British Defence Doctrine* (London 1997).
Ministry of Information, *They Sought out Rommel. A Diary of the Libyan Campaign*
    (London 1942).

War Office Publications:
    Training Regulations (1934) (London 1934).
    Notes on Certain Lessons of the Great War (London 1934).
    Notes on Certain Lessons of the Great War (London 1936).

Memoirs and edited collections of original documents

Captain Sir Basil Bartlett, *My First War. An Army Officer's Journal for May 1940* (London 1941).

Tim Bishop, *One Young Soldier: The Memoirs of a Cavalryman* (Norwich 1993).

Brian J. Bond (ed.), *Chief of Staff. The Diaries of Lieutenant-General Sir Henry Pownall* (London 1972).

Stephen Brooks (ed.), *Montgomery and the Eighth Army: A Selection from the Diaries, Correspondence and Other Papers of Field Marshal the Viscount Montgomery of Alamein, August 1942 to December 1943* (Army Records Society 1991).

Sir Arthur Bryant, *The Turn of the Tide, 1939–1943* (London 1957).

—, *Triumph in the West, 1943–1946* (London 1965).

Field Marshal Lord Carver, *Out of Step. The Memoirs of Field Marshal Lord Carver* (London 1989).

Winston S. Churchill, *History of the Second World War* (London 1948–1956).

Terry Copp (ed.), *Montgomery's Scientists: Operational Research in North West Europe* (Waterloo, Ontario 2000).

Alex Danchev and Daniel Todman (eds), *Viscount Alanbrooke, War Diaries 1939–1945* (London 2001).

Anthony Deane-Drummond, *Return Ticket* (London 1953).

Denis Forman, *To Reason Why* (London 1991).

Martin Gilbert (ed.), *Churchill War Papers II. Never Surrender May-Dec 1940* (London 1977).

Lewis Golden, *Echoes from Arnhem* (London 1984).

Sir John Hackett, *I was a Stranger* (London 1979).

Michael I. Handel (ed.), *Stategic and Operational Deception in the Second World War* (London 1987).

Mark Henniker, *An Image of War* (London 1987).

Sydney Jary, *Eighteen Platoon* (Carshalton Beeches, Surrey 1987).

Otto John, *Twice through the Lines. The Autobiography of Otto John* (London 1972).

Thomas Jones, *A Diary with Letters 1931–1940* (Oxford 1954).

Howard Kippenberger, *Infantry Brigadier* (Oxford 1949).

Ernest Lampard, *Gentlemen of the Royal Corps* (Privately printed 1999).

Captain Basil. H. Liddell Hart, *The Memoirs of Captain Liddell Hart* (London 1965) Volumes 1 and 2.

— (ed.), *The Rommel Papers* (London 1953).

Pete Littlewood, *Life as a Wireless Operator with Phantom, 1943–1945* (Caversham 1996).

Colonel Roderick Macleod and Denis Kelly (eds), *The Ironside Diaries, 1937–40* (London 1962).

G. Le Q. Martel, *Our Armoured Forces* (London 1945).

Field Marshal Viscount Montgomery, *Memoirs* (London 1958).

Field Marshal Sir Bernard L. Montgomery, *Eighth Army. El Alamein to the River Sangro* (Printed in Germany by Printing and Stationery Services. British Army of the Rhine 1946).

General Sir Frederick Morgan, *Peace and War: A Soldier's Life* (London 1961).

Lieutenant-General Sir P. Neame, *Playing with Strife: The Autobiography of a Soldier* (London 1947).

E. S. Nicholson, *The Adventures of a Royal Signals Despatch Rider* (Leicestershire 2003).

Colonel Donald Portway, *Memoirs of an Academic Old Contemptible* (London 1971).

Stan Procter, *A Quiet Little Boy Goes to War* (Tadworth 1997).

Harry Ramsbottom, *Memory Diary. An Account of his Service from June 1940 to May 1943 with 4 Squadron Middlesex Yeomanry (Signals)* (Epsom 1995).

Anthony Rhodes, *Sword of Bone* (1942, paperback 1986).

Major-General G. P. B. Roberts, *From the Desert to the Baltic* (London 1987).

Christopher Seton-Watson, *Dunkirk – Alamein – Bologna* (London 1993).

Sir Edward Spears, *Assignment to Catastrophe* (London 1954).

Staff Officer of a Division, 'A Diary of Events in France and Belgium', *Army Quarterly*, April 1941.

Richard Tregaskis, *Invasion Diary* (New York 1944).

Lieutenant-General Sir F. Tuker, *Approach to battle, A Commentary: Eighth Army November 1941 to May 1943* (London 1963).

Major-General Roy E. Urquhart, *Arnhem* (London 1958).

Major-General D. A. L. Wade, 'Those Early Days', *Journal of the Royal Signals Institution*, Vol XV(1) (1981), 47–8.

Ashton Wade, *A Life on the Line* (Tunbridge Wells 1988).

Theodore A. Wilson (ed.), *D-Day 1944* (Kansas 1994).

Published secondary sources

Ronald Addyman, *The 51st Royal Tank Regiment: Morley, Tunisia and Italy, 1939–1945* (Leeds 2004).

David S. Alberts and Richard E. Hayes, *Power to the Edge* (Washington 2003).

—, *Understanding Command and Control* (Washingtom 2006).

Stephen E. Ambrose, *Eisenhower. Volume 1, Soldier, General of the Army, President Elect 1890–1952* (New York 1983).

Brigadier Robert C. B. Anderson, *History of the Argyll and Sutherland Highlanders 1st Battalion 1939–1954* (Edinburgh 1956).

Anon, *War History of the 7th Battalion, The Black Watch* (Fife 1948).

Stephen Ashley Hart, *Montgomery and 'Colossal Cracks'. The 21st Army Group in Northwest Europe, 1944–45* (Westport 2000).

Ronald Atkin, *Pillar of Fire: Dunkirk 1940* (London 1990).

Donald H. Avery, *The Science of War: Canadian Scientists and Allied Military Technology during the Second World War* (Toronto 1998).

Stephen Badsey, *Arnhem 1944: Operation Market Garden* (London 1993).

—, *A Bridge too far: Operation Market Garden* (Oxford 2000).

—, *Weapons of Liberation* (London 1996).

Brigadier Cyril N. Barclay, *The History of the Duke of Wellington's Regiment 1919–1952* (London 1953).

A. J. Barker, *Dunkirk. The Great Escape* (London 1977).

Correlli Barnett, *The Desert Generals* (London 1960).

Niall Barr, *Pendulum of War: The Three Battles at El Alamein* (London 2004).

Andre Beaufre, *1940: The Fall of France*, Translated by Desmond Flower (London 1967).

Frank Beckett, *'Prepare to Move'. With the 6th Armoured Division in Africa and Italy* (Grimsby 1994).

Gordon Beckles, *Dunkirk and After* (London 1940).

Sandra Bell and Rebecca Cox, *Communications Inter-Operability in a Crisis* (London: RUSI 2006).

Ralph Bennett, *Ultra and Mediterranean Strategy* (New York 1989).

Shelford Bidwell and Dominick Graham, *Fire Power: British Army Weapons and Theories of War 1904–1945* (London 1982).

—, *Tug of War. The Battle for Italy 1943–1945* (London 1986).

Gregory Blaxland, *The Buffs* (London 1972).

—, *Destination Dunkirk* (London 1973).

—, *The Plain Cook and the Great Showman: The First and Eighth Armies in North Africa* (London 1977).

—, *Alexander's Generals. The Italian Campaign 1944–1945* (London 1979).

Martin Blumenson, *Sicily. Whose Victory?* (London 1968).

—, *Salerno to Cassino* (Washington 1969).

Rudolf Boemler, *Monte Cassino* (London 1964).

Brian Bond (ed.), *Fallen Stars: Eleven Studies of Twentieth Century Military Disasters* (London 1991).

Brian Bond, *Britain, France and Belgium 1939–1940* (London 1990).

—, *British Military Policy between the Two World Wars* (London 1980).

Brian Bond and Nigel Cave (eds), *Haig. A Reappraisal 70 Years on* (Barnsley 1999).

Brian Bond and Michael D. Taylor (eds), *The Battle for France and Flanders 1940. Sixty Years On* (Barnsley 2001).

Clifford A. Borman, *Divisional Signals* (Wellington 1954) (Part of *The Official History of New Zealand in the Second World War, 1939–1945*).

Douglas Botting, *The D-Day Invasion* (Richmond, VA 1998).

—, *The Second Front* (Alexandria, VA 1978).

Michael Brander, *The 10th Royal Hussars* (London 1969).

John M. Brereton, *A Guide to the Regiments and Corps of the British Army on the Regular Establishment* (London 1985).

Stephen Brooks, *Operation Overlord: The History of D-Day and the Overlord Embroidery* (Southampton 1989).

Colin Bruce, *Invaders: British and American Experience of Seaborne Landings, 1939–1945* (London 1999).

George Bruce, *Second front Now!: The Road to D-Day* (London 1979).

William F. Buckingham, *Arnhem 1944* (Stroud 2004).

Christopher Buckley, *Second World War, 1939–1945* (London 1951).

John Buckley, *British Armour in the Normandy Campaign 1944* (London 2004).

Stephen Bungay, *Alamein* (London 2002).

Brigadier Burden (ed.), *The History of the East Lancashire Regiment in the War 1939–1945* (Manchester 1953).

Robert Frederick Burk, *Dwight D Eisenhower, Hero and Politician* (Boston 1986).

James R. Montagu Butler, *Grand Strategy II* (London 1957).

—, et al, *History of the Second World War: United Kingdom Military Series* (London 1976–1987).

Paul Carell, *Invasion-They're Coming!* (New York 1964).

Tim Carew, *The Royal Norfolk Regiment* (London 1967).

Lieut-Colonel R. M. P. Carver, *A Short History of the Seventh Armoured Division October 1938-May 1943* (The Printing and Stationery Forces MEF 1943) (in the Tank Museum Archive reference RH.4 7AD).

—, *Second to None. The Royal Scots Greys 1919–1945* (Glasgow 1954).

—, *Tobruk* (London 1964).

—, *El Alamein* (Lomdon 1962).

—, *Dilemmas of the Desert War. A New Look at the Libyan Campaign, 1940–42* (London 1986).

Central Statistical Office, *Statistical Digest of the War* (London 1951).

Alun Chalfont, *Montgomery of Alamein* (London 1976).

Guy Chapman, *Why France Collapsed* (London 1968).

George F. Cholewczynski, *Poles Apart: The Polish Airborne at the Battle of Arnhem* (New York 1993).

Lloyd Clark, *Arnhem: Operation Market Garden* (Stroud 2002).

Tim Clayton and Phil Craig, *The End of the Beginning* (London 2002).

Joseph F. Cody, *21 Battalion* (Wellington 1953).

—, *New Zealand Engineers, Middle East* (Wellington 1961).

Basil Collier, *The Defence of the United Kingdom* (London 1957).

Richard Collier, *D-Day: June 6th 1944: The Normandy Landings* (London 1999).

Sir John R. Colville, *Man of Valour. The Life of Field Marshall, The Viscount Gort* (London 1972).

John Connell, *Auchinleck* (London 1959).

Terry Copp, *Fields of Fire. The Canadians in Normandy* (Toronto 2003).

Robert Coram, *Boyd. The Fighter Pilot who Changed the Art of War* (Boston 2002).

James S. Corum, *The Roots of Blitzkrieg* (Kansas 1992).

Major G. Courage, *The History of 15/19 The Kings Royal Hussars, 1939–1945* (Aldershot 1949).

Jeremy A. Crang, *The British Army and the People's War* (Manchester 2000).

Martin van Creveld, *Command in War* (Cambridge MA 1985).

—, *Technology and War* (New York 1991).

—, *The Art of War. War and Military Thought* (London 2000).

—, *Supplying War. Logistics from Wallenstein to Patton* (Cambridge 2004).

Alex Danchev and Daniel Todman (eds), *Field Marshal Lord Alanbrooke, War Diaries 1939–1945* (London 2003).

John D'Arcy-Dawson, *Tunisian Battle* (London 1943).

Brigadier D. Dawnay (ed.), *The 10th Royal Hussars in the Second World War* (London 1948).

Carlo D'Este, *Bitter Victory: The Battle for Sicily 1943* (New York 1988).

—, *Fatal Decision: Anzio & The Battle for Rome* (London 1992).

—, *Decision in Normandy* (New York 1994).

Donald S. Detwiler (ed.), *World War II German Military Studies* (New York 1979).

Tony Devereux, *Messenger Gods of Battle: Radio, Radar, Sonar: The Story of Electronics in War* (London 1991).

David Divine, *The Nine Days of Dunkirk* (London 1964).

Richard Doherty, *Only the Enemy in Front (Every Other Beggar Behind. . .)* (London 1994).

Theodore Draper, *The Six Weeks War: 10th May – 25th June* (New York 1944).

Colonel Trevor N. Dupuy, *A Genius for War. The German Army and General Staff, 1807–1945* (London 1977).

Eve Eckstein, *Operation Overlord* (Southampton 1988).

David Edgerton, *Britain's War Machine: Weapons, Resources and Experts in the Second World War* (London 2011).

David Eisenhower, *Eisenhower at War, 1943-1945* (New York 1986).

Major Lionel F. Ellis, *Victory in the West*. Vols I and II, (in Sir James Butler (ed.), *The History of the Second World War* (London 1962)).

—, *The War in France and Flanders, 1939-1940* (London 1953).

John Ellis, *Cassino: The Hollow Victory: The Battle for Rome January – June 1944* (London 1985).

Bernard Fergusson, *The Watery Maze* (London 1961).

John Ferris (ed.), *The British Army and Signals Intelligence during the First World War* (London 1992).

Ernest Fisher, *Cassino to the Alps* (Washington 1984).

David Fletcher, *The Great Tank Scandal: British Armour in the Second World War. Part 1* (London 1989).

—, *The Universal Tank: British Armour in the Second World War. Part 2* (London 1993).

Ken Ford, *Battleaxe Division* (London 2003).

George Forty, *Desert Rats at War: North Africa* (London 1977).

—, *Battle for Monte Cassino* (London 2004).

George Forty and John Duncan, *The Fall of France: Disaster in the West 1939-40* (Tunbridge Wells 1980).

Major R. C. G. Foster, *History of the Queen's Royal Regiment Volume VIII, 1924-1948* (Aldershot 1953).

David Fraser, *Alanbrooke* (London 1982).

—, *And We Shall Shock Them: The British Army in the Second World War* (London 1983).

David French, *Raising Churchill's Army. The British Army and the War against Germany 1919-1945* (Oxford 2000).

Robert L. V. french Blake, *The 17th/21st Lancers 1759-1993* (London 1993).

Arthur L. Funk, *The Politics of TORCH* (Kansas 1974).

Bernard Ferguson, *The Black Watch and the King's Enemies* (London 1950).

Juliet Gardiner, *D-Day: Those Who were There* (London 1994).

W. J. R. Gardner, *The Evacuation from Dunkirk: Operation Dynamo, 26 May – 4 June 1940* (London 2000).

Eleanor M. Gates, *End of the Affair: The Collapse of the Anglo-French Alliance, 1939–1940* (London 1981).

Norman Gelb, *Desperate Venture. The Story of Operation TORCH. The Allied Invasion of North Africa* (London 1992).

Norman H. Gibbs, *Grand Strategy, I. Rearmament Policy* (London 1976).

Stan Gibilisco, *Handbook of Radio and Wireless Technology* (New York 1999).

Michael Glover, *The Fight for the Channel Ports, Calais to Brest 1940: A Study in Confusion* (London 1985).

John Gooch (ed.), *Decisive Campaigns of the Second World War* (London 1990).

Ian Gooderson, *A Hard Way to Make a War: The Italian Campaign in the Second World War* (London 2008).

Dominick Graham, *Cassino* (London 1970).

John Griffiths, *Radio Wave Propagation and Antennas. An Introduction* (Englewood Cliffs 1987).

Pascal Griset, 'Les industries d'armement: l'exemple des transmission', in Christine Levisse-Touze (ed.), *La Campagne de 1940. Actes du colloque du 16 au 18 novembre 2000* (Paris: Editions Tallandier 2001), pp. 330–45.

Francis de Guingand, *Operation Victory* (London 1947).

Jeffery A. Gunsberg, *Divided and Conquered. The French High Command and the Defeat of the West 1940* (Westport 1979).

Nicholas Hagger, *Overlord: the Triumph of light 1944-45: An Epic Poem* (Shaftesbury 1995).

Tony Hall, *Operation Overlord: D-Day: Day by Day* (Hoo 2003).

Nigel Hamilton, *Monty: The Making of a General, 1887–1942* (New York 1981).

—, *Master of the Battlefield: Monty's War Years, 1942–1944* (New York 1983).

—, *Monty: Final Years of the Field Marshal, 1944–1976* (New York 1986).

William K. Hancock and Margaret M. Gowing, *British War Economy* (London 1949).

Nicholas Harman, *Dunkirk. The Patriotic Myth* (New York 1980) (published in London 1980 as *Dunkirk: The Necessary Myth*).

Russell A. Hart, *Clash of Arms: How the Allies Won in Normandy* (Boulder, Co 2001).

Stephen Ashley Hart, *Montgomery and 'Colossal Cracks': the 21st Army Group in North West Europe, 1944–1945* (Westport 2000).

Guy Hartcup, *The Challenge of War* (Newton Abbot 1970).

—, *The Effect of Science on the Second World War* (Basingstoke 2003).

John P. Harris, *Men, Ideas and Tanks. British Military thought and Armoured Forces, 1903-1939* (Manchester 1995).

Timothy Harrison Place, *Military Training in the British Army, 1940–1944* (London 2000).

Max Hastings, *Overlord: D-Day and the Battle for Normandy* (London 1989).

Michael Herman, *Intelligence Power in Peace and War* (New York: Cambridge University Press 1996).

Christopher Hibbert, *Anzio. The Bid for Rome* (London 1970)

Des Hickey, *Operation Avalanche: The Salerno Landings, 1943* (London 1983).

Reginald. John T. Hills, *Phantom was There* (London 1951).

Francis H. Hinsley et al, *British Intelligence in the Second World War: Its Influence on Strategy and Operations,* Vols I and II (London 1979, 1981).

Francis H. Hindley and Alan Stripp (eds), *Code Breakers* (Oxford 1993).

—, *Code Breakers. The Inside Story of Bletchley Park* (Oxford 1993).

Anthony Hockley, *Airborne Carpet: Operation Market Garden* (London 1970).

K. S. Holmes, *Operation Overlord: The Sea-Borne Invasion of North-West Europe, 1944-45* (London 1984).

Richard Holmes, *The D-Day Experience: From the Invasion to the Liberation of Paris* (London 2004).

Alistair Horne, *To Lose a Battle: France, 1940* (London 1969).

Alistair Horne and David Montgomery, *The Lonely Leader. Monty, 1944-1945* (London 1994),

Michael Howard, *British Intelligence in the Second World War*: Vol. V (London 1990).

—, *The Mediterranean Strategy in the Second World War* (London 1993).

Michael Howard and John Sparrow, *The Coldstream Guards, 1920-1946* (London 1951).

Julian Jackson, *The Fall of France: The Nazi Invasion of 1940* (Oxford 2003).

Robert Jackson, *Air War over France, May – June 1940* (London 1974).

William. Godfrey Fothergill Jackson, *Battle for Italy* (London 1967).

—, *Alexander of Tunis as Military Commander* (London 1971).

—, *'Overlord': Normandy 1944* (Newark 1978).

Brigadier W. J. Jervois, *The History of the Northamptonshire Regiment, 1934-1948* (London 1953).

Brian Jewell, *Overlord: the War Room Handbook Guide to the Greatest Military Amphibious Operation of All Time* (Harrogate 1994).

Vincent Jones, *Operation TORCH. Anglo-American Invasion of North Africa* (New York 1972).

Philip Jordan, *Jordan's Tunis Diary* (London 1943).

Lieutenant-Colonel H. F. Joslen, *Orders of Battle. Second World War, 1939–1945* (2nd Edition, London 1990).

Basil Karslake, *1940, The Last Act* (London 1979).

John Keegan, *The Mask of Command* (London 1987).

—, *Six Armies in Normandy: From D-Day to the Liberation of Paris, June 6th – August 25th 1944* (London 1982).

—, *The Second World War* (London 1989).

Orr Kelly, *Meeting the Fox: The Allied Invasion of Africa from Operation Torch to Kasserine Pass to Victory in Tunisia* (New York 2002).

Lieut-Commander Peter K. Kemp, *The History of the Royal Norfolk Regiment, 1919–1951, Vol. III* (Norwich 1953).

Robert J. Kershaw, *D-Day: Piercing the Atlantic Wall* (Shepperton 1993).

Elizabeth Kier, *Imagining War. French and British Military Doctrine Between the Wars* (Princeton 1997).

Robert H. Larson, *The British Army and the Theory of Armoured Warfare, 1918–1940* (Newark 1984).

Jon Latimer, *Alamein* (Cambridge 2002).

Richard Lamb, *Montgomery in Europe, 1943-1945: Success or Failure?* (London 1983).

Ronald Lewin, *Man of Armour: A Study of Lt-Gen. Vyvyan Pope* (London 1976).

—, *Ultra Goes to War* (London 1978).

—, *The Chief. Field Marshal Lord Wavell Commander-in-Chief and Viceroy, 1939-1947* (London 1980).

Basil H. Liddell Hart, *The Other Side of the Hill* (London 1993).

—, *History of the Second World War* (London 1970).

Bradley Lightbody, *The Second World War: Ambitions to Nemesis* (New York 2004).

Eric Linklater, *The Campaign in Italy* (London 1977).

Walter Lord, *The Miracle of Dunkirk* (Ware 1988).

Bill McAndrew, *Normandy 1944: The Canadian Summer* (Montreal 1994).

Kenneth Macksey, *The Shadow of Vimy Ridge* (London 1965).

—, *Crucible of Power (The Fight for Tunisia, 1942-43)* (London 1969).

Fred Majdalany *Cassino: Portrait of A Battle* (London 1966).

Karel Margry (ed.), *Operation Market Garden* (London 2002).

Carol Mather, *When the Grass Stops Growing* (London 1997).

Barton Maughan, *Tobruk and El Alamein* (Canberra 1966).

Ernest R. May, *Strange Victory: Germany and the Defeat of France 1940* (Cambridge Mass 2000).

C. R. Mepham, *With the Eighth Army in Italy* (Ilfracombe 1951).

Charles Messenger, *The Tunisian Campaign* (London 1982).

Louis Meulstee, *Wireless for the Warrior. Vols. 1 and II* (Broadstone Dorset 1995).

Viscount Montgomery of Alamein, *A History of Warfare* (Glasgow 1968).

C. J. C. Molony, *The Mediterranean and Middle East Vol. V* (in Sir James Butler (ed.), *The History of the Second World War* (London 1973)).

Samuel Eliot Morison, *Sicily-Salerno-Anzio, January 1943 – June 1944* (Boston 1954).

—, *Operations in North African Waters, October 1942-June 1943* (Boston 1950).

—, *The Invasion of France and Germany, 1944-1945* (Boston 1957).

Eric Morris, *Circles of Hell: The War in Italy, 1943–1945* (London 1993).

Williamson Murray, *The Change in the European Balance of Power, 1938–1939. The Path to Ruin* (Princeton 1984).

—, *A War to be Won: Fighting the Second World War* (Cambridge 2000).

Frederick Myatt, *The Royal Berkshire Regiment* (London 1968).

Major-General R. F. H. Nalder, *The History of British Army Signals in the Second World War. General Survey* (London 1953).

—, *The Royal Corps of Signals. A History of its Antecedents and Development (c. 1800–1955)* (London: Royal Signals Institution 1958).

Robin Neillands, *The Desert Rats: 7th Armoured Division 1940-45* (London 1991).

Captain Nigel Nicolson and Patrick Forbes, *The Grenadier Guards in the War of 1939-1945* (Aldershot 1949).

Nigel Nicolson, *Alex: The Life of Field Marshal Earl Alexander of Tunis as Military Commander* (London 1971).

Lt-Col. Philip R. Nightingale, *The East Yorkshire Regiment (Duke of York's Own) in the War, 1939/45* (Goole 1998).

Douglas Orgill, *The Gothic Line: the Autumn Campaign in Italy, 1944* (London 1969).

Terence Brandram H. Otway, *Airborne Forces* (London 1990).

S. W. C. Pack, *Operation Husky: The Allied Invasion of Sicily* (Newton Abbot 1977).

—, *Invasion North Africa* (London 1978).

Albert Palazzo, *Seeking Victory on the Western Front* (Lincoln, Nebraska 2000).

Matthew Parker, *Monte Cassino* (London 2003).

Roger Parkinson, *Blood, Toil, Tears, and Sweat* (London 1973).

—, *The Auk: Auchinleck, Victor at Alamein* (London 1977).

Angelo Pesce, *Salerno 1943 'Operation Avalanche'* (Napoli 2000).

Barrie Pitt, *The Crucible of War. Western Desert 1941* (London 1980).

Major General Ian Stanley O. Playfair, *The Mediterranean and Middle East Vols. I-IV* (in Sir James Butler (ed.), *The History of the Second World War* (London 1966)).

Lieut-Colonel Donald Portway, *Military Science Today* (Oxford c.1943).

Michael. M. Postan, *British War Production* (London 1952).

Raymond E. Priestley, *The Signal Service in the European War of 1914–1918 (France)* (S.I. 1921).

Robin Prior and Trevor Wilson, *Command on the Western Front* (Barnsley 2004).

David Potts (ed.), *The Big Issue: Command and Combat in the Information Age* (Great Britain: Strategic and Combat Studies Institute 2002).

Public Record Office, *Battlefront: Operation Market Garden; The Bridges at Eindhoven, Nijmegen and Arnhem* (2000).

—, *Battlefront: D-Day* (1999).

Cyril Ray, *Algiers to Austria. The History of 78th Division in World War II* (London 1952).

Peter Riley, *Royal Signals* (Cheltenham 1995).

Sebastian Ritchie, *Arnhem: Myth and Reality: Airborne Warfare, Air Power and the Failure of Operation Market Garden* (London 2011).

David Rolf, *The Bloody Road to Tunis: Destruction of the Axis Forces in North Africa, November 1942 – May 1943* (London 2001).

Royal Corps of Signals Association, *A Short History of Signals in the Army* (London c. 1948).

Cornelius Ryan, *A Bridge too Far* (London 1975).

Rowland Ryder, *Oliver Leese* (London 1987).

Keith Sainsbury, *The North African Landings 1942: A Strategic Decision* (Delaware 1979).

Martin Samuels *Command or Control? Command, Training and Tactics in the British and German Armies, 1888-1918* (London 1995).

Tim Saunders, *Operation Varsity. The British and Canadian Airborne Assault* (Barnsley 2008).

John Sawyer, *D-Day. (The Story of Operation Overlord, June 6th, 1944)* (London 1960).

John D. Scott and Richard Hughes, *The Administration of War Production* (London 1955).

Christopher Seton-Watson, *Dunkirk – Alamein – Bologna* (London 1993).

Bruce Shand, *Previous Engagements* (London 1990).

Gary D. Sheffield (ed.), *Leadership and Command. The Anglo-American Military Experience Since 1861* (London 1997).

Gary Sheffield, *Forgotten Victory. The First World War: Myths and Realities* (London 2002).

Gary Sheffield and Dan Todman (eds), *Command and Control on the Western Front* (Staplehurst 2004).

Gilbert A. Shepperd, *The Italian Campaign, 1943-45* (London 1968).

William L. Shirer, *The Collapse of the Third Republic. An Inquiry into the Fall of France in 1940* (New York 1969).

Hugh Skillen, *Spies of the Airwaves. A History of Y Sections during the Second World War* (Pinner 1989).

—, *Four years of war-time wit and humour in the Royal Signals/ATS/Intelligence Corps* (Pinner 1993)

Major Edward B. Stanley Clarke and Major Alan T. Tillot, *From Kent to Kohima. Being the History of the 4th Battalion The Queen's Own Royal West Kent Regiment (TA), 1939-1947* (Aldershot 1951).

Captain Patrick F. Stewart, *The History of the XII Royal Lancers*, Vol. II (London 1950).

Mark A. Stoler, *The Politics of the Second Front: American Military Planning and Diplomacy in Coalition Warfare, 1941-1943* (London 1977).

Captain William Alfred T. Synge, *The Story of the Green Howards, 1939-1945* (Richmond 1952).

John Terraine, *The Smoke and The Fire. Myths and Anti-Myths of War, 1861-1945* (London 1980).

—, *White Heat. The New Warfare, 1914-1918* (London 1982).

George Raynor Thompson and Dixie R. Harris, *The Signal Corps: The Test*, in US Army in World War II (Washington GPO 1966).

—, *The Signal Corps: The Outcome*, in US Army in World War II (Washington GPO 1966).

Reginald W. Thompson, *Montgomery the Field Marshal: A Critical Study of the Generalship of Field Marshal The Viscount Montgomery of Alamein KG, and of the Campaign in North-West Europe, 1944-1945* (London 1969).

Barbara Brooks Tomblin, *With Utmost Spirit: Allied Naval Operations in the Mediterranean 1942-1945* (Lexington 2004).

Peter Tooley, *Operation Quicksilver* (Romford 1988).

Patrick Turnbull, *Dunkirk. Anatomy of Disaster* (London 1978).

Wynford Vaughan-Thomas, *Anzio* (London 1963).

Gerald L. Verney, *The Desert Rats: the History of the 7th Armoured Division 1938 to 1945* (London 1954).

Bruce Allen Watson, *Exit Rommel: The Tunisian Campaign, 1942–1943* (London 1999).

Philip Warner, *Auchinleck. The Lonely Soldier* (London 1981).

Russell Frank Weigley, *Eisenhower's Lieutenants: The Campaign of France and Germany, 1944-45* (Bloomington 1981).

Lieutenant-Colonel Oliver Geoffrey W. White, *Straight on for Tokyo? The War History of the 2nd Battalion, The Dorsetshire Regiment, 1939–1948* (Aldershot 1948).

Arch Whitehouse, *Amphibious Operations* (London 1964).

John Williams, *The Ides of May: The Defeat of France May–June 1940* (London 1968).

Hugh Williamson, *The Fourth Division 1939 to 1945* (London 1951).

Patrick Wilson, *Dunkirk: From Disaster to Deliverance* (Barnsley 1999).

Harold R. Winton, *To Change an Army. General Sir John Burnett-Stuart and British Armoured Doctrine, 1927-1938* (Kansas 1988).

Stephen L. Wright, *The Last Drop. Operation Varsity March 24-25, 1945* (Mechanicsburg, Pa 2008).

Articles in Journals

Larry H. Addington, 'Operation Sunflower: Rommel Versus the General Staff', *Military Affairs*, 31(3), (Autumn 1967), 120–30.

Martin S Alexander, 'The Fall of France, 1940', *Journal of Strategic Studies*, 13, (1990), 10–44.

Anon, 'The British Resistance Organisation', *The Wire*, (June 1999).

Lieutenant-Colonel A. G. Armstrong, 'Army Manoeuvres 1935', *RUSI Journal*, LXXX, (1935), 805–12.

'R. M. A.' (full name not supplied), 'A Commander Royal Signals in Action', *Journal of the Royal Signals Institution*, VII(5), (Summer 1966), 222–6.

Abraham Ben-Zwi, 'Hindsight and Foresight: A Conceptual Framework for the Analysis of Surprise Attacks', *World Politics*, 28(3), (1976), 381–95.

—, 'Intention Capability and Surprise: A Comparative Analysis', *Journal of Strategic Studies*, 13(4), (1990), 19–40.

John Berry, 'Communications at the Battle of Arnhem: a Modern Day Technical Analysis', *Solutions in Radiocommunications* (February 2004) (*www.atdi.co.uk*).

Michael Carver, 'Disaster in the Desert', *Times Literary Supplement*, (4 November 1977), 1289.

Major Richard C. Trench, 'Signal Communications in War', *RUSI Journal*, LXXII, (1927), 295–313.

Robert Citino, 'Beyond Fire and Movement: Command, Control and Information in the German Blitzkrieg', *Journal of Strategic Studies*, 27(2), (June 2004), 324–44.

John Ferris, 'The Usual Source: Signals Intelligence and Planning for the "Crusader" Offensive 1941', *Intelligence and National Security*, 14(1), (1999), 84–118.

Captain Leo Framery, 'Campaign of Flanders 1940', *Field Artillery Journal*, Sept, Oct, Nov, Dec 1941.

David French, 'Doctrine and Organisation in the British Army, 1919-1932', *Historical Journal*, 44(2), (2001), 497–515.

—, 'Colonel Blimp and the British Army: British Divisional Commanders in the War against Germany, 1939-1945', *English Historical Review*, 111, (1996), 1182–201.

Nikolas Gardner, 'Command and Control in the "Great Retreat" of 1914: the Disintegration of the British Cavalry Division'. *Journal of Military History*, 63(1), (Jan 1999), 29–54.

—, 'Command in Crisis: The British Expeditionary Force and the Forest of Mormal, August 1914', *War and Society*, 16(2), (October 1998), 13–32.

Brad Gladman, 'Air Power and Intelligence in the Western Desert Campaign, 1940-43', *Intelligence and National Security*, 13, (1998), 144–62.

Emily O. Goldman, 'Introduction: Information Resources and Military Performance', *Journal of Strategic Studies*, 27(2), (June 2004), 195–219.

Major John W. Greenacre, 'Assessing the Reasons for Failure: 1st British Airborne Division Signals Communications during Operation "Market Garden"', *Defence Studies*, 4(3), (Autumn 2004), 283–308.

Jeffery Gunsberg, 'The Battle of the Belgian Plain, 12-14 May 1940: The First Great Tank Battle', *Journal of Military History*, 56(2), (1992), 207–44.

Brian Hall, 'A Practical, Reliable and Safe Means of Communication? The Telephone and the British Army, 1877-1914', *Mars & Clio*, (22), (Summer 2008), 34–7.

Stephen Hart, 'Montgomery, Morale, Casualty Observation and "Colossal Cracks": 21st Army Group's Operational Technique in North West Europe, 1944–45', *Journal of Strategic Studies*, 19(4), (1996), 132–53.

David Kahn, 'Codebreaking in World Wars I and II: The Major Successes and Failures, Their Causes and Their Effects', *Historical Journal*, 23(3), (Sep 1980), 617–39.

Joseph P. Kutger, 'Irregular Warfare in Transition', *Military Affairs*, 24(3), Irregular Warfare Issue (Autumn 1960), 113–23.

Commander C. H. N. James, 'Communications the Vital Thread of War', *RUSI Journal*, LXX, (1925), 436–41.

Captain Basil H. Liddell Hart, 'Army Manoeuvres 1925', *RUSI Journal*, LXX, (1925), 647–55.

W. P. Lunn-Rockcliffe, 'The Tunisian Campaign', *Army Quarterly*, 98(1–2), (1969), 228–35.

Lieutenant John A. McDonald, 'Communications between Army Formations and Aircraft', *RUSI Journal*, LXXII, (1927), 122–8.

Captain F. S. Morgan, 'The Development of Communications and Command', *RUSI Journal*, LXXVI, (1931), 128–36.

—, 'Modern Communications and Command', *RUSI Journal*, LXXVI, (1931), 411–9.

Samuel G. Myer, 'The Fourth Arm', *Military Affairs*, 8(3), (Autumn 1944), 169–72.

Keith Neilson, 'The Defence Requirements Sub-Committee, British Strategic Foreign Policy, Neville Chamberlain and the Path to Appeasement', *English Historical Review*, 118(477), (2003), 651–84

Stephen T. Powers, 'The Battle for Normandy: The Lingering Controversy', *The Journal of Military History*, 56(3), (July 1992), 455–71.

Brigadier Philip Pratley, 'Lifeline, Pipeline and Occasional Noose? How the British Army's Communicators Looked Back on World War II', *Mars & Clio*, (22), (Summer 2008), 38–42.

Glyn Prysor, 'The "Fifth Column" and the British Experience of Retreat, 1940', *War in History*, 12(4), (2005), 418–47.

Major P. Richards, 'Armoured Command Vehicle', *Journal of the Royal Signals Institution*, XVI(4), (Spring 1984), 177–83.

Commander John A. Slee, 'Control of Radio-Telegraphy in Time of War', *RUSI Journal*, LXXI, (1926), 34–7.

R. H. S. Stolfi, 'Equipment for Victory in France in 1940', *History*, 55(183), (Feb 1970), 1–20.

Timothy. H. E. Travers, 'The Offensive and the Problem of Innovation in British Military Thought 1870-1915', *Journal of Contemporary History*, 13, (1978), 531–53.

Major-General D. A. L. Wade, 'Those Early Years', *Journal of the Royal Signals Institution*, XV(1), (1981), 47–8.

Chapters in published collections of essays

Mary Kathryn Barbier, 'Deception and the planning of D-Day', in John Buckley (ed.), *The Normandy Campaign 1944. Sixty Years On* (Abingdon 2006).

Brian Bond, 'Arras 21st May 1940: A Case Study in Counter Stroke', in A. Trythall (ed.), *Old Battles and New Defences* (London 1986), pp. 61–84.

—, 'The British Field Force in France and Belgium 1939-40', in P. Addison and A. Calder (eds), *Time to Kill: The Soldiers Experience in the West 1939–1945* (Pimlico 1997), pp. 40–49.

—, 'Commentary on Military Operations to Defeat Germany', in Charles F. Brower (ed.), *World War II in Europe. The Final Year* (London 1998).

Brian Bond and Williamson Murray, 'The British Armed Forces 1918-39', in A. R. Millett and W. Murray (eds), *Military Effectiveness*. Volume II, The Interwar Period (London 1988), pp. 98–130.

Brian Bond and Martin S. Alexander, 'Liddell Hart and De Gaulle. The Doctrines of Limited Liability and Mobile Defence', in Peter Paret (ed.), *Makers of Modern Strategy: From Machiavelli to the Nuclear Age* (Princeton 1986), pp 78–101.

John Buckley, 'British armoured operations in Normandy June – August 1944', in John Buckley (ed.), *The Normandy Campaign 1944. Sixty Years On* (Abingdon 2006).

R. A. Doughty, 'The French Armed Forces, 1918-1940', in A. R. Millett and W. Murray (eds), *Military Effectiveness*. Volume II, The Interwar Period (London 1988), pp. 49–54.

John Ferris, 'The British Army, Signals and Security in the Desert Campaign, 1940-42', in M. Handel (ed.), *Intelligence and Military Operations* (London 1990), pp. 255–91.

Jurgen Forster, 'Evolution and Development of German Doctrine 1914–45', in John Gooch (ed.), *The Origin of Contemporary Doctrine* (Strategic and Combats Study Institute 1997).

Paddy Griffith, 'British Armoured Warfare in the Western Desert 1940-43', in J. P. Harris and F. N. Toase (eds), *Armoured Warfare* (London 1990), pp. 70–87.

W. Heinemann, 'The Development of German Armoured Forces 1918–1940', in J. P. Harris and F. H. Toase (eds), *Armoured Warfare* (London 1990), pp. 55–69.

Robin Higham, 'Technology and D-Day', in Eisenhower Foundation, *D-Day. The Normandy Invasion in Retrospect* (Kansas 1971), pp. 80–97.

Brian Holden Reid, 'War Fighting Doctrine and the British Army' (annex A to Chapter 1 in *Army Doctrine Publication Volume 1, Operations*) (General Staff June 1994).

John Hussey, 'Portrait of a Commander–in-chief', in Brian Bond and Nigel Cave (eds), *Haig. A Reappraisal 70 Years On* (Barnsley 1999), pp. 12–36.

John Kiszely, 'The British Army and Approaches to Warfare since 1945', in Brian Holden Reid (ed.), *Military Power. Land Warfare in Theory and Practice* (London 1997), pp. 179–206.

Bradford A. Lee, 'Strategy, arms and the collapse of France 1930-40', in R. T. B. Langhorne (ed.), *Diplomacy and Intelligence during the Second World War: Essays in Honour of F. H. Hinsley* (Cambridge 1985), pp. 43–67.

Nigel de Lee, 'American tactical innovation in Normandy, 1944', in John Buckley (ed.), *The Normandy Campaign 1944. Sixty Years On* (Abingdon 2006).

Williamson Murray, 'British Military Effectiveness in the Second World War', in A. R. Millett and W. Murray (eds), *Military Effectiveness, III: The Second World War* (London 1988), pp. 90–135.

—, 'May 1940: Contingency and fragility of the German RMA', in M. Knox and W. Murray (eds), *The Dynamics of Military Revolution 1300–2050* (Cambridge 2001).

M. R. H. Piercy, 'The Manoeuvre that Saved the Field Force', in Brian Bond and Michael D. Taylor (eds), *The Battle for France and Flanders 1940. Sixty Years On* (Barnsley 2001), pp. 53–72.

Gary D. Sheffield, 'The Australians at Pozieres: Command and Control on the Somme, 1916', in David French and Brian Holden Reid (eds), *The British General staff. Reform and Innovation c.1890-1939* (London 2002), pp. 112–26.

Peter Simkins, 'Haig and the Army Commanders', in Brian Bond and Nigel Cave (eds), *Haig. A Reappraisal 70 Years on* (Barnsley 1999), pp. 78–106.

Hew Strachan, 'The British Army, its General Staff and the Continental Commitment 1904-14', in David French and Brian Holden Reid (eds), *The British General Staff. Reform and Innovation c.1890-1939*, pp. 75–94.

Harold R. Winton, 'Tanks, Votes, and Budgets. The Politics of Mechanisation and Armored Warfare in Britain, 1919-1939', in Harold R. Winton and David R. Mets (eds), *The Challenge of Change. Military Institutions and New Realities, 1918–1941* (Nebraska, 2000), pp. 74–107.

Unpublished Theses

Brad Gladman, 'Air Power and Intelligence in the Western Desert Campaign, 1940-43' (PhD University of London 2001).

Simon Godfrey, 'Command and Control in the Western Desert: The case of Wireless Communication in the British Seventh Armoured Division between Operation BATTLEAXE and the Battle of El Alamein' (MA Thesis, University of London 2003).

Simon Godfrey, 'Command and Communications in the British Army in Europe and North Africa c.1919–1945' (PhD University of London, 2009).

David I. Hall, 'The Birth of the Tactical Air Force: British Theory and Practice of Air Support in the West, 1939-1943' (D. Phil University of Oxford 1996).

Patrick Rose, 'British Army Command Culture 1939-1945. A Comparative Study of British Eighth and Fourteenth Armies' (PhD University of London 2008).

Index

British Army Formations and Units

Armies

Brigades

Corps

Divisions

Regiments

Other Formations

US Army Formations and Units

British Wireless sets (by letter/number)

US Wireless Sets

Lightning Source UK Ltd.
Milton Keynes UK
UKOW06f0333030817
306596UK00003B/74/P